We're Still Not Alone

Also by Peter Haines and Clive Birch

So You Think We're Alone?
Maturity and Chi Gong – A Perfect Partnership

And by Peter Haines

The Clarion Resource
A Matter of Public Interest
Priory

We're Still Not Alone

Peter Haines and Clive Birch

Higher Ground Publishing

First published in the United Kingdom in 2012
by Higher Ground Publishing

ISBN 978-0-9571304-0-1

Produced by
The Choir Press, Gloucester

Contents

Introduction

Tom Stoppard said of writing, 'The hard part is getting to the top of page 1.' Fortunately, for us that was not a challenge. We, that's Clive Birch and Peter Haines, acknowledge that the world has moved on since we wrote *So You Think We're Alone?* The decision to write a sequel was easy. Indeed, this decision was influenced in no small measure by the responses from readers, of which more later.

We have written this latest offering in the third person in an attempt to keep confusion to a minimum. We hope we will be forgiven for the lack of a more personal presentation.

On the subject of beginning, Stephen Bayne has some words of wisdom: 'I am rather like a mosquito in a nudist camp; I know what I ought to do, but I don't know where to begin.'

Birch says that inspiration and insights come to him at the most unexpected moments. He had a deep spiritual insight while standing at a photocopier. A similar experience struck him when he was conducting his ablutions in his bathroom. The first book was in preparation with his good friend and co-author Peter Haines. Suddenly the intuitive impression struck Birch that this would be the only book that he would write. He was disappointed by this thought. He was beginning to enjoy the process and working with such a skilled wordsmith and story development expert as Haines.

Disappointment turned to puzzlement as the first book went off to the publishers and work commenced on a second one. As the second book began to take shape and the whispers of a third one entered his mind, the puzzlement refused to abate. Then one day, as he worked on his morning meditation, he was struck by the intuitive insight that the reality from a cosmic overview perspective was that all three books were part of the same whole. They were all part of Birch's story, therefore, in that sense, they were one book. Thereafter puzzlement subsided and Birch was able to proceed with confidence and inner comfort.

Birch jokes with Haines that, whereas Haines has a three-book deal with his publisher for his novels, Birch has a three-book deal with the cosmic for the inspiration of the three books.

In this offering we have concentrated much more on storytelling, where the stories are relevant to Birch's journey, relevant to his work or just plain interesting, which links with John Mortimer's comment, 'The only rule that I have found to have any validity in writing is not to bore oneself.' We have tried to follow this advice in writing this book. We have not been afflicted by the problem where 'You do your best to delay the moment of creation – Laurie Lee used to copy out all the shipping news from *The Times* before he started a poem.' More good sense from John Mortimer.

Birch simply goes away and does something else when inspiration dries up. This makes things very easy for him as he has an attention span just above that of a gnat, or so he says. He is blessed with many interests and the funds to ignore conventional employment. His inspiration is the world and people around him, and he can thus avoid the source of Terry Pratchett's inspirations: 'I get my ideas from a warehouse called Ideas R Us.' Hopefully we all know Pratchett was joking.

Both this and the first book, *So You Think We're Alone?*, are based around the stories of Birch's travels. When some men reach middle age they buy a sports car. Birch is not particularly fond of this mode of transport, and he hates those little blue peaked caps that men of a certain age wear in order to keep their bald heads warm when driving open-topped cars. Other middle-aged, menopausal males acquire a mistress or change their partner. Now that really is looking for trouble. Birch, on the other hand, started travelling outside Western Europe for the first time at age 56. This was his psychological middle-age menopause, although he sees it as a way of breaking out from the mainstream into the phenomenal.

We hope that the publisher does not offer the following Samuel Johnson quote: 'Your manuscript is both good and original; but the part that is good is not original, and the part that is original is not good.' We don't agree with the Olin Miller quote, 'Writing is the hardest way of earning a living, with the probable exception of wrestling alligators.' We are certainly not in the power position of Winston Churchill when he said, 'History will be kind to me, for I intend to write it.'

We present a penultimate quote before we start the book proper. This is from *The Placebo Response* by Howard Broady.

> A prominent psychologist, Jerome Brunner, has concluded that the major way we make meaning of our lives is to tell stories. Stories have a beginning and an ending; they have structure; things happen that cause

> other things to happen in a way suggesting we can predict and control certain events.
>
> We are so used to thinking in stories, we can easily forget that the raw data with which the world presents us often lacks clear beginnings, endings, causes and effects. Those are generally things we construct with our minds and our stories, not things the world hands us on a platter. We construct our image of the world in a way that attaches meaning to things in our lives.

The following quote struck Birch as being apposite for anyone reviewing information which was new for them, or which possessed a degree of controversy. The Lord Buddha has said,

> That we must not believe in a thing said merely because it is said; nor traditions because they have been handed down from antiquity; nor rumours, as such; nor writings by sages, because sages wrote them: nor fancies that we may suspect to have been inspired in us by a deva (that is, in presumed spiritual inspiration); nor from inferences drawn from some haphazard assumption we may have made; nor because of what seems an analogical necessity; nor on the mere authority of our teachers or masters. But we are to believe when the writing, doctrine, or saying is corroborated by our own reason and consciousness. 'For this,' says he in concluding, 'I taught you not to believe merely because you have heard, but when you believed of your consciousness, then to act accordingly and abundantly.
>
> *The Secret Doctrine*, vol. III, page 401

Some names have been changed to save blushes. Many have not.

The authors would like to thank many for their contribution. This book would not be the same without them. However, there are so many to thank, and if there are any omissions it is the fault of Haines and Birch. We apologise now.

Stephen Bayne, Cecilia, Sue, Michelle, Fred, Madelaine, Chet, Kallista, Tony, Sheena from the Malta/ Brittany tour, Doug, Karine Guevorkian and James Valles, Hazel, Audrey, Faye, Judith, Robert M Hutchins, Jaqueline, Samuel Johnson, Dr Tsion Kanchen, Barbara Marciniak, Mother Meera, John Mortimer, Terry Pratchett, Jacques Rangasamy, Louise, Ian, Shaun, 'Roger', Tom Stoppard, Eduard Sure, Margaret White, mind.net, www.sceptic.com, www.plim.org, www.tpub.com.

Specific texts to which the authors owe thanks: *Afterwards, You're a Genius* by Chip Brown, *The Placebo Response* by Howard Broady, *The*

Cathar Prophecy, *Spiritual Nutrition and the Rainbow Diet* by Dr Gabriel Cousens, *Suicide of the West* by Richard Koch and Chris Smith, *Something in This Book Is True* by Bob Frissell, *The Crystal Bible* by Judy Hall, *Anna, Grandmother of Jesus* by Claire Heartsong, *The Spiritual Practices of the Ninja* by Ross Heaven, *DNA Pirates of the Sacred Spiral* by Dr Leonard Horowitz, *The Gentle Art of Blessing* by Pierre Pradervand, *The Disappearance of the Universe* by Gary R Renard, *Demons of the Inner World* by Alfred Ribi, *Don't Underestimate the Power of Your Blood* by Karen S Clickner, *Futhark* by Edred Thorsson, *Autobiography of a Yogi* by Paramahansa Yogananda, *The Ancient Secret of the Flower of Life* vol. 1 by Drunvalo Melchizedek, *Egypt* from the Lonely Planet series of travel guides and *The Secret Doctrine* vol. III.

In the preparation of this book we would like to thank Miles at Choir Press for his patient and wise counsel. We also thank Harriet for her brilliant editing, a major reason for turning our manuscript into a book. Also thanks to the other staff at Choir Press for their contribution.

A Very Peculiar Ceremony

Nuptials of a very different nature

Nervously, the tall, grey-haired gringo, an Englishman, stood in front of the judge who was shuffling his papers on his large mahogany table. The gringo was vaguely aware of sounds from the outside world.

As the minutes rolled on the Englishman shifted his weight from one foot to the other: a sure sign of discomfort. A dribble of sweat slowly rolled down the centre of his forehead and on down the not inconsiderable length of his nose. A dewdrop formed on its end. The gringo wiped it away. *OK, relax. Take the pressure off myself,* he thought.

He went through a series of exercises to remove the mental strain. *Breathe deeply, stretch and relax the muscle groups.* He was sweating profusely in the airless room, and was wishing that he had not put on the heavy business suit in that hot climate.

Forget about it. Just relax and concentrate on the issue that is to come.

Suddenly the judge stopped shuffling his papers, looked up and cleared his throat. He stared at the Englishman over the top of his spectacles, unblinking and silent for what seemed an eternity, but in hindsight it was probably only a few seconds.

'Clivay Terrencay blah, blah, blah blah.'

The Englishman understood not a word. The judge was speaking in his native Spanish. This was Mexico.

'Clivay Terrencay blah blah blah blah.'

The Englishman jumped as he felt a jab in the ribs. Not only was the judge speaking to him, but he was also expecting a response.

Clivay Terrencay? Oh, that's me. Clive Terence Birch.

Birch was dragged back to the there and then. This was his wedding day and he was in a town hall in Mexico City for the civil ceremony. To his left stood his prospective sister-in-law, to his right his soon-to-be wife, Jaqueline. To Jaqueline's right was her mother, Victoria Robles.

Jaqueline hissed in Birch's ear, 'Just say "si".'

Birch duly did so. 'Si,' he responded, feeling strangely comfortable with the sound of the unfamiliar language. *This Spanish language isn't so bad after all. I can do this.* He was soon to be disabused as the ceremony rolled on.

Questions and responses continued in this most bizarre of weddings. Birch responded with 'Si' each time he was jabbed in the ribs. For all Birch knew he could have been in a court of law, accused of any number of crimes which would have incarcerated him in one of Mexico's notorious jails. He understood not a word apart from 'Clivay Terrencay' and 'Si'. It was a start; not much of a start, but a start nonetheless.

It was just as well that he trusted those around him. All this was most disconcerting. But the end of the ceremony was reached and Birch and Jaqueline signed on the dotted line, shook hands with the judge and marched out of the room. Birch's head was spinning. Jaqueline's Mexican friends and relatives were there, all Spanish speakers. Birch was the only Anglophone; no friends or family from far-off England to support him. He almost felt like an observer at his own wedding; a strange and unnerving experience.

Smiles, hugs, kisses and handshakes were exchanged. Birch felt it best to exclude the judge from this process. The party moved to the outer office, where the final document was pounded out by muscular Latino ladies on the most ancient of typewriters. The typewriters were huge, thus the need for the powerfully built ladies. Birch wondered if the women had started their working life slim and trim, then muscled up through their daily exertions. At the end of the pounding, the women tipped the ancient machines forward to give themselves room to relax and converse with their neighbours. The typewriters looked as though they had come from the 1930s, all cast iron. The noise was redolent of heavy engineering, perhaps shipbuilding. The ladies hammered the keys in order to make suitable depressions on carbon and official paper. Of necessity, these items of plant rested on substantial desks, ancient and solid.

They could have been rescued from the Titanic or Queen Victoria's drawing room, and perhaps the original design was by Isambard Kingdom Brunel, thought Birch. He made sure that he kept his thoughts to himself; little point upsetting his generous host's family and friends. If one of the ancient machines had been dropped on a foot, a poor unfortunate would most certainly have sustained serious injury. Administration complete, the party left and made to the feast.

So what were the circumstances leading to a civil wedding in that most Catholic of countries?

'Mama. I am going to marry the Englishman Birch,' said Jaqueline to her mother.

'That's nice, dear, but he is a little old for you. Why hasn't he been married before and is he a good Catholic?'

'He is divorced. No, he is not a Catholic; he is a mystic.'

One cat immediately found itself among the pigeons. Here was Senora Robles' youngest and finest, proposing to marry a divorcee, a heretic, and an older man to boot. This had not been part of the plan, at least in the mind of Mama, the head and strong will of the family.

Weeks of wrangling, arguing, wheedling, persuasion and pressure followed. Jaqueline had to abandon this reckless and foolhardy adventure, or so the family thought. Jaqueline held firm. The marriage went ahead. At one point, Mama was not going to attend the ceremony. When she saw that not even that threat would deter her daughter, she relented and, at the last, attended with good grace.

Before the nuptials could go ahead, there was one final hurdle to overcome. An audition took the form of a family meeting where the prospective bridegroom was to be interviewed by a senior member of the family. The remainder of the family was present to judge the suitability of the intended. This event was held in Mama's house with a son as interviewer because Jaqueline's father was dead.

Birch now had a clue what Daniel might have felt as he entered that den of felines. The underwhelming welcome with which the prospective marriage had been met gave little cause for optimism. However, the interview started well. The questions were relatively friendly and innocuous as elder son addressed the gringo. As the question and answer session continued, the inquisitor warmed to his task with various derogatory remarks about England and the English.

At first Birch kept his cool, answering politely if a little icily. He was aware that friends and supporters were thin on the ground. Then came a point where Birch snapped. The straw that broke the camel's back was the statement concerning the high number of prostitutes in England, according to elder son. Precisely on what evidence this statement was made remained unclear.

Red cheeks and bulging eyes from the Englishman switched Jaqueline on to the deteriorating atmosphere; she interrupted to calm matters.

Birch struggled to calm himself. *No point in making things worse,* he said to himself. Thereafter the interview settled and was fairly quickly terminated.

The final chapter of this event was when Jaqueline confided in Birch that the family's rule book decision about Clive would have made no difference to her decision to marry the English gringo.

To cap it all, Mama insisted that an attempt be made to arrange the wedding in the Catholic Church. This would require our somewhat flawed hero, Birch, being baptised. As part of the negotiation, Birch bowed to the heavy pressure and agreed to this, much against his wishes. Fortunately, the aforesaid Catholic Church decided that it could do without the divorced, heretical gringo being welcomed into its bosom. Birch breathed a sigh of relief.

So, bring on the judge.

Travels Alone Part 1

One man, a map and a hire car – Carcassonne to Perpignan

July in Carcassonne, France. Delightful. The French taxi driver gesticulates at the traffic management and one-way systems. Repetition of the word 'merde' and other words unknown to the English passenger punctuate the stream of French that Birch, sitting uncomfortably in the rear seat, finds impossible to follow. Occasionally the driver even puts his hands back on the steering wheel. He also decides to watch the road and the aforementioned hated traffic system from time to time, rather than directing his invective by turning to address Birch.

Welcome to France, Birchy.

Birch does his usual soothing peacemaking from the back of the taxi, within the confines of his limited French. It is with great relief that he climbs out of the taxi, intact.

Carcassonne; the castle of this city is the most impressive fortified mediaeval structure in the south of France. Its history goes back 2,000 years. The majority of the modern town is on the plain in the lee of this UNESCO World Heritage Site. No matter what direction you are coming from, you can't miss the imposing silhouette of the city of Carcassonne. (So says the advertising blurb. It fails to take into account arriving by air, as Birch did.)

Pepin the Short, king of the Franks, captured most of the south of France, defeating the Saracens in 760, but he didn't take back Carcassonne. As in time past, it remained an impregnable fortress. The Franks settled down to starve out the defenders. Dame Carcas, widow of the castle lord, planned to fool the Franks. She fed a pig with the last sack of grain in the redoubt. The fattened animal was thrown from the ramparts: an act which successfully persuaded the attackers that there was plenty of food available for the castle's defenders. Thus they concluded that there would be no early surrender, so the Franks left and the siege was lifted. Dame Carcas celebrated the survival of the city by ringing the bells for a day.

It is said that 'Dame Carcas sonne' (Dame Carcas rings) became the name of the city from that day. The Saracens had such bad press in the West; it is good to see the underdog triumph.

First evening, and Birch imbibed a 'comfortable' French wine, purely medicinal to help sleep, you understand? Birch liked the style of French waiters. They took a pride in what they were doing: just small things such as bringing a fresh bottle of water, without being asked, when the previous one was finished. Yep, Birch was going to like Carcassonne.

There were a lot of British people in Carcassonne. Birch heard French spoken only once in the Carousel area. He couldn't help noticing the many pink faces and pink heads on the middle-aged, caused by the sun. That probably included Birch.

Birch was struck by the contrast of dark and light forces. A tourist guide talked proudly of the construction of a canal during the eighteenth century, to transport goods and increase prosperity. Within eighty years the revolution had brought chaos and bloodshed.

From maps and other information, Birch had selected various castles and other places to visit. They were selected because they felt right to visit. Most, if not all, were places of slaughter and suffering. Perhaps there would be healings there?

In a healing situation, who is the healer and who is the healed? Birch realises that this sounds much like a Zen saying: what is the sound of one hand clapping? He is, in this case, attempting to convey the idea that, in a healing situation, the healer is receiving a gift also. This may be in the form of satisfaction at a job well done, or simply joy in the experience.

OK, Birchy, you have been here twenty-four hours. Get your act together, playtime over. Time to get your rear in gear, pick up the rental car and hit the road.

His first stop was Béziers, after a visit to a small village called Villeneuve on a tourist part of the Canal du Midi. Relaxation was still on the agenda as Birch continued to slow down towards holiday mode. As he sat relaxing by the cool and calm water, he eavesdropped on some local old men. They were not speaking French, but a local language, maybe, or a strong regional patois. The locals, apparently happy in their togetherness, ignored the foreigner.

Béziers is located on a small bluff above the River Orb about six miles from the Mediterranean. The Canal du Midi crosses the River Orb as an aqueduct called the Pont-Canal (Canal Bridge) de l'Orb. Successive waves of Neolithic peoples, Celts, Romans and Moors lived in the city. Béziers was a stronghold of Catharism, which the Catholic Church exterminated when it called for the Albigensian Crusade. Once inside the city, the victorious Catholic commander ordered the slaughter of every person with the phrase, 'Kill them all. God will know his own.' Nice man. Birch wondered if he was kind to small animals and children.

In the repression following Louis Napoleon's coup d'état in 1851, troops fired upon and killed republican protesters in Béziers.

Tradition has it that Saint Aphrodisius, first bishop of the city, arrived on a camel. From this arose the custom of leading a mechanical camel in the procession on the feast of the saint. The city is twinned with Stockport in northwest England. Birch considered whether Stockport paraded a mechanical camel through the streets; somehow he doubted it. That would not seem to be attractive to a hard-nosed English northern town.

Birch drove through the town: a chaos of traffic, parked cars and narrow winding streets. A parking place opened for him. He strolled past crumbling tenements and through streets filled to overflowing with brown-skinned residents. He wondered, as the people here were speaking a language he did not recognise, if they were from North Africa. The only French he heard was in the tourist information office.

The city made the traffic of Birch's home town of Cheltenham look almost relaxed. There were wall-to-wall cars on the roads and parked against the pavements.

There was something oppressive about the looming tenements, as he made his way to the cathedral overlooking the river. Perhaps it was the closeness of the buildings to each other, a cramming that made him feel a little nervous, or perhaps it was the obvious poverty. Another reason could be the massed and milling example of humanity jammed in between the buildings. He shuddered, telling himself to get a grip.

Birch wondered if his feelings about this place were possibly caused by the slaughters that had occurred, the energy trapped in by the ugly buildings. He reached the cathedral, an unprepossessing building from the outside. It was locked, which increased his chagrin. The only joy to be had there, it seemed to him, was the view from the wall next to the cathedral, gazing down a 150-foot drop to the river below. There was a panorama of green countryside opposite.

This wasn't working. There wasn't much point in staying in that oppressive environment. The tourist information office was unable to suggest any other building of historic interest to visit. So it was with a feeling of some relief that he left the city with no definable heart. Many French cities that he had visited had well-laid centres with parks and spacious public buildings. This town planning model seemed to have bypassed the city fathers here. Perhaps he was being unfair, but Béziers didn't work for him. Much later, when reviewing this part of the journey, he felt impelled to perform a healing on behalf of this seemingly chaotic place. Whatever the cause, the town needed as much spiritual help as it could get.

That evening, with Béziers behind him, a meditation gave Birch insight into a deeper energy in the landscape. It felt similar to friends, Joan and Mary's, visit to Crete, where they had been inspired to work on the 'skin' of Christianity which covered the deep and ancient spiritual heart of that land. Maybe the purpose of his visit there was to attune himself with the Cathar vibration of the Languedoc, the first of many sites of slaughter. A visit by this 'crazy mystic' (Birch's words) may have been enough to change the energies. However, he had had experiences of being inspired to visit certain places, then being disappointed by lack of feedback afterwards.

The next day our traveller drove to Minerve, another site of slaughter of Cathars. On the drive, an insight came to him. Minerva was a Roman goddess of crafts, poetry and wisdom and the inventor of music. Accounts were heavily influenced by Greek mythology and the figure of Athena. Minerva was the daughter of Jupiter and was not born in the usual way. Jupiter had a headache. Vulcan opened up his head and out came Minerva, fully grown and dressed in armour. Birch felt as though there had been a temple at Minerve dedicated to Minerva.

As he walked down into a deep limestone valley just below the town, two enormous caves, the mouths opposite each other, opened up. One had a closed back that felt very male and the other had an opening at the far end that was distinctly female, or perhaps it was the other way round. It didn't matter; the two were of a different and opposite balancing vibration. As Birch sat between the mouths of each, the energy was so powerful there was no need to go into meditation. All that was necessary was to sit, switch off the thinking engine and allow the energy to wash over him. It was stunning and powerful. As he walked between the two caves, and into them, it felt as though the whole trip was worth it, just to experience the amazing energy. Marvellous.

This is from Wikipedia:

> In 1210 a group of Cathars sought refuge in the village after the massacre of Béziers during the Albigensian Crusade. The village was besieged by Simon de Montfort, 5th Earl of Leicester. The attacking army besieged the village for six weeks before it capitulated. They set up four catapults around the fortification: three to attack the village, and the largest, Malevoisine, to attack the town's water supply. Eventually the commander of the 200-strong garrison, Viscount Guilhem of Minerve, gave in and negotiated a surrender which saved the villagers and himself after the destruction of the town's main well. However, 140 Cathars refused to give up their faith and were burned to death at the stake on 22 July.
>
> http://en.wikipedia.org/wiki/Minerve,_Hérault

Birch was not aware of the extent of the slaughter of Cathars at Minerve until some time after his visit. In his view this was another example of being in a place that needed a healing presence, not necessarily a healing ritual.

As Masaaki Hatsumi, the thirty-fourth Ninja Grand Master, wrote,

> In every encounter there is potential for gaining enlightenment, the possibility of finding that one missing piece of the puzzle that brings about illumination. It is our own mind that brings about the experience.
>
> *The Spiritual Practices of the Ninja*, Ross Heaven

Birch now regrets that he never returned there. He was certain that inspirations and intuitions would be heightened in that incredible place.

Birch visited the Musée Archéologique with its very old-fashioned glass case displays and musty, dusty interior. The woman looking after the place, in reply to Birch's question, said that scientists had dismissed the link of the name with Roman or Greek sources and that the name was linked to a herb. He much preferred the goddess link. (There again, he would, wouldn't he?)

The Michelin Guide told of an ancient dolmen close to Minerve. Birch thought it worth a visit without expecting any spiritual work to be done. As he arrived, the lone car in the car park left. Good, he would be alone. As things turned out, the cosmic had set out to give Birch the space to work undisturbed.

A dolmen is a Neolithic stone formation comprising a horizontal stone supported by two or more vertical stones. We are left to wonder how ancient people were able to transport and position such mighty stones, some weighing many tons. What technology did they have? Some believe they are the remnants of a tomb. There is nowhere better to see them than in Brittany in northwest France, especially around Carnac. Indeed, the word dolmen is thought to come from the ancient Breton language, *tol* meaning table and *m?n* meaning stone.

Birch walked up the very large mound surrounding the dolmen. The cicadas chirped their evocative racket, the energy building then breaking before starting to surge upward again. The mound and dolmen were surrounded by dark fir trees crowding in. This focussed even further the very strong energies.

Birch walked into the dolmen and stood under the capstone. The energies pressed down on his head. He was struck by the power. He felt guided to tile the dolmen, walking anti-clockwise. He sensed that this walking meditation dispersed the stuck energy, allowing it to be transmitted out. As he perambulated around the site, the cicadas were making and breaking their crescendos. On two occasions the crescendos were reached at the same point on his walk around the dolmen. These peaks were both close to the entrance.

Birch sensed that the insect kingdom was in complete harmony with the Earth energy; all three – insects, place and Birch – interacted to complete the task of tiling.

After three circuits of the tiling to focus energy in this incredible place, Birch walked away, back to the car. The energy, in the end, had been as much as he could stand. This was most unusual. Normally he tried to raise vibrations further. Birch felt that he had contributed as much as possible. This work had come completely out of the blue, another example of work being presented to him with no pre-planning on his part.

Tiling is an old mystic idea. Simply walking around a building, room or area can change the energy inside, for better or worse, retaining and focussing internal energy, keeping out discordant external energies, funnelling in positive ones. The conscious attitude of the tiler is also significant. By using sound, group energy and constant repetition, a standing wave of energy can be built up. The human element is key.

Birch watched the World Cup football final on television one evening. The chant of 'Allez France' did not work on this occasion. Italy won. Now in

Quillan, Birch enjoyed this typically French event. Many people, including Birch, sat outside a town square bar, relishing the occasion. Although exciting, somehow the atmosphere was more relaxing watching the big match outside. Perhaps the open air helped disperse the emotional energy? Perhaps also the good humour of the people played its part? There was no male aggression as one may experience on similar events in England.

Now we jump to the mystery surrounding the parish priest of Rennes-le-Château, Bérenger Saunière, and how he obtained very large sums of money to refurbish the church and grounds at the end of the nineteenth century. The mysterious priest may have had a considerable sense of humour, as he is said to have left clues to his sudden wealth.

Part of the mystery surrounds Jesus and the hypothesis that he was married to Mary Magdalene. Hints to the mystery are also allegedly shown in some of the paintings of Nicolas Poussin. Various hoaxes around hidden treasures have been perpetrated which have not enhanced the credibility of the mystery, but have certainly not deterred those with a psychic and mysterious interest in the place. Many visitors poke around the countryside looking for clues to mysterious happenings, much to the delight of the local tourist trade.

Saunière, it is alleged, died in poverty after being accused of amassing a fortune from the sale of Catholic masses. How much of the official story is truth or spin is now impossible to tell. Abbé Saunière allegedly only confided in Marie Dénarnaud, his housekeeper and lifelong friend. It is argued that both took their secrets to the grave. It is difficult to believe, however, that the Catholic Church was unaware of, and did not collude in, the bizarre designs in the church and the equally bizarre behaviour of its abbé. The Catholic Church is not known for its moderation in dealing with what it considers heresy. Ask the Cathars. (Not all may be aware that the Office of the Inquisition is still in existence.)

Rennes-le-Château is beloved by those who love these intriguing mysteries. The name became globally recognised after publication of Dan Brown's *The Da Vinci Code* book and the subsequent film. Birch wondered why he had found himself directed there. The visit was not part of his planned itinerary. In fact he had no interest in it initially. There was a small problem with the rental car, and it was not until he was on the road to this place that the apparent fault cleared up. He had been on the road back to his hotel and he had suddenly seen the sign to Rennes-le-Château. Anyway, there he was in this hill-top village.

Through the door of the church he saw a very strong statue of the devil which was shocking in its power and unexpectedness. The devil had a bowl on his head which held holy water. Birch's mother had a saying: to truly loathe something was like 'the devil loving holy water'. Here were two antithetical elements: the church and the devil, cheek by jowl.

On the left-hand side of the church in Rennes-le-Château, up the short nave, is the figure of St Germaine as a young woman. At her feet are two sheep: symbols of modesty and grace. The circular window above the altar has the image of Jesus with a halo. He is talking to four men. At his feet is a woman. Could it be Mary Magdalene? She is washing Jesus' feet with her hair: the biblical sign of marriage.

To the left and right of the altar are the figures of Joseph and Mary holding up the infant Jesus. His arms are spread in a mature fashion, as though giving a blessing. His head is slightly cocked to one side, looking down. This is not a very baby-like pose. It is the body language of a very aware person.

This is a most interesting church, full of symbolism that doesn't seem to rest easy with Catholic teaching. It is particularly interesting that the church allows this apparent heresy to be so openly displayed. Perhaps the Catholic Church knows the full meaning of the symbolism? But why display this alternative symbolism here when it cracks down on other conflicts with its dogma elsewhere? There is a mystery here that has not been answered yet. Perhaps the church is of the view that the mystery is so well hidden that no one will discover it?

Birch didn't feel much in the way of special energies there. There again, the place was full of tourists whose energies may have overlaid any that would have been of interest to him. Maybe it was a special place of energy, maybe not. It is not very often that Birch is ambivalent about centres of supposed special energy. The only remarkable thing for him was the way that he had been drawn there.

In 1985, a huge pentagram was found in the Rennes-le-Château landscape. Its geometrical points are on ancient sites, now mostly marked by Christian churches. The figure was found to be part of an incredibly complicated geometrical pattern, requiring a very sophisticated knowledge of mathematics. It was laid out thousands of years ago, probably before the birth of the present civilisation.

There are also legends of giants in the area. The Phoenicians referred to the nearby Pyrenees as the home of the Titans, a race of giants.

Arguably Montségur is the most powerful monument to the Cathar religion, and the next port of call on Birch's journey. Set on a high looming crag 3,000 feet up, fifty miles southwest of Carcassonne, it lies in the heart of France's Pyrenees region. The walk up to the ruined castle is a physical challenge for all but the fittest.

The Cathars believed in a simple way of living. They criticised the Catholic Church, particularly for its corrupt, negligent clergy and power-hungry officialdom.

In the final battle for the castle, hundreds of Cathar defenders were battered into surrender by the forces of the Albigensian Crusade. Two hundred and twenty were burned to death as they chose not to renounce their faith. Before the final surrender, it is alleged, several defenders escaped carrying an unknown treasure. This has never been identified or discovered. Is this another good story for the tourists, or something more deserving of serious research? The present ruins are the remains of a castle built after the Cathar surrender.

The Nazis showed a great deal of interest in Montségur, as part of their revolting racial drivel. Some sources say that in 1944, on the 700th anniversary of the fall of Montségur, German aircraft were seen close by, flying in strange formations similar to Celtic crosses and swastikas. Quite what the claimed connection was between that perverted philosophy and the simple Cathar religion is something of a mystery. Elements in the Nazi hierarchy were very interested in the Holy Grail legend, which some commentators claim is also connected to this place. Some claim that Alfred Rosenberg, an ideologue in the Nazi Party, was aboard one of the aircraft that made that bizarre flight in 1944.

A forty-five minute climb is needed to reach the redoubt. One enters a keep surrounded by high walls. The area at the top of the mount is surprisingly small for the 600 Cathars who allegedly sheltered there: the last redoubt of the heresy. It must have been extremely crowded. At the end when the castle fell, the last of the Cathars walked out, singing as they went to their fate of being burned alive.

Birch walked to the left side as viewed from the keep entrance, quietly looking down on the countryside spread below. As he moved back to the keep, his solar plexus started to vibrate strongly. He gave healing to himself and this place. Behind Birch, a French couple was talking at machine-gun speed; they could talk for France.

Birch's second visit there was preceded by the climb. On that occasion, his leg muscles coped better. At the keep he received the psychic message to work at healing the painful memories in order to allow the powerful vibrations underneath to burst forth. Indeed, this was a message for the whole of this part of the journey. Using meditation, he was encouraged to release the stuck energy in these castles and ancient places.

That night, Birch felt comfortable with the idea of returning to this special place. Perhaps there would be more healing, more insights. So back he went, for this third visit. After his arrival at the top of the castle, a very noisy group of people also arrived: kids and noisy adults. Everywhere, there were wall-to-wall people. It was difficult to find a quiet place. Maybe that was the plan?

Some people go there for a nice day out, some for a challenging climb up the hill, some for the history and some for the vibrations. As Birch reached the bottom of the hill for the last time, it came to him that the energy forms, the violent ones as a result of the atrocities that had been perpetrated there, sat like scabs over the energy points. He was reminded of Prince Charles's remark about buildings that are insensitively altered. How it seemed like the appearance of a carbuncle on the face of a well-loved friend.

There are those who believe that Montségur is the fabled Montsalvat: the location at which the Holy Grail, the vessel fabled to contain Christ's blood, is hidden. It is now the symbolic centre of the movement which seeks independence for Occitania, the old langue d'oc-speaking region. Some modern historians and theologians suggest that while the Holy Grail might exist, it is not a vessel at all.

This explanation of the Cathar faith is taken from www.russianbooks .org:

> The dualist Cathar heretic religion has been over time both demonized and romanticized. At the peak of their existence in 13th century Europe, primarily in France and Italy, they were characterized as satanic demon worshipers. Today the Cathars are most often portrayed as pacifist vegetarian feminists; mediaeval New Agers who were ruthlessly put down by a supposedly reactionary and corrupt Catholic Church. While there are elements of some truth in these portrayals, the reality of the Cathar faith falls somewhat short of the fuzzy-warm puppy-loving reputation attributed to it.
>
> The origin of Cathar beliefs has never been precisely identified, but most historians link them to the dualist Bogomil sect in the Byzantine

> sphere. Like the Bogomils, Cathars were Christian dualists – a doctrine that has existed in various forms as long as there has been Christianity and before. The dualists attempt to confront the question of how can a God that is all powerful, merciful and good, allow monstrous evil to exist. Their response is that there must be two equally powerful gods – one good and one evil. Unlike Christianity, which demoted Satan beneath God's authority, dualists see the forces of evil and good as equally powerful.
>
> According to the Cathar approach to dualism, a good god made the heavens and the human soul, while an evil god entrapped that soul to suffer in the flesh of the human body and in material and worldly things of the earth – an evil place. Salvation, according to the Cathars, lay in the human soul's escape to the spiritual realm from its prison of flesh in the material world.
>
> http://www.russianbooks.org/montsegur/montsegur1.htm

Château de Termes is built on a high bluff and protected on three sides by deep ravines. The castle was defended by the Cathar Raymond de Termes for four months after the fall of Minerve. Following an exceptionally dry summer and autumn, the empty water tanks persuaded Raymond to consider surrender. As the crusaders prepared to occupy the castle they were met by a hail of arrows. A heavy overnight storm allowed the defenders to hold out a little longer. Later, weakened by dysentery and exposed to fire by siege engines, the defenders attempted to escape at night. They were caught and butchered.

The castle was rebuilt in the thirteenth century, one of the five castles defending the border with Spain and Aragon and known as the 'five sons of Carcassonne'. When the border moved further south, the castle was no longer needed. After being taken over by brigands who terrorised the area, it was demolished in order to curb this excess. The bill for blowing up the walls was 14,922 livres and 10 sous. Even in those days, accounting was a powerful tool of authority. Some things don't change.

Perhaps just being there, in that place of past violence, was enough to set new energies in motion. Birch moved around the piles and broken walls, offering thoughts of healing into the past. Although there was a small tourist office manned by a bored young man, no work had been done to repair the ancient pile.

As Birch walked back towards the car park, he passed a wonderfully cool-looking stream. He would have loved to put his feet in the water. The water was teeming with life. Hundreds of tiny fish were moving around. Water boatmen were skating on the surface. A snake about ten inches long, having been sunning itself on the bank, slid off its rock into the water and hid under a submerged stone. Birch assumed that the serpent had heard the vibrations in the ground created as he walked. He decided not to disturb all this and to put up with his aching feet. He stood on the bank instead, and communed meditively with the cool water. It helped him to feel better.

Birch likes the idea, in a future world, of the honouring of sacred places so that one would have to earn the right to visit. The performance of spiritual ritual would keep the vibrations at a high level in such places. Without the right to visit, people would be restricted to historical sites and learning environments.

Changing tempo and entering the realms of the mundane, Birch managed to charge his MP3 player in an Internet café. While the player was being charged in a computer, the boy responsible for the place played the most wonderful classical guitar music. It was beautiful and Birch was transfixed by it.

Back to the car and Birch found himself on the road to Prades, a base for the next leg of his exploration and work. Prades is capital of the Conflent region where the plains meet the mountains. It was first mentioned in historic documents in AD 843. It has many hours of sunshine and claims to have a micro-climate. This claim amuses Haines, a Francophile and home owner in France. It is difficult to find any town, village or bay which does not claim a pleasant micro-climate. This fine setting lured Pablo Casals to choose Prades as his second home when he left Franco's Spain. He is honoured each summer during the renowned Pablo Casals Chamber Music Festival. The photograph on the town's website shows the charming church, minus the ubiquitous cars that normally clog the town square.

Birch found the local Logis de France hotel managed by a charming, friendly young man. Birch promised to recommend this hotel upon returning to Angleterre. By mentioning it in this book, Birch has delivered on his promise.

This area of Languedoc has a distinct feeling. It is as though it is protected by a benign female energy. The surrounding mountains act as a buffer from the remainder of the Languedoc. It seems more peaceful here, less traumatised by the pain and suffering of the past, quite a different vibration. Birch spoke to a waitress in the hotel: a third-year English student. It was her vibration, an emanation from the benign female energy source, that triggered Birch's connection with the divine female energy there. He spent a little time aligning with this energy.

On two occasions during his visit, a mirror gave him a shock. Birch saw a different face, suddenly and without warning, staring back at him. The image was of a person younger than Birch, a broader face, muscular features, fair wavy hair. He dismissed it until one day he was driving through the lower reaches of the Pyrenees, towards Prades. Another person came into his consciousness and began a startling conversation.

'Are you another aspect of me?' Birch opened the conversation.

'Of course,' came the reply. 'But then we are all connected.'

'Are you in physical manifestation?' Birch continued as he drove down the winding road.

'What is physical?' The other consciousness picked up that Birch wasn't happy with his answer and so qualified it. 'I am in a different dimension or density and I was in physical manifestation during the crusades. I wanted to make a relationship, along with those around me, with Muslim intellectuals and religious leaders. The attempt failed because the kings and pope on the Christian side had too much vested interest in maintaining distance. After my life I passed into other realms.'

'Why are you contacting me?'

'You have a certain wiry, flexible strength which will help the work that would be useful for you to do.'

'Could I have more evidence of your existence?'

'What do you want, a postcard?'

'That would do nicely,' Birch continued this bizarre exchange. 'I am quite happy to work with you, but cleverer people than me have been fooled by discarnate entities. I have a lot of time on this trip for this work but I don't wish to waste time on meaningless side issues.'

Ignoring Birch's reservations, Roger, for that was his name, pronounced the French way, told Birch that it was important that he go to the château of the last white Cathar, Guillaume.

'Are you connected to the place or the person?' Birch asked.

'Guillaume is with me in this density,' came the echoing reply.

Birch was reading a book on the Gospel of Judas at the time. The Gospel of Judas was written in early Christian times but excluded from the Bible. It claims that Jesus asked Judas to betray him. There are a number of theories: the Christian one that Jesus died on the cross, several mystical ones wherein he didn't, and this Judas proposal. Birch asked the honourable Roger which theory was correct.

'They all are,' answered Roger. 'We are constantly creating our reality forward, backward and in the present moment. If fifty people saw the crucifixion or knew the causes, there would be fifty versions of it. If they each told five people of their experiences, the next day there would be 250 versions. This is how reality works in the so-called third dimension. There is no straight-line reality. We are all points of consciousness creating our past, present and future all the time. There is no one-time version of any action or event. We humans, if we did but know it, are playing with this plastic reality constantly. If we did this more consciously we would be more empowered.'

'Mmmm, I could have come to that conclusion,' Birch replied.

'I told you that I am an element of your consciousness.' Roger had the last word. He also offered the information that he had lived close to the Pyrenees when in physical form, which had made it easier for him to make initial contact with Birch.

It was a hot, 75-mile journey to the château of the last white Cathar. Guillaume had suffered death at the hands of the orthodox Christian authorities by being burned at the stake for his beliefs.

The castle had been very well renovated with sophisticated audio-visual guidance aids in several languages, including English. Birch found the tour interesting and instructive. In addition, his solar plexus was vibrating, not for the first time on this trip, as he walked around. He felt distinctly shaky. Whether this was something to do with the energies or had a purely physical cause, he never found out. However, this reaction tended to be connected with psychic events or places of power that Birch was visiting. He didn't feel it necessary to go into meditation to do any healing. It was simply enough to be there.

As Birch listened to one of the taped stories in an inner room, an internal door next to him slammed shut with a loud bang. He jumped. There was no one in either room, no wind either, just the slamming of a very large oak door. It was scary at first; goose-pimples erupted on his arms. Later, this reminded him of his experience when he had been returning from Stoke Orchard Church, years before. He had been working meditively there with ex-partner Brigid. This fascinating story is told in *So You Think We're Alone?*

As Birch rationalised this event, it came to his attention that Roger was telling him that the work was done and he could now go. Birch having done the work asked of him, Roger returned to the Englishman's consciousness briefly on a later occasion.

After the tour, Birch sat in a café recovering in the company of a glass of Orangina. His solar plexus gradually settled down and he began to feel better. He reflected that the location, as did others, contained memories that were blocking the upsurge of the new vibrations. In such a situation the energy needs to come through gently, otherwise pressure will build up from below, creating an explosive situation. This is not ideal for man or beast. Although quite how the explosive situation would manifest in this case was hidden from the traveller.

On the tour he had felt very connected to the place. Was he experiencing vicariously the events of the past, or connected to these events through his DNA? Maybe the connection was through his contact with Roger, or was there some other reason? Perhaps one day he will find out.

The following day, Birch sat in a park in Tautavel, about one hour from Prades, waiting for the Musée Archéologique to open at 11.30 am. It was 10.30 and already very hot. He wouldn't be sitting in the sun for very long. This was the first park he had seen in France. Green spaces for the public were not big on the agenda. Problems with a lack of water were certainly an issue. The grass was dry and the ground undulating. Staying there, one could do chi gong in the mornings on the flat concrete parts. Well, one could if one were so inclined.

Birch thinks one of the reasons that movement systems, such as tai chi, are not big there, at least in the towns and cities that he has visited, is that the bodies of the locals are well served in so many ways: the climate, the food, the relaxed lifestyle. People can spend much time outside, so they receive much energising force naturally. Cycling is big there. There are many cyclists' touring clubs on the road. One group of thirty souls was in Birch's hotel. The food generally is much healthier than in England, in his view.

But hold on there, Birchy. Haines remakes his point here. He needs to stand up for English food. French food may be healthier, perhaps, but Haines, like Birch, travels widely, and he believes that English food can be among the best. Its global reputation for poor quality, blandness and lack of variety is probably based on the culinary status of the 1950s, 60s and 70s. Food then was not an adventure to be relished, but a necessity that had to be endured.

And another thing. French restaurants are not as marvellous as the French think they are: good value, yes; world quality, no. English restaurants are much better than the French claim them to be. But then again, as Birch warns, Haines has a passion for cheeseburgers. Enough said?

Anyway, back to the park. It sits in a bowl surrounded by a semi-circle of wonderful rock formations. A smelly, scummy river runs behind, or rather sits behind because, at the time of Birch's visit, no water flowed. The two rocky prominences at the top of the surrounding hills represented to Birch a crab, Cancer symbol, on the left; on the right, a physically very powerful watching angel. The two figures seemed to be protecting the bowl of land below, in which Birch was standing. The female energy was alive and well in Tautavel. The war memorial was especially interesting. It was the first time he had seen a female form on such a monument.

Birch reflected on the door slamming in the castle the previous day. He now felt much happier with the contact, less threatened and suspicious. He reasoned that if he viewed the contact as part of himself and filtered any information through his intuitive self, then he would not be fooled.

When not in a positive situation vis-à-vis psychic communication, Birch felt a lowering and depressing of the spirit. This was a warning sign to him. One reason for this lowering of energies may have been because the work at the castle had marked the exact halfway point of this journey, in time at least.

Birch spent an interesting hour in the museum at Tautavel. This one was also very well supported by audio-visual as well as conventional displays. There was a sheet in English for a framework background: very useful for Birch's limited French.

Tautavel is a small town of 800 souls in the Roussillon region. In a wine-growing area, it sits in the foothills of the Pyrenees. It became famous when ancient human remains were found in a cave near the town in 1971. 'Tautavel man', so dubbed, was one of the most ancient sets of remains found in Europe up to that time. The bones are said to be 450,000 years old. Prehistoric humans exploited this area as a seasonal hunting ground, most likely. Tautavel man is said to be an ancestor of Neanderthal man and exhibits characteristics of European *Homo erectus*. The rock in this area is limestone and the caves were created by running water. The caves provided shelter for our early ancestors.

Much later, when revising this text before publication, Birch received a profound intuitive shock. He became aware that it was in this place that he had been incarnated, for the first time, in human form. He had, indeed, been born into a *Homo erectus* body.

Some Pleiadian commentators claim that each hominid grouping was a creation of stellar beings. The museum led Birch to ponder whether humanity was now on the cusp of a similar creative process. In his view, *Homo sapiens* has reached the end of the road in social development terms. The Earth can't and won't sustain this abuse, this lack of working in harmony.

There are a number of possibilities. The Earth and its inhabitants will remain. Some mystics are saying that old animal forms, such as the dodo, are returning in remote areas. Animals will get on with their development without man's involvement. A new consciousness is bursting forth among the mystics, environmentalists and the young. We will see what the future brings. It would be pleasant to be here on Earth to see at least some of the positive changes come to pass.

While at Tautavel, Birch felt that he had released something, some blockage, but he didn't know what it was. Perhaps this was connected to his *Homo erectus* life. The town and immediate area had something special energetically. It seemed as though he were in France plus. If Birch ever spent some considerable time in France, he would be happy to base himself there.

The Albigensian Crusade, the cause of the destroyed castles in which Birch was working, was a twenty-year military campaign, 1209–1229. It was initiated by the Catholic Church to eliminate the heresy of the Cathars in the Languedoc. Pope Innocent III declared a crusade, offering bribes of land to any noblemen willing to take up arms.

Birch has an alternative version of the Albigensian Crusade. In his version, a new and charismatic Cathar leader arose at the beginning of the incursion by the crusaders. He realised that the attempt to defend the land by withdrawing into the castles was doomed: a self-destruct strategy. So he developed guerrilla tactics. He set up camps high in the mountains, well stocked with men, arms and fuel and close to a water supply. He fought only at night. Each night he captured or killed a limited number of invaders. In silence, he took the same number each night. The Japanese used the same psychological strategy during World War II. They would creep into the Allied camps at night and slit the throat of one guard only. Each night was the same. Imagine the tremendous psychological pressure on the opposing side. *Will I be the next victim?* This would be extremely unsettling, frightening and destabilising, shattering to morale.

As the crusaders penetrated deeper into Languedoc territory, the individual troops were worried that the number of night deaths would increase. They wouldn't withdraw, of course. So the pressure increased. In addition, the invaders were worried that for every citizen they killed, ten of their number would die at night. For every animal they stole, every house they burned, a like retribution would occur. This was another promise and pressure from the defenders. The defenders also kidnapped and held for ransom any senior member of the invading force, no matter what their role.

The invaders progressed and the defenders carried out their promise, scrupulously keeping count and letting the invaders know that they were keeping count. With no withdrawal the pressure on the attackers increased. The quantities were doubled, trebled. Daylight attacks were carried out to vary the tactics. Any ordinary soldiers that were captured were spared being killed or tortured. They were interrogated, without pain, for information concerning the attacking force. Those that could be so persuaded were invited to join the defenders in freedom and honour, without pressure to change their religion.

The defenders had to be prepared to fight this sort of war for years. If the attackers used a scorched-earth approach, then the defenders would have to do the same, burning and destroying the baggage trains of the invaders. The defenders set up food dumps so that those citizens forced out of their livelihood by the attackers could be cared for.

Attempts were made to spread the conflict to the attackers' home territory. The defenders first sent spies and then tried to recruit local dissidents. Next, utilising good intelligence, they raided the homes and lands of the leaders of the attacking force. After years, the attackers might have been prepared to negotiate. The Russians in Afghanistan, the Americans in Vietnam and Iraq found themselves in unwinnable wars. The crusaders had to be persuaded to think the same of this conflict. This is creating history backwards. Why not? Reality is ever expanding, forwards and backwards. As we've said, there is no straight line from then until now, unless that is what we choose to create.

Seeing all these broken castles created these thoughts in Birch's mind. If one side sets up strong, fixed forces, then the other side will rise to counteract them. Flexible strategies and tactics are far more powerful with potential for movement. With a fixed system there is no movement. That is why the Christian religion is dying on its feet, or so Birch believes. It is not moving with the consciousness of the people. The French set up the Maginot Line before World War II with very powerful guns, emplacements and barriers. In 1940, the Germans simply went round these defences through Belgium.

Back to the Albigensian Crusade. The attackers, led by King Louis IX and the pope, would want negotiation like a hole in the head. They had invested their reputations on this misadventure.

Message from Roger: 'I like your version of the crusade.'

Before negotiation, the king and the pope, just like current politicians, must have become heartily sick of the cost and the damage to their reputations. This is a prerequisite. When this time comes, the negotiation must include an offer. The offer: withdraw all your forces and we will allow the introduction of papal and king's representatives into the province. They would be given ostensible power with a governing role and titles. Thereby, the king and the pope could claim to have won the war to their subjects.

The real power, however, would remain with the Languedoc hierarchy. They would continue to practise their religion, albeit giving it a lower profile in terms of external politics. The Languedoc hierarchy would give nominal leadership to the king but would keep their own day-to-day power. Effectively, they would run things as before without interfering with papal representatives, perhaps even giving the king an annual tithe. No one would appear the victim. There need be no losers in the long term.

That version would play back to the present. Birch brought it into consciousness and sent it back through time. Now it is a reality in the thirteenth century. The events and repercussions would now work their way forward, rippling through time. Amazing what you can create in thought when you have time and inspiration.

The idea really came to a head after Birch read some of the history of the Château d'Aguilar that he visited. Having been defeated in the Albigensian Crusade, the count of the castle gave it up to the king. He then fought bravely in the crusade; Birch assumed that this was in Palestine. He was awarded the castle back as a reward. Ten years later, the count sold the castle to the king. Is this good long-term planning and business or what? 'Stay flexible and get in a good bargaining position' was, and is, the name of the game. This is no different from the practices of today.

In 1210, the château was invaded and occupied by Simon de Montfort, whose soldiers took the owner, Raymond de Ternes, and imprisoned him in a dungeon in Carcassonne. The castle subsequently served no military purpose until Raymond's son, Oliver de Ternes, took it back in a brief revolt against the crusaders thirty years later. Aguilar became a refuge for many Cathar knights and lords and, in 1246, a point for supervision of the Aragonese border. When the border was moved south, the castle lost its importance; it was abandoned in 1569 and is now listed as a *monument historique* by the French Ministry of Culture.

The real story of the Albigensian Crusade is one of poor military performance, attempts to fight and defend from fixed positions, and then inevitable collapse, changing the religious, political and social context of the Languedoc for ever. It struck Birch how badly the defending Albigensian forces had fought in open battle against the crusading invaders. The castle defence strategy had only occurred after the open field defeats. Had they fought more effectively, the results might have been very different.

So play it long; the game of life, that is. Birch is reminded of the Pilgrims' Walk in Chartres Cathedral. Two steps forward, one step back. This can be a metaphor for life. Sometimes a backward step is the only way. That is fine as long as the eventual goal is kept in mind and in focus.

Birch's next visit was to Perpignan and he was not overly impressed. There was not much there for a 'crazy mystic'. Well, not this one anyway. He bought a present in the Moroccan market bang in the middle of a crumbling ghetto. This reminded him of the ghetto in Béziers. Vibrant trading and energy pervaded the square, with not much sign of white people apart from himself and the wary police on the periphery. There was no street lighting. Birch wouldn't want to walk through there late at night. Perhaps he was being over-sensitive to a strange place and culture.

Birch walked into Perpignan Cathedral as a baptism was taking place. He sat at the back. Everything was said by the priest, who was dressed all in white. The parents, children and guests were passive observers apart from one bout of clapping near the end. This was an interesting view of the religion and the adherents' relationship with it.

As he sat there marvelling at the soaring vaulting and curved panels of the ceiling, he wondered if the original planners of the building would have settled for what went on there now. Would they be happy? Perhaps they were planning a deeper, more mystical outcome for the ceremonies in the buildings; perhaps not. He wondered if those who now occupied or owned these wonderful gifts to the spirit had any real understanding of their forebears. Perhaps they were so far into their own present perspective that this version of the past was not in their consciousness.

In the final analysis, perhaps it does not matter. Everyone who respects this place, and other places, will have their own perspectives, bring their own energy and make their own contributions to the vibrations.

Travels Alone Part 2

The sea, mountains, castles and more – Collioure to Chartres

The time had arrived for our traveller to recharge his near-exhausted batteries. He had the opportunity to go to the coast for two days to honour and work with the water energy, and to take a break from driving for a while. It was a very calm evening, quite cool with a slight breeze coming off the mountains. He would miss this climate when his eventual return to England came about. *Tant pis*! OK, back into the trusty mechanical chariot.

Just south of Perpignan, Collioure is close to the Spanish border. Glory be; a parking space presented itself right outside the hotel. There were ten spaces for thirty beds. Initially Birch went into the car park. It was full. As he drove round, a car pulled out. Fortune favoured the Brit.

Birch relished the Mediterranean. He relaxed on the beach, enjoyed the water energy, swam and communed with the element. The water was clear and clean. The little public beach felt quite cosy. There was a flat concrete area over to his left. If he was really ambitious he would get up early, go down for a swim and then maybe do a little chi gong. Simply relaxing, enjoying the shade: this was top quality chill-out. As someone said nearby (in English), the water was not warm; it was refreshing.

France is such a country of contrasts. On the one hand, everyone eats healthily outside; on the other, dogs leave a considerable mess on the street and no one cleans it up. Does anyone get sick? Who knows?

Birch was sitting in a very narrow pedestrian alley, eating a midday meal. The food was nothing better than average, unlike some restaurants in France. People promenaded up and down so he inevitably started people-watching: all shapes and sizes and different shades of brown. In Birch's case, the patches of pink had the odd patch of brown.

Two vehicles drove through the alley. Both had just enough space. The second car touched the back of a woman's chair as she sat in the restaurant. No one seemed concerned. C'est la France.

Next on the agenda, a tour of the building that passed for a castle, providing the *pichet de vin rouge* and food allowed his free movement. The people walking past looked hot and tired and he was glad he'd stopped for a meal.

What is it about males that dictates that when they get on a pebble beach they have to skim pebbles over the surface of the water? Ducks and drakes. Would that be a function of testosterone, or do they just need something to do? Maybe sitting and being is not enough? Recently, Birch heard on the radio that the world record for skimming a stone on water had been broken with fifty-two skims. Ah well, Birch supposed that in these times there were world records for almost everything.

It was a pleasant late evening on the beach. The crowds had dispersed back to hotels, food and wine. The beach was very relaxing. The Knights Templar 'passed through' there, according to the official guide. By that they must mean the knights stayed for a very short time. However, a warning. Birch and Haines take official guides with a substantial pinch of salt. This extract is taken from Birch's contemporary notes: 'I have rarely (if ever) come across a city, town or village, coastal or inland, lowland or mountainous, which does not claim to have a micro-climate. Furthermore, this micro-climate will claim to elevate the location in question in some very special way from all others in the locality, department, country or rest of Europe.' Sound familiar?

Then there's *la cuisine*. It is not possible to find any human settlement of any size, anywhere, which does not claim to have a culinary speciality which is the very best of its kind in the world. Well, good for them. There can be no harm in local pride.

A TV chef, who is French but owns a restaurant in London, tells this story which exemplifies the difference between French and British attitudes to food. His father, who started the business, would import food from France by buying it and bringing it in himself. He was always very careful to ensure the correct forms were completed for UK Customs and Excise, which would otherwise confiscate and destroy it. Much later, he exported food the other way, taking exotic British food such as wild salmon and grouse to his restaurant in France. Again he was very careful to ensure the correct forms were completed for French Customs, otherwise he knew the French customs officials would have confiscated it and eaten it.

Back to Knights Templar: Birch could picture the dhow-type sailboats in the harbour bringing goods, information, troops and people. This place had been an important port for the Templars at one time, he felt. It was so easy to take oneself back to those times with the backdrop of the spectacular Templar castle overlooking the beach and sea.

It was the second day at Collioure. It was still early and Birch was relaxing, having risen at 7.10 to swim in the little cove he'd discovered the previous day. No one else was around, apart from a few fishermen ambling home. Again the water was refreshing. He paddled around for fifteen or twenty minutes… great! Spying a flat piece of concrete nearby, he relaxed into dragon's gate (chi gong movements) and tai chi chuan. Just as he finished, the bin men arrived. The peace was gone. No matter, he'd had a great start to the day.

He returned to the hotel just in time for breakfast at 8 am and found himself alone. Orange juice, tea, cereal, croissants, a roll: a very enjoyable repast. He bought two English newspapers for entertainment and enlightenment. A walk around the bay, a *café au lait* at a pavement café, an English newspaper, a meander around the shops: a mystic on his holiday.

During the previous night, as he had done the Bruce Frantzis water meditation, Birch had received a flash, a vision of men sitting, straight-backed, either in or next to water. He had perceived that there were water lilies also. The intuitive impression had suggested that these were beings in another density (dimension) either working with or having responsibility for the water energy.

Birch was enjoying the breeze coming off the sea: a calming experience. He sensed that the water energy, when properly used, could be of great benefit in cooling down conflicts without suppression, which, as the Yugoslavian break-up has shown, only delays the final madness and slaughter.

He was feeling that the reason he had come here was to experience a pleasant foil to the previous activities and places: a relative quiet between two storms, energetically speaking. There seems to be a deep psychological contract at the human level. We work and then we reward ourselves with play, e.g. holidays. It seems so ingrained that it would need an enormous trauma at the level of the race to change it, hopefully to make it more transcendental, developmental. On the face of things, we are stuck in a loop without the imagination or the desire to progress out of it. What to do next? Perhaps there are underlying changes. At the level of the race the changes are difficult to perceive. Perhaps the answer is to concentrate on changing ourselves, then our changes might influence the whole. As someone once said, it is better to light a candle than curse the darkness. It may be that the underlying vibrations are creating changes in the psyche of humanity which can transmit to the level of consciousness that will change reality.

The wind had strengthened during the early evening. The sun was still strong. It was a combination of the sea (water), wind (air) and sun (fire). When invoking these three elements, together with the earth element for magical purposes, perhaps it would be best to ask which element would be most favourable in the circumstance that presents itself. It is important to always remember to make an act or speak a word of gratitude during or after such work.

Invoking the energy of the four elements is a powerful magical tool. This is sometimes supplemented with the fifth element which can be equated with the chi for the Chinese, prana for the Indians. It has many names. Birch wonders if humanity is sensitive enough to ask the elements, in an appropriate manner, for help, and if the elements are gracious enough for energy to be given directly for the normal needs of human society.

Collioure has been a key location for centuries because of its opening to the Mediterranean and the two bays which are easily defended. Phoenicians, Romans and Greeks travelled there and left a rich archaeological heritage. In AD 673 Collioure was occupied by Wamba, king of the Visigoths. He named the place Caucoliberis.

The Château Royal was built on Roman foundations and is the centre of Collioure fortifications. Most of it was built during the reign of the counts of Roussillon and kings of Aragon between 1344 and 1376. Later, the Majorcan court lived in the castle. It was then occupied by the Spanish until 1642 when it fell into French hands. Vauban had the outer city wall built and the rampart flattened. Today it's a car park. In 1951 the castle was sold to the General Council of the department of the Pyrenees-Orientales.

It was time for Birch to move on. He drove up into the lower Pyrenees, to Amélie-les-Bains, a spa town in the Pyrenees-Orientales department. It was named after Queen Amelia, wife of Louis Philippe I. The traffic was painfully slow but not heavy. Classical piano music played on the radio, and the feminine energy of the sea slowly turned into the masculine of the mountains, creating a magical atmosphere. This reminded Birch of the journey made with Hazel and Marissa in Hawaii, and that last journey to the magical place past the mountains when he became aware of the male spiritual twins that joined the trio. This incident is recounted in *So You Think We're Alone?*

A session in the thermal baths fascinated Birch. He immersed himself in a pool of hot water; jets in the wall pushed out streams of water which, when his body was pushed against them, acted as a massage. The jets played up and down. Birch was advised to avoid the chest and belly area because the water pressure was so intense. This water massage lasted for maybe fifteen minutes. Next came what could best be described as a mud bath. It comprised pink liquid so thick that it was impossible to sink; very relaxing, a bit like floating in the Dead Sea. Soft music played in the background. Birch was there for about twenty minutes, regretting that the experience didn't last longer. It was so relaxing and therapeutic. He repaired to a café after the excellent physical experience. It was good, so much so that he considered going for the forty-five-minute session the following day. His skin felt so smooth. This was a real lift. He had been feeling a little down just before the spa session. It was mentally tough making this journey in a country where English wasn't the first language. When Birch launched into his limited French, sometimes people thought him more linguistically capable than he really was. That was when the whole thing would fall down. With his limited learning through studying abilities, he would need to live there for some time to acquire a better grasp of the language. Occasionally he felt a little isolated. He felt better after the water jet massage and mud bath. It had lifted his spirits. The next day, the spa drew him back for a repeat dose, plus a massage. The temperature was very comfortable and the air clear, being so good close to the mountains. What with the air, the waters, the sun, Birch was building up more health and vitality.

The French do love their dogs, all shapes and sizes. This town did seem better in the *merde* on the pavement issue. Birch didn't see any. That was very unusual on this trip.

That night Birch had a dream. He was in a house with other people when aircraft-type spaceships flew overhead, very fast, one after the other. Birch knew that they were alien and he felt concerned. The spaceships then flew very much closer as though preparing to land. In the next scene, Birch and other humans were lining up, or being lined up, in rows. Birch placed himself at the end of one of the rows. In the next scene, the humans, including Birch, were near an isolated stone church. The land around was covered in a mist-type cloud. Suddenly, it cleared and close to the church a very futuristic building appeared. Birch knew that it had been constructed by the aliens. His impression was that they had demolished human buildings in order to make the space for it. In the next scene, an alien in human form was standing in front of Birch. She was making pulling movements with her arms. Birch suddenly realised that she was showing him how to use the bell-rope of the church. This last point, Birch felt, was about being influenced regarding how best to utilise the existing communication potentials in the third dimension. Birch believed that this information came from his inner-self. The other parts of the dream were about how humanity was increasingly being influenced by cosmic and extra-terrestrial sources.

Before leaving Amélie, Birch had planned a particular route that would have taken him past some interesting ancient stone circles. Having missed them, or been unable to find them, he eventually drew up close to Quéribus. But why this place in particular? He had not planned to visit and work in this château. Quéribus, like many other châteaux, is perched on a high crag. It was the last of the Cathar strongholds to fall in 1255. It is probably the best preserved of the border castles, and the most inaccessible.

These romantic sites are not only Cathar castles. They are memorials to a kingdom that never was, a culturally united realm of Catalans and Occitans. The splitting of Charlemagne's empire between his three feuding sons in the ninth century ensured that the kingdom never became a reality. Instead Languedoc became a prize to be fought over by Aragon and France, with France the ultimate winner after the Albigensian Crusade. Today the memory is kept alive by the small number of Occitan militants and the more politically powerful Catalans.

A queue had formed at the entrance. An English-speaking young couple had insufficient funds to enter the castle and were discussing their plight with the non-English-speaking receptionist in the payment booth. The French people behind the couple, bless them, waited patiently. After a few minutes Birch broke the impasse, stepped up to the mark and provided the extra euros. The couple stepped through the entrance without any sign of gratitude. *Tant pis*!

Birch felt the need to conduct a healing meditation within Quéribus's château wall. In that open space, and with no crowds of tourists, a young woman entered the space and stood a little apart from him. There were just the two of them. Birch realised that the energy needed this male-female bi-polarity. He was pretty sure that the female was unaware of the healing going on. No matter. She was playing her part, unaware as she was. After a few minutes, her male partner appeared and the magic was cut. The work was complete.

Significantly, Birch wasn't able to do any significant healing at Peyrepertuse, his originally planned destination; he was too tired or it wasn't necessary. He visited the castle and left without performing any healing. Bizarrely, he can remember nothing about it. It is almost as though he went through it in a dream. It may be that the following day's unbalanced physical feeling was a reaction to whatever Birch sensed during this unconscious visit. Perhaps he hadn't needed to be there at all?

The next morning Birch made a slow start; he didn't feel so good. Perhaps it was the large amount of sun he had absorbed the previous day or perhaps his diet had not been controlled over the last couple of days. Perhaps the energies in his body were unbalanced by his work and negative stuff had surfaced. Or maybe it was the region, or a combination of things. Sometimes one can overdo the psychic work and the body will react by becoming slightly sick. Still, no serious damage was done, so it was just a recovery period that was needed.

Time to move on, this time to Foix, another town that Birch had not intended to visit in his original plan. He seemed pushed to visit it by driving a route not intended. As he arrived, the castle in the middle of the town loomed over the surroundings. As Birch drove towards it he felt the energy in his body move to a higher vibration. If he had been a musician he might have described it as an octave rise. *Ah! This is why I am here.*

Birch booked into the local Logis hotel. Suitably refreshed, he walked around the town to familiarise himself with his surroundings. He visited a large Catholic church near the hotel. It was a very impressive building. As he walked in the organ was playing Bach's *Toccata and Fugue in D minor*. Birch slipped quietly into the back row, transfixed by the wonderful music. People were gathering in the church, obviously for a service. Someone was lighting candles on the altar. Realisation dawned in Birch's consciousness concerning the importance of the divine in all our lives. He had been completely focussed on energy work and, until then, had completely forgotten the place and meaning of deep spiritual practice and belief. He realised that living the spiritual was vital, not simply being aware of it. Listening to the wonderful music in that impressive place brought it back to him with a bang. When the last strains of the music died away, Birch walked quietly out of the church before the service began. Sometimes spiritual upliftment is more important to one's being than eating.

Walking down the street away from the church, he saw an advertisement for *Brokeback Mountain*, the film about cowboys who have a gay relationship. The ad said something like, 'The great film of the year'. Jaqueline saw it and said that it was nothing special. So why did it have all this attention if the film was fairly modest in quality?

One reason may be because it is an icon-breaker. It broke the myth, or at least challenged it, of cowboys being the model of the macho culture. As Jacques Rangasamy said, 'Those that would change or destroy a society try to break its icons.' The example that he gave was that of the 2001 attack on the Twin Towers. The myth/icon of the unbreakable financial/business/material society in the USA was very badly shaken. This is an extremely interesting subject for further thought. Are these icon breakers always extremely negative, as in the case of 9/11, or can they be challenging in more positive ways? Perhaps *Brokeback Mountain* was challenging the polarised male/female role perspective in Western thought. Perhaps governments and other powers utilise icon breaking in a more subtle way. Staying open to this idea and looking for examples would be good, Birch thought to himself.

Sitting on a bench and watching the world go by reinforced what a society of doers humanity was to Birch. Those in the Western world work like crazy then have to play like crazy as the antidote. Most people do not address the internals of their beings unless or until crisis hits and they are forced to consider this area. This accounts for all the mental, psychological stress we see around us, Birch thinks.

Perhaps this society is in a crisis of being. Perhaps this society needs some more icon breaking for it to move into balance. What is an icon? It is an exemplary model of human action, behaviour or material structure. Perhaps the mass consciousness, in order to break out, can initiate icon breaking. Some examples of attempted icon breaking that didn't work: the hippie movement, the green political movement (arguably). Maybe they are steps on the way?

During his first evening in Foix, Birch went to the town square where there was some energetic dancing taking place. People whirled, twisted and turned, using and creating energy by their movements and their happiness. It was such a positive scene. Birch just sat, watched and absorbed.

A young woman broke off from the dancing and stood just in front of him. After a couple of minutes she turned, looked at him and then came and sat next to him. She said nothing; neither did Birch. His French certainly wasn't up to an in-depth conversation and he definitely didn't want to enter a situation in which he couldn't communicate effectively.

He looked around, seeming to be the only unaccompanied male in the square. So it wasn't his charm and personality that were of interest, only his apparent availability.

He might have said, *Désolé, mademoiselle, je suis mariée.* Birch didn't bother; he just sat quietly and watched the dancing. Eventually the young woman gave up and moved away. This incident reminded Birch of Henry Allingham, at the time Britain's oldest man at 112 years and survivor of World War I. He was asked for the secret of his great age and why his mind had remained so sharp. 'Keep your eyes and ears open, and say nowt,' was his reply. Birch had taken his advice.

He had an interesting visit to the castle at Foix the next day. The town had been an independent entity from 1001 to 1290. There was plenty of explanatory information on the well-preserved château. Because it had been used for different purposes throughout history, it was not a ruin like so many in which Birch had worked.

It had been a prison and bore witness to the extreme tension and terror between Catholics and Protestants in the seventeenth century. In one horrible event, Protestants had been dropped to their deaths from a high cliff. This immediately brought to mind Birch's own discomfort when peering down to the ground from a great height. So much so that, when peering over the wall of the battlements, he felt electrical shocks going up the backs of his legs, as well as panic gripping his intestines. He clung to the wall as waves of nausea washed over him. Was this the reprise of his death on a castle wall when speared to death in a previous life? This story is fully told in *So You Think We're Alone?* Perhaps in another lifetime he had been thrown to his death and this irrational fear was a reaction to that terrible event.

OK, so Birch is a bit of a wimp when it comes to heights.

So this introduced our traveller to two potential healing needs at this site: first, the suffering of prisoners, and second, the suffering of

Protestants, and possibly some Catholics, in the religious war. There was also another war that scarred the psyche of the place and peoples: the Hundred Years' War between France and England.

During the afternoon Birch returned to the castle for a guided tour in English, after which he found a quiet spot on top of one of the towers. There he meditated. During the course of this meditation our trusty mystic was joined briefly by a young woman. He was reminded of his meditation at Quéribus, when a young woman had been there as he had conducted the healing meditation. In both cases it appeared a balance of the male and female energy was needed for maximum effect. So the work at Foix Château was done. Again Birch had been guided there rather than pre-selecting it as part of the tour.

The next day was to be the last with the rental car. It had taken care of our traveller so well he couldn't have done what he had without it. He was grateful to it and the cosmic for such a gift. Another thank you was for his humble sandals. He had worn nothing else since arriving there, all those hills to climb and stones to climb over. Both had been great. A further thank you went to Logis Hotels where he had stayed most of the time, modest and within his price range, another support to him for which he was truly grateful.

That evening Birch sensed a real end of term, even end of school year, this fourth and last day in Foix. Content as he made his last walk around the inner old town, he wondered if this might even be the end of the Clive Birch project. He was told, pretty strongly, *No.* Birch says that he would like to be around for winter equinox 2012 to see what happens and play his part in events leading up to it.

In his end of term feeling, Birch drove from Foix to Saissac, which is now just a pile of old stones really. Some reparation work was going on and two rooms had been restored. Birch walked around, opening out to the healing energies. He entered a church which had been quite tastefully restored, not over the top as some he had seen. It was a very pleasant atmosphere in there, quiet and peaceful. As he walked out he wondered how many churches he had still to visit in his life's adventures, in other lives as well as this.

The next part of the journey was by train from Carcassonne to change at Bordeaux, change again at Paris Montparnasse and finally arrive at Chartres. So there he was again: another visit to Bordeaux, however brief. He'd thought he had finished with that city after the visit to his father's grave and crash site that features in Haines and Birch's previous book.

At this point, Birch wondered if all this travelling, healing and being in these places was of benefit. Wouldn't it be nice to have a progress report from cosmic sources?

The Carcassonne to Bordeaux train service arrived one minute early. Take note, British railway system. The French rail service, in Birch's experience, is far superior to the British. It is well run and travellers feel they are receiving a service. It is, of course, heavily subsidised by the state.

Birch stood at Bordeaux station waiting for the Paris train. The platforms and seating were crowded with people waiting for connections. There was no space to sit or rest. What to do? No problem. Our man faced the oncoming track and dropped into the chi gong stance to relax and enter another conscious space: knees bent, feet facing forward, back straight, coccyx tucked in, arms and shoulders relaxed, head up, gaze relaxed, into another time space, cut out the mêlée around.

After a few minutes his awareness was breached by someone watching him on the left. He couldn't see the watcher, just sense their presence and energy. Birch ignored the apparent interest. After a short interval he sensed the watcher move in a semi-circle and stand in front of him. It was a blue-shirted, nondescript man. His body language was the antithesis of chi gong man. He stood stiff-legged, arms locked across his chest, hands under his armpits, chin thrust forward. His stare towards Birch was challenging, intrusive. He seemed to be asking, *Why are you standing like that, you crazy foreigner?*

The two men stood for some time, facing each other approximately ten feet apart, Monsieur le Blue Shirt in his aggressive stance facing Birch, Birch in his chi gong stance, eyes unfocussed, not connecting with the other man. Yet there was a connection, for a brief moment, that felt timeless. All the while, people swirled around the two men. Were these busy people aware of the little drama playing itself out between the two standing men: the chaos around the still centre? Birch neither knew nor cared. He was in his internal world.

After an indeterminate time M. le Blue Shirt stepped back and away from the energy field created by both men in their separate spaces. Perhaps he was disconcerted or simply bored. For a short time Monsieur leaned against a post, still watching. At last he moved away and out of Birch's vision. The latter remained in stance until the Paris train arrived; it had been a bizarre experience.

On the train from Paris to Chartres Birch met with a number of the Temple Study Group from back home in Cheltenham. It was just great to be talking English again, especially to likeminded people. Birch had forgotten how much he enjoyed using his own language in a coherent fashion.

This trip brought to mind the place of the trickster in spiritual and mystical living. The trickster is the use of humorous or slightly shocking events or people to bring into our awareness those elements of knowledge that we aren't absorbing any other way. This trickster energy or person invariably manifests when we are least expecting it. Sometimes it is a last resort wake-up call. This energy manifests in the tarot pack in the form of the fool.

So it was with some surprise, on a previous trip to Chartres, that a number of the Temple Study Group encountered such energy on a walk around midnight. As they walked towards the cathedral they were met by a clown in full regalia: big coloured shoes, whitened face, striped baggy clothes, the lot. There was much hilarity at this apparent chance meeting with the archetypal figure of the trickster, and debate as to what this meeting at this bizarre time of day meant. The clown only spoke French, so verbal communication wasn't possible.

The following morning a number of the group, including Birch, went to the cathedral grounds to perform a *salutation to the dawn* ritual and then into the cathedral maze: the Pilgrims' Walk. Birch walked the maze twice. The first time he completed at a normal slow walk. On the second occasion he was taken into a different psychological and spiritual space. He lost track of time. As Jacques Rangasamy said, the maze is a microcosm of our life, so completing the Pilgrims' Walk means concentrating on the now. The immediacy and rhythm of it gave concentrative powers which helped Birch to temporarily leave objective consciousness and turn inwards. Any distractions, such as people crossing in front or overtaking in the maze, he perceived not as a distraction but as a microcosm of life.

Before the walk, Jacques had talked to the group about the insights he had concerning its purpose and symbolism. There was a direct geometric relationship between the maze and the rose window above. One could lie on the other and create a perfect fit. The rose window was representative of the sun, and the maze of the moon. The latter represented the lunar cycle and life. The number of stones in the maze was equal to the number of days in the human gestation cycle. The constant forward or backward direction of the walking replicated the forward and backward movement in our lives. The backward steps represented the inner conflicts that we all have to deal with in order to progress, so it was a microcosm of life. The combined width of one forward and one backward step on the maze's pathway was twenty-eight inches, equal to the number of days in the lunar cycle.

Jacques suggested, once having made the walk, standing in the middle of the maze and making the connection with the rose window above: as above, so below.

Jacques encapsulates so much in his discourses to the fortunate listeners that Birch tends to feel almost buried in the psychic truths. Perhaps it is best just to let the whole thing be absorbed at other levels rather than attempt to make intellectual sense of it all. It is, after all, an initiatory experience primarily. Birch spent some time sitting in front of the cathedral: an overwhelming initiatory experience in itself. What Jacques was doing was focussing the group's mental, psychic, spiritual attention on this initiation instrument to give them some tools to move forward without being buried in the enormity of it all.

Birch says that, for him, the maze walk is a microcosm of our physical life. So those people who walk across the maze-walkers, or don't give the maze sufficient respect, or the kids that are running around, need to be treated as though they are part of the pattern rather than being resisted or resented. For isn't that the way that life works? Life is not a result of a planned pattern. We each pull into existence those elements that are important for our growth at any given time, for apparent positive or apparent negative experiences. That weekend was about taking the group on one step from the previous year's Temple Study Group retreat, which gave those present the information about the place of the spirit and the soul in this initiatory journey we call life. That step forward is about starting to live that reality.

One of the geniuses of Chartres was that it was built on hermetic principles as an initiation instrument. Christians could, and can, take over, look after, ignore the deeper meanings and vibrations in the place. They perform their own rituals. This leaves the deeper aspects of initiation to the now burgeoning numbers of mystics and seekers. These take away their requirements and, in return, leave their own energetic contribution.

Birch has been troubled by the hostility of the Catholic adherents to the maze-walkers. They display a lack of tolerance, a grumpiness, as they pass to and from their worship. He always thought it strange that the church authorities permitted the mystically-based maze-walkers to continue their activities, although the chains were removed to allow access to the maze on only one weekend each year. Many of the maze walkers were pilgrims and could be adherents of the Christian faith. Later, Birch discovered that since the revolution, cathedrals in France had been owned by the state rather than the Catholic Church. So this was why this practice was allowed to continue. It was a decision by the state and not the church.

Birch subsequently discovered that a portable copy of the Chartres labyrinth, on canvas, was laid out in Gloucester Cathedral each August. He was thus able to walk the labyrinth more regularly, experiencing a heightened exhilarating consciousness. Drunvalo Melchizedek, in *The Ancient Secret of the Flower of Life* vol. 1, is able to put into words succinctly what the labyrinth can do for one:

> a sevenfold labyrinth. This is found all over the world – everywhere from China to Tibet to England to Ireland to Peru to the American Indians ... You'll find this labyrinth on the floors of many of the churches in Europe. The same form is on stone walls everywhere. It must have been of great importance to ancient mankind. There are seven regions in it, which relates to the torus and to the beating of the human heart. Later on I'll be talking about the ancient Druid mystery school on the Island of Avalon in England. To get to the top of the hill there, you have to walk through the same labyrinth, going back and forth through this motion. While I was in England, I spoke to Richard Feather Anderson, who is an author and expert on labyrinths ... He'd discovered that when you walk through it [a labyrinth], you are forced to move through different states of consciousness, giving you a very specific experience ...
>
> When you walk this labyrinth, unless you block the experience, you will automatically move through these changes. Even if you don't know about these things, you will go through the experiences anyway. People all over the world have found this to be true and it is true that those changes did happen for me. He [Mr Anderson] feels that this particular labyrinth is related to the shape of the Holy Grail and to its secret knowledge. From my experience this feels right, but I am keeping an open mind. I don't know about this yet; it may be true.

On the latest occasion that Birch walked the labyrinth in Gloucester, he was confronted with one of his own demons. As he moved around, he cut out from his awareness the two children who played in this sacred space. Their raucous screeching reached such a pitch that Birch felt compelled to turn to the mother who watched in silence, remonstrating with the words, 'This is a place of contemplation and prayer, not a children's playground.' He then continued his walk, fighting the rising anger in his throat. Mother and children departed. It took a couple of minutes for Birch to regain his composure. As said before, walking the labyrinth is a microcosm of life experiences.

It is well documented in these books that Birch is not the greatest friend of Roman Catholicism. However, in one regard he does hold respect for this sect of the Christian faith. He experiences a greater degree of reverence by visitors in Catholic places of worship compared to those of Protestantism. An example of this is in his perambulations around the labyrinths of Chartres and Gloucester. In the former, there is an air of respect by those who are obviously tourists. In the latter, many treat the sacred building as though it is merely another leisure place and playground for children, to be visited without giving much thought to its true purpose.

Birch feels that Chartres Cathedral will work at whatever level the aspirant or potential aspirant is at at any given time. The only thing that is necessary is for the aspirant to be open to positive, spiritual influence.

So there they were, English mystics working in the French heartland. This belies George Bernard Shaw's quotation, 'The English are not a spiritual people so they invented cricket to give themselves a perspective of eternity.' GBS was an Irishman, 1856–1950, living at a time when his country was still mired in the business of empire; the Republic of Ireland came into existence within his lifetime. This may help to explain his acerbic and faulty dig in the metaphorical ribs of the English.

OK, time for Birch to return to base Angleterre; time had run out. Back to dear old Blighty, this time through the Tunnel.

There is a misconception in England that the French don't like the English. Nothing could be further from the truth in Birch's and Haines's experience. They have always been treated with courtesy and friendliness. This is a myth that ought to be squashed. There is a national trait of the French that is attractive to both Birch and Haines; that is their tendency to flout over-zealous authority. Any new legislation by the French government or the all-powerful EU that is unpopular with the masses provokes a very strong reaction. This reaction can be a deliberate flouting of the law or, if the legislation is sufficiently unacceptable, barricades and marches on the streets. This reaction approach is in contradistinction to the comatose reaction of many nations to high-handed authority. Haines, who himself is not the most acquiescent of citizens, tells the following story. On a ride on his Harley through France towards the family home in the south, he pulled into a service station for a break. Gasping for a cigarette, he lit up right next to a *Défense de Fumer* sign. Almost immediately a police car arrived bearing two gendarmes. *Oh no*, groaned our intrepid hero. *I am for the high jump now*. The two gendarmes approached him, nodded in greeting and duly lit up their own cigarettes! This is not a defence or otherwise for smoking, but one of numerous examples of French attitudes. The EU, which has its advantages and disadvantages, has more legal complaints against the French than against all the other nations combined.

There is a place, in the view of Birch and Haines, for the individual to fight bureaucracy that is against the best interests of the people in their own way. Harnessed and co-ordinated this can be a powerful instrument.

The French, it appears to Birch, are extremely proud of their nationality, and rightly so. A speaker on BBC Radio 4 recounted a tale of a trip on a cross-channel ferry between England and France. There was a football match on the TV between France and Senegal. The latter was not a major force in world football, whereas France was, at the time. The almost unthinkable happened and Senegal won the match. The response of the French bar staff was to refuse to serve drinks to passengers. Le sulk was in operation and lasted for the duration of the trip. It is unlikely that this would happen with English bar staff, particularly as the England football team has not engendered great confidence of victory in their supporters in recent times. Increased drinking to the point of collapse would probably be the order of the day for England supporters. Victory or defeat would probably not affect the alcohol consumption. Aggression, rather than sulking, would probably be the predominant emotion among such so-called supporters. Birch's wife, Jaqueline, suffered some of the worst racial abuse that she has been subjected to in this country when she came across drunken English football supporters after a match.

Au revoir, la belle France!

Baja

Fun and adventure in desert and city

And now a few stories that may not be seen as spiritual, yet they illustrate the triumph of people over adversity: individuals and groups using their power to fight abuses.

The first tale concerns a trip which started as a conventional holiday but developed into something deeper as the journey progressed.

As Jaqueline and Birch prepared to leave England, the phone rang. Jaqueline's sister told them that there had been earthquakes in Baja California, Mexico, where they were bound. People were sleeping in the streets for fear that buildings, not least their homes, would fall on them. *Mmmm…* Birch thought, *that seems interesting. I wonder how we will be welcomed and by what?*

As Birch and Jaqueline sat on their LA-bound aircraft, Birch pondered the notion that God is everything in terms of consciousness in the universe, both positive and negative. *Hell's bells, God, get your act together. Surely there have been enough negative experiences for you. It must be time, on this Earth plane, for a lot more positive and a lot less negative. Ordinary people on the planet are fed up with negative experiences and challenges. Give us some rest, peace and a little angelic input. That really wouldn't go amiss.*

Then he realised that we are all God: you, your partner, the dog that walks by and, most difficult to appreciate, the enemy, whatever you perceive that to be, as well as all aspects of the environment. Thus, for Birch, attempting to place responsibility other than on himself is spurious. The state of being here, in this third-dimension reality, is the responsibility of all of us. Part of our current failure is the ignoring of that responsibility: our responsibility.

Los Angeles immigration control and Birch got the fascist, not for the first time, as some readers may recall. Here he was, yet again facing the arrogant egomaniac. As the pair walked to his desk, the set of his face made Birch feel uneasy. He looked as though he had escaped from the

Titanic and been saved by the *Marie Celeste.* Mr Stone Face asked Birch questions, all the while looking at Jaqueline through narrow slit-like eyes. *Yes, Mr Hitler, she is brown.*

'Do you have business cards?' he barked.

Why did they have to be so rude? Birch sensed that he was looking for an opening before driving the verbal stiletto into their mental ribs. *No, Mr Hitler, we are on holiday, V-A-C-A-T-I-O-N!*

'Where are you going?' Rubber-gloved fingers starting to twitch in anticipation of landing the big one here: an al-Qaeda operative at least.

'San Diego and then the Baja, Mexico,' Birch replied in his most keep-the-bastard-happy tone of voice.

'Ah, the Baja and Mexico,' he said. That made his mind up. They must be drug smugglers, his eyes were telling Birch. He marked a big A on the couple's entry forms and banished the duo to the heavy mob to have their bags checked, item by item. As they left his bunker, Birch was sure Mr Stone Face was thinking, *Have a lousy day.*

Their baggage was put through another scanning system and hand baggage checked by hand. One banana was confiscated. *Big criminals; no doubt about it.* Jaqueline and Birch looked at each other meaningfully; staying cool was the order of the day. The whole thing was so surreal they couldn't get too excited by it. The heavy mob let the two travellers through when they realised that Birch had a visa on his passport. Jaqueline and Birch passed through, with him thumbing his nose metaphorically at the back of Mr Hitler.

That attitude was balanced by a lovely black, smiling, friendly guy as the two went through yet another security check. This event was only mildly marred by the confiscation of their English bottled water.

Ah, the hit squad missed the really important stuff, Birch thought triumphantly.

'I like your trainers,' the friendly guy said to Birch before waving them through.

As they prepared to take the flight to San Diego, Birch felt like running back to Mr Stone Face and confronting him with, *Why don't you stop killing Muslims, then we could all cease from going through this farce?* Then, of course, he would not have the outlet of abusing foreigners as compensation for his bruised libido. Birch thought better of returning. There was no point in being thrown into jail and then thrown out of the country: wasted time, energy, effort and money.

Birch made a mental note to stop putting himself in those negative immigration situations when entering the US; after all, most of his connections in this great country were entirely positive.

Haines told Birch later that the two of them fitted the profile of possible terrorists. It was inevitable, therefore, that they would attract considerable unwelcome interest. Birch felt that their destination had also been part of the reason for the suspicion; Baja was on the drug smugglers' route from Mexico into the US.

The pair arrived at San Diego. Ah, the warmth of the evening air helped them both relax after the trauma of the flight and the immigration fiasco. San Diego County lies just north of the Mexican border, south of Orange County, and shares a border with Tijuana. It has miles of beaches, a mild Mediterranean climate and sixteen military facilities hosting the United States Navy, the US Coastguard and the United States Marine Corps.

In 1847, San Diego was a destination of the 2,000-mile march of the Mormons. After the end of the Mexican–American War and the gold rush in 1848, San Diego was incorporated as a city in 1850. With a population of 1.2 million, San Diego is now a major centre for the biotechnology industry.

This is a city of great contrasts. There are enormous skyscrapers in the downtown area, many bearing the names of financial institutions. Birch wondered if any money from these palaces of Mammon were fuelling the arms trade. Or was any used to suppress the indigenous peoples around the globe?

The city showed tremendous growth since he had last been there in 1999. Buildings had shot up with amazing speed. Birch did and still does like this city a lot. Along with Austin, Texas, it is his favourite in the US. The wide boulevards, the grid-like plan, as in all US cities that he knows, help to give it a relaxed feel. Folks walk around, even at night, with no sign of danger or stress even though there are many down-and-out street people. Birch had seen around thirty the previous night, as he and Jaqueline had walked back from the Gaslight restaurant area to their hotel.

The central Gaslight area was throbbing with life, restaurants serving many different types of food, thousands of people walking or eating outside, although it was a pretty cool 16°C that evening.

San Diego is not a typical US city, Birch reckons. The city fathers have encouraged residency in the city in an attempt to reduce the urban sprawl. This has contributed to the vibrant and energetic Gaslight area. There is not the manic stress of other cities there. The people stroll, not rushing in that eye-popping, stiff-legged, strained way that many do in big business areas.

Jaqueline and Birch ate in an excellent Mexican restaurant, complete with mariachi band: trumpets, violin, guitar, great atmosphere.

The US is not short of its extroverts. As our travellers strolled downtown, they passed two men talking. 'I am from Dallas,' Birch heard one say. The speaker was wearing the most extraordinary dark orange check suit straight out of the 1950s. Atop he sported an overlarge obligatory ten-gallon hat. *Only in America.*

Birch was once castigated by his Mexican wife for calling the US 'America'. 'America is the whole continent, Birchy.'

'We gringos have always called this country America,' responded Birch, rather lamely.

The last word came from Jaqueline. 'You should realise that America consists of thirty-five countries, not just the one that considers itself superior. America is more than gringoland.'

Birch saw the logic but chose to remain silent. Um, yeah, wise choice.

Baja California is a narrow peninsula running south, joined to the Pacific west coast of California, USA. It is 760 miles long and 30–50 miles wide. Except for two large coastal plains on the Pacific side, it consists largely of mountain ranges. The Baja, as it is usually called, is divided into two Mexican states, Baja California Norte (North) and Baja California Sur (South). The population includes white European, Mestizo, and others of East Asian, Middle Eastern, African and indigenous descent. There are also large immigrant populations from the USA and Central America. The peninsula is bounded by the Pacific Ocean to the west and the Gulf of California to the east.

The first humans came to the peninsula more than 11,000 years ago, allegedly, probably following the Pacific coast down from Alaska. Europeans reached the north in 1539 when Francisco de Ulloa explored the peninsula's east coast on the Gulf of California and the west coast as far as Cedros Island. The discovery of Baja California Sur is credited to Fortún Ximénez, despatched by Hernán Cortés in 1533. There were, of course, indigenous peoples in the Baja long before the Spanish invasion. It is likely that they were less than thrilled to be discovered, given the Western European diseases that were introduced by the conquerors. This was not the first, or last, occasion when imported diseases had a disastrous impact on indigenous populations.

The Jesuits founded a permanent mission at Loreto in 1697. They were followed by Franciscans and Dominicans. The population of the south at the 2005 census was 512,170 and the north 2,844,469.

Hollywood movies fail to inform us that the army of the United States was defeated near the town of Mulege by Captain Manuel Pineda in the Mexican–American War. The US invaders were forced to withdraw from the peninsula. The US could not lay claim to it as part of the new territories acquired through the Treaty of Guadalupe Hidalgo of 1848. Birch finds an odd satisfaction in this. Perhaps it would have been different if John Wayne had been there at the battle?

Jaqueline and Birch took the trolley, a train-like transport system, to the Mexican–US border. As they travelled closer to Mexico, at the various stops the number of white faces thinned out and the Latino ones increased.

Entering Mexico was a little like walking through a steel wall. The security fence was enormous. Birch paid $20 for the privilege of entering the country. This was the first time that he had had to pay. Perhaps his lack of Spanish was the main reason. It was commented on by an immigration officer.

Breakfast in Ensenada was well cooked. Birch asked the waitress for a *jugo de naranja* in his cracked Spanish. This caused much merriment to the waitress and Jaqueline. It seemed he'd asked for a jug of spiders instead of orange juice. The waitress was a strongly built girl, with a pleasant open face. Jaqueline said that she spoke well with customers: polite and diplomatic.

As the two waited to get on the coach to take them to their next destination, one of the passengers who alighted was dressed as a Nazi with swastikas, enormous bovver boots, black clothes and a balaclava covering his face. It was disconcerting because it was so unexpected in the heart of Latin America to see this symbol of the dark past of Europe. Mexico doesn't have the same unhappy memories of Nazism. It tends to look at it with a degree of fascination, without the revulsion and pain that Europeans feel.

Oh! Oh! The two were losing items, à la poltergeist. In the first two hotels, the electronic keys disappeared. One morning, Birch put his remaining dollars in his trouser pocket after giving Jaqueline enough to cover the breakfast bill. These also disappeared in San Diego only to reappear later in the Baja. He believes that there is some connection between his being distracted when handling items and their disappearance. This had happened before this trip. Somehow his consciousness dismisses items when handling them and, lo and behold, they disappear. Distraction occurred in the handling of both keys just before they were lost.

There were also the cracking noises which occurred in the hotel room in San Diego. Birch heard them when he retreated to the bathroom to complete his notes, in the early hours of a disturbed night. These noise phenomena have been a common occurrence throughout his life.

While this particular phase of phenomena was going on, Jaqueline looked at him quizzically and said half jokingly, 'Are these strange phenomena caused by you being an alien?'

'What do you mean?'

'Well, you have the strangest navel that I have ever seen and it looks, to me, as though you were hatched from an egg.'

Birch responded rather liverishly, 'I think that my navel is perfectly fine and normal,' not forgetting to cover his abdomen area with his hands in defensive posture, despite the fact that he was fully dressed. 'Anyway, if there was anything truly odd, my mother and the nurses would have commented.'

'I think that you were born from an egg,' was the final word from Jaqueline. She is still not totally convinced that he didn't originate from an alien source. Birch feels, for the most part, very human.

Now it was time for Birch to do some inner work. While resting in their hotel room in Ensenada, Birch was musing on the fact that the hotel had been a Spanish mission. He assumed that this was the case, given its name and its apparent archaeological structure, although it had been modernised: Hotel Mission Santa Isobel. Birch lay on his bed musing and feeling distinctly uneasy for no reason that he could satisfactorily explain. He had the impression that the Spanish had built the mission on the site of an older spiritual centre for the indigenous people. He felt that there was blocked energy from that time. He tuned in and felt that he should align his heart with the heart of the place. He meditated for a few minutes, after which he felt much better. Something had been cleared, Birch believed. He couldn't help wondering what would happen next … never a dull moment.

Jaqueline bought a magazine during the day. It was one of the few genuinely investigative journals, from a political point of view, in Mexico. It detailed horrible violence being perpetrated by the military in Oaxaca, Mexico, against the indigenous people who were trying to defend their rights and their land against powerful developers. People were killed; others disappeared. Torture is endemic for those held incommunicado, or so it is alleged. One man with broken ribs and a broken shoulder from a severe beating received no medical treatment. The abuse of women would certainly be worse.

Jaqueline and Birch conducted a healing meditation at night in an effort to replace the extreme negative conditions with those of the light, compassion and love. They believed that they had come to Ensenada to be given this work. The disappointment of cold weather and barely acceptable environment paled into insignificance. Later in the trip, Birch did some more healing meditations for the people of Oaxaca who were being persecuted by the army in the pursuit of the interests of the rich and powerful.

After an eighteen-hour bus journey down the peninsula of Baja, the pair staggered into the Hotel Loreto, Loreto town, at 3.30 am. Jaqueline started to negotiate reductions in cost with the night receptionist. Birch dissuaded her from pursuing her negotiations further. He was too tired for these high-level talks and the prospect of bed was more agreeable than the saving of a few pesos.

The journey had been a mixture of boredom and interest. The first part of the desert had been full of ribbon development, industrial buildings and wind-blown trash: all typical of the worst of Mexico. Later it had brightened up with varieties of different desert conditions, from flat pans of sand to heaped broken rocks in interesting piles, to areas of cacti, brush and aloe type plants.

As the sun had sunk below the horizon, the beautiful orange and red hues had merged into the darkening sky. This is one of the most attractive sights in the desert: beautiful. The lack of cloud much of the time creates wonderful twilight conditions.

One of Birch's issues on these long journeys is the availability of toilets. Most coaches have them but sometimes they are broken. Jaqueline, on the other hand, has the water retention of a Bactrian camel so is relatively untroubled.

Loreto was once the capital of territory stretching from California to

Texas. It is at the heart of the Sea of Cortez. It provides refuge for mother of pearl, starfish, sea urchins, fan coral, killer and blue whales, dolphins and sea lions.

The dry heat was tempered by the cool sea breeze that blew off the Sea of Cortez. The climate is agreeable all the year round, hence the presence of numerous gringos. At last, the duo had found substantial sun now that they were in the south of Baja, relaxing in open air cafés and eating delicious food.

Loreto is a centre for whale watching, which would have been fun. The waters are conducive for the mating of these wonderful and mysterious animals. Unfortunately the duo arrived there a month before the whales.

As they walked along the seafront, Jaqueline and Birch met a pleasant, sociable American farmer from Idaho. He was visiting friends. He was a Republican. They had an illuminating debate about Iraq and Mexican society. The farmer had an interesting slant on the character of Hillary Clinton. He said that the personal treatment handed out to her by Bill Clinton was a disgrace. She put up with it for reasons best known to herself. The farmer believed that a leader demonstrating courage would have high-tailed it out of there and, because of this, she was not leadership material. That was his view, anyway. This was in 2005. He was quite a character with a ZZ Top beard.

It is strange how simple everyday facts can be missed. Jaqueline and Birch watched the rollers come in to shore. Jaqueline asked Birch about the cause of this. He told her that it was the gravitational pull of the Moon on the Earth, and that the Moon also had a subtle effect on us, or perhaps not so subtle. He pointed out the influence of the full moon on lunatics and on women's menstrual cycles. One wonders what changes there would be to the Earth if the Moon disappeared. The loss of the binary system would be devastating. The tides must be part of the sea cleansing process. Perhaps creatures are affected by the gravitational force of the Moon, as we are.

Birch told Jaqueline the story of the lunatic behaviour of one of his fellow workers in the multi-national company where he had once worked. He was an adequate employee except at the full moon. He would act quite bizarrely, walking around laughing to himself and calling directors of the company by their Christian names. Not at all the thing to do back in those far-off days of the 1970s.

Birch subsequently found the following on the Internet:

> For many single-cell organisms living in water the force is always against them. The classic example is the slipper-shaped paramecium, which consistently swims harder going up than going down, just to keep from sinking. Now physicists Karine Guevorkian and James Valles of Brown University have worked out a way to turn gravity on its head and see how the creatures respond.
>
> ... so Valles and Guevorkian were ... able to create conditions simulating zero gravity and inverse gravity.
>
> By dialling the magnetic field up or down, the researchers could change the swimming behaviour of the paramecia drastically. In high gravity, the organisms swam upward mightily to maintain their place in the water column. In zero gravity, they swam up and down equally. And in reverse gravity, they dove for where the sediments ought to be [the sea bed].
> http://www.brown.edu/Administration/News_Bureau/2006-07/06-024.html

Discounting the first day of travel, the two had been on this trip for four days. Each day one item had disappeared. Day one was a hotel electronic key, day two the same, day three Birch's last remaining dollars, day four his sunglasses. Birch felt that poltergeist activity was the cause. He thought that there must be a potent, positive use for this energy; perhaps ritual or meditation could help.

Stranger and stranger: Birch woke Jaqueline from an afternoon nap. She leapt from the bed to discuss something with him. After talking for maybe three minutes, she looked across the bed and pointed. Birch shouted, 'My sunglasses!' Where Jaqueline had been lying on the bed were the said sunglasses. If they had been there before, Jaqueline would have been lying on top of them; she would certainly have felt them under her body, and most likely have crushed them. These phenomena were precisely the same as in the Danny poltergeist era during Birch's childhood. At that time, the events were elements of his burgeoning psychic energy.

During the late afternoon they walked along the beach following the line of surf, very pleasant but surprising how cold the Pacific was at that time of year. The vast sea seemed to stretch into infinity. As one looked at it for any length of time, it pulled the watcher out of their narrow objective awareness. One could lose oneself in the immensity of it, becoming part of the sea in a vast spread-out way, losing the singularity of human awareness.

Birch was brought back to awareness of the drugs issue when he heard an American complaining to one of the shopkeepers about how his camper van had been invaded by policemen and sniffer dogs at the border. Everything of his had been turned topsy-turvy. No doubt they didn't replace the disturbed items.

As the two bought their coach tickets in Loreto bus station for the next leg of the journey to La Paz, a woman looked at Birch's T-shirt. She spoke to Jaqueline, asking her if the strange man was Canadian.

'No, he is British,' Jaqueline replied.

'Ah, he doesn't look like the gringos around here,' the Mexican woman continued. She meant Americans. It is interesting to speculate on the subtle, and not so subtle, differences between Americans and Britons. The Americans wear their well-recognised baseball caps and their T-shirts which tend to be US specific. There is a swagger and self-confidence that surrounds US citizens as befits their culture. Certainly that is the perception there.

If we look for differences between the two, we may find subtle rather than the obvious ones. There is quietness in the demeanour of British people in the Americas, compared to their American cousins, Birch had noticed. This may have something to do with the energy of the continent. The British are not indigenous and do not belong there. White US citizens have been on the continent for generations and have adjusted.

The continent of Europe has a different vibration which requires adjustment when moving from one continent to another. This continental energy adjustment may account for the quietness mentioned above, at least in part.

This is a personal, intuitive feeling of Birch's. He feels sensitivity to the energies of places he visits. Other people could and do feel the same. Perhaps some are not as aware of this energy interaction between person and place. Nevertheless, it is present and there will be a human response, both overt and subtle.

There are societal causes adding to these more subtle projections of energy. In Britain it is deemed good to be demure, self effacing, modest. In the US, 'putting it out there' is an equally valued human trait. These values are inculcated from a young age and become ingrained in our persona (Greek for 'as you seem').

On the first night in La Paz the two walked along the promenade, stretching their legs after the long journey. The sea along the front was calm due to a parabola-shaped isthmus protecting it from the rollers. They stopped at a statue to La Reina del Mar, the Queen of the Sea. The text explained that the queen protects life forms in the water from all attack. Birch found this extremely interesting considering his work with Mary and Joan on the Theos animal consciousness and energy development (see *So You Think We're Alone?*). Thus the female energy is performing the nurturing and supporting role in this context.

The previous day, Jaqueline had recounted another example of this female spiritual energy in Mexico. The Saint of the Dead was a belief in a spiritual entity from a long time before the Spanish invasion. It was responsible for the cycle of birth and death. This belief also stipulated that death was a journey into another life. Believers were encouraged not to be frightened by death as it was not the end. The Catholic Church attempted to suppress this belief. When the Spanish arrived, they destroyed the chapels associated with the saint and built their own constructions over them. They failed to suppress it totally, and the Catholic Church had to accommodate this belief within its own religion, creating small altars within its churches. Birch wonders if the Catholic hierarchy swallows hard on this one. Perhaps not.

For those who believe the Catholic Church is a progression of the Roman Empire, this absorption is synonymous with the ancient Roman practice of incorporating the gods and customs of conquered peoples into their society. This served a clear social purpose of developing and maintaining the loyalty and peaceful behaviour of conquered peoples.

Jaqueline recounted two stories of the adventures of believers. In one, a man, a simple worker, wore a believer's amulet, always cleaning it at the end of the day. He would leave it on his altar overnight. A committed and active believer was he. One day, returning home from work, he was stopped by two men demanding money. He only had three pesos, which he gave them. The robbers, very unhappy with their haul, pushed the believer to the floor and he feared for his life. As the attacking robbers stood over him, the believer saw some people approaching.

One of the robbers pulled a knife, and the believer's hand moved to his heart in defensive mode. He felt his hand grasp his amulet as he did so. The men grappled with him, thinking that he was holding something of value. The approaching people drew close. At the front of the group was a woman dressed in black, hooded so that her face could not be seen. The robbers were frightened and ran off. As the believer recovered and spoke with the group, he saw that the hooded figure had disappeared. Strangely, the people in the group had not seen her, nor had they any knowledge of the woman.

Back to hols. After a stomach-filling breakfast of eggs, ham, beans (Mexican), pancakes (American), orange juice and coffee, the duo walked onto the pier to watch the birds diving for fish. Large pelicans with enormous beaks dived towards the water to catch fish, or simply to have fun, it seemed to Birch. A flock of smaller pelicans with white underbellies flew in echelon, like a squadron of warplanes, along the line of the surf. Small black seabirds dived under the waves seemingly for ages before reappearing on the surface. And what were those small pigeon-like seabirds? Many of the birds were moving in couples. Birch was reminded of the fact that some types of birds in England mated for life, unlike many humans, including him.

Birch saw a jellyfish just under the surface, its transparent body held together by lines of white. Perhaps the presence of such creatures was the reason that no one was swimming in the sea. But then, as far as the locals were concerned, it was winter. The temperature was around a wind-chilled 18°C, although the sun was very strong.

The doughty travellers could see small shoals of fish gathering around the stanchions and pylons of the pier, obviously the objects of interest for the birds.

Another Saint of the Dead story involves a woman, abandoned at birth, brought up by her grandmother who was a believer. As in the first story, the woman would clean her necklace of the saint every day, offering up prayers to the saint. In time, her grandmother, by then aged seventy, fell very ill. The believer was distraught. She cried out and prayed to the saint for the recovery of her mum, because that was who the grandmother had become. The doctors gave up all hope and told the believer to prepare for the worst. The believer refused to accept the doctors' opinions and redoubled her prayers. The story has a happy ending. The grandmother did, indeed, recover, much to the amazement of the medical authorities, and she is still living into her vigorous nineties.

The book from which Jaqueline obtained these stories, written in Spanish, outlines the rituals and contents of an altar which can be used to set up an atunement with the saint. Jaqueline feels drawn to set this up. Birch encourages her because it is a way for her to access a greater reality, which she has not done before. In the past she has lived entirely in the mundane, the world of family, employment and studying. This work will open a doorway for her. Birch and Haines will watch her progress with interest and no small measure of expectation. The two men talk about how the Saint of the Dead faith works in terms of the apparent fantastic results achieved by believers. Birch says that any belief system co-ordinates or pools mental, psychological and psychic energy which then becomes available to all those believers. He also believes that there is a synergistic process going on with the universe giving the belief system boosts of energy. This can be a positive or negative process. However, over time the negative will tend to work against the laws of the universe, causing eventual collapse.

In objective consciousness, humans tend to switch from one energy system to another rather than using a co-ordinated holistic approach to all available energies. They pick and choose, selecting some that appeal at the time while avoiding or ignoring others. There must be a whole book, potentially, on the co-ordination of such energies.

The egregore (from the Greek meaning 'watchers'), the collective group mind or pool of energy that was in existence for the Rosicrucian Order, AMORC, was believed to be the sum total of all the Rosicrucian thought and psychic energy which could be accessed by attuned members of the Order. Members believed that discarnate beings were also attuned to AMORC, contributing to the sum total of the resource. Birch worked with this energy pool for years. It was extremely powerful until withdrawn by the cosmic powers at the end of the 108-year cycle of external work of the Order. Or was it the fact that he was preparing to leave AMORC and had distanced himself from the egregore? Others he knows have had the same experience of the egregore being withdrawn.

In relationship to the female energy, particularly in places of perceived high energy, Birch remembers an experience that he had a few years ago. On a trip to Yucatán, Jaqueline and he saw a lone woman. First they saw her in a bus station, then in two of the pyramid cities. Each sighting was hundreds of miles apart. The sightings could have been coincidence, except that she was on her own each time, an uncommon experience for a single Mexican woman. Excursions are conducted in family groups. She spoke to no one and did not appear interested in her surroundings; she just walked. Birch called her the shadow.

One evening the travellers ate caldos in the market. This is a rich soup containing vegetables and pieces of chicken, completed by a sprinkling of lime juice; very nutritious. Just what the doctor ordered. Birch spoiled it later by eating an enormous wedge of sticky cake. Still, this was a holiday.

The missing dollars re-appeared in a pair of jeans that had been checked several times. The person washing them found them in the pocket. They had been checked before going to the laundry. This caused Birch to speculate further on the disappearance phenomenon. He mused that if this transfer of three-dimensional objects could be controlled in some way, then energy, actions, material things could be transferred in and out of this reality at will. Perhaps Jesus used something similar to feed the 5,000? Given Birch's belief that there needs to be a balance energetically between giving and receiving, then the process, when effective, should not only be used for selfish purposes. It could be used to balance negative forces wherever they manifest in this 3D world. In some ways it is the extension of the laws of cause and effect and the law of karma in which circumstances, conditions and people that one needs for development and growth are magnetically attracted. Perhaps the poltergeist element enables Birch to strengthen already existing usage of the cosmic flow and assist in the manifestation of physical objects. Spencer Lewis and his successor as leader of AMORC, Ralph Lewis, were both required to manifest objects materially from the cosmic realm when they took the leadership.

When the 108 years were completed, the great mystics were no longer in the Order, in Birch's view. At a convention later, Birch's good friend Doug asked a contemporary leader of the Order which initiations he had performed and which psychic manifestations he had completed in order to gain the leadership. By the leader's reaction it was obvious that he didn't have a clue what Doug was talking about.

The other energetic elements which might be beneficially utilised are the noises, cracks and bangs in the duo's flat and other places that Birch visits, which he sees as a leakage of energy. If this could be harnessed, then an increase of energy and power might boost the performance of the positive work of mystics. The night after this insight, Birch worked with the creation of a field of opportunity in order to attempt to contain and use this energy creatively.

The male receptionist in their hotel, Birch called a 'reverse Ahmed'. This story begins in Gloucester, at Ahmed's Fish Bar (name changed to protect the innocent). Birch and Jaqueline enjoy Ahmed's fish and chips often. When they make their purchase in the shop, Ahmed always speaks to

Birch, ignoring Jaqueline totally. He is perfectly sociable, but where Jaqueline stands appears to be empty space in his world. Probably this is a cultural issue. The hotel receptionist here was the reverse of Ahmed. It was as though Birch were standing in free space. The receptionist chatted animatedly and socially with Jaqueline as the two guests passed in and out of the hotel reception. Birch knew that this was because of his very limited Spanish. The receptionist did suggest to Birch that he was lazy in this regard. He was right. Birch thinks it unlikely that a guest would receive such bluntness from British hotel staff, apart from at Fawlty Towers, that is.

Haines's wife, Jacqui, finds a similar problem. In their business travels, they often meet people from cultures very different from those to which we are accustomed in the UK. Jacqui is not at all amused when she is ignored, while Haines gets all the attention. On one recent occasion in London, conference delegates from an Eastern European country were having a buffet lunch. Jacqui stood, holding her plate and balancing her glass of wine. An Eastern European male pushed her out of his way so he could secure a chair. The guest meant no harm or disrespect in his terms. It was just that Jacqui was a female and was standing in his way.

Haines does much work in a Balkan country which he has come to love, yet he struggles with the attitude towards women. They are treated badly by the men in the community and, typically, Haines kicks against what he believes is wrong and unacceptable. He insists on walking on the outside of the pavement (such as they are) when walking with a female. He holds open doors for them and enjoys using female translators and lawyers whenever he can. This has caused business problems. One partner company refused to discuss business with his female lawyer. Haines's response was predictable (for those who know him): deal with it, or the business is off. The business arrangement did not continue. Birch says that even traditional societies immured in male dominance will be forced to change by circumstances. The female energy is on the rise. The universe will ensure that in the future there will be a balance of both forms of energy. This may be very painful for some.

On another occasion, Jacqui and Haines were amazed at a dinner party at their English home. Dear friends, a husband and wife from Roermond in the Netherlands, were staying. It seemed like a good idea to throw a dinner party and invite an English friend and her Dutch partner, Vim. Haines cooked the meal and, as he started to serve it at the table, Vim said,

'Why are you doing this? You have cooked it and now you are serving it.' He then nodded in Jacqui's direction. '*She* should be doing all this.'

The Haines family found his reaction odd, not least because they view the Dutch as being progressive, polite, cultured and sophisticated. Well, maybe that doesn't go for all of them?

Perhaps it is best to leave to readers' imaginations what Haines's reply to Vim might have been.

The travellers came across a beggar woman in the street; not very common in this city, although very common elsewhere in Mexico. Birch was not going to give any money. As they approached the beggar, Birch had his hand in his pocket with fingers curled around the pile of coins that was there. Guilt was his immediate reaction. He had so much and she had so little. He gave her one peso: so very little for him, but more important for her. There was no need for the guilt either. Victor Mansfield in *Synchronicity, Science and Soul Making* describes beggars wandering the streets as projections of our own homelessness, abandonment and poverty rather than someone with an equal right to a quality of life: a symbol of one's own deficiencies.

The following morning the two ate a nutritious breakfast to set them up for the day. They were approached by a young boy, maybe twelve years old. He was selling chocolate. He told Jaqueline that he was selling in order to fund his school expenses: books, pencils. He asked for twelve pesos for a chocolate bar. Birch offered him ten pesos (50p), which the boy accepted. His selling point was that he had brought his school results with him to show how he was working. After he left, Jaqueline said cynically, Mexico City style, 'He has probably borrowed the school results from his brother.'

The boy had a fine face and Birch preferred to take the less cynical view.

Our travellers went to a bank to change some pounds into pesos. They had each brought £200 because they were certain that a good rate of exchange could be obtained in Mexico. The first bank was not interested in *libras* (Spanish for pounds). At the second bank Jaqueline was told that the exchange could only be made for foreigners. Standing in a queue, Birch turned to see Jaqueline waving her British passport in the face of the bank teller in protest at this ruling. The assistant merely shrugged his shoulders. She still couldn't get her pounds changed.

This was the first time that Birch had seen any sign that Jaqueline had any pride in being British. She has both Mexican and British citizenship and is terrifically proud of her Mexican heritage. Perhaps she is a mite less proud of her adopted country because Britain is not embedded in her cells, in her DNA. Birch laughed hugely at Jaqueline protesting so strongly for her Britishness.

On a subsequent visit to the pier, they saw an interesting exchange between the birds. One small white seabird was attacking a second, in the water. The second bird was crying out in distress. Three large pelicans that had been floating nearby flew over to the fighting avians, separated them and then floated between the two until calm was restored. A second attack was broken up by another bird, brown and larger than the fighting birds.

So there must be a sense of natural justice and sensitive awareness in certain sectors of the bird kingdom. The fights looked like those in any British town or city on a Friday or Saturday night, except that the protagonists there are human. Here there was no alcohol and the minimum of violence.

There is a plaque at the entrance to the pier commemorating the landing of HM Queen Elizabeth II and her husband on their official visit to Mexico in 1983. They landed there, presumably, on their luxury yacht funded by the British taxpayer. QEII, the woman not the boat, shed a tear when the yacht, the Royal Yacht *Britannia*, was eventually taken out of service. Birch, on the other hand, smiled. There was at least a little less cash going from the poor to the rich. Jaqueline, coming from a republican country, finds the idea of royalty strange and old-fashioned.

Just to balance up the royalist rant a little, Kingsley Martin in the *New Statesman* said,

'We should note the warnings of history, if we drop the trappings of monarchy in the gutter … Germany has taught us that some guttersnipe … may pick them up.' No messages from angry royalists, please. Birch will never be a royalist; some people will never be anti-royal. Best to leave it there.

Jaqueline read to Birch from a magazine. The story concerned the abuses in the drugs trade in Mexico. Allegations were made that over 50% of the police in the country were involved with the transfer of the drugs through the country and that the biggest traffickers were senior police officers. She also read of the terrible tortures that were perpetrated in order to further the trade.

It seemed to Birch then, as now, that the work with energies that he and others were doing was of even greater importance. He believes that humanity's positive thoughts and energies, particularly in these times, have a greater impact than the negative, on a one-to-one basis.

Now for two stories with a nautical flavour. The authorities responsible for some fishing villages decided to tax the fishermen. This provoked an outburst of illegal fishing by the already poor fishermen. One group, illegally fishing, encountered a great storm. The storm was so severe that they were swept away from their known fishing grounds and out into the open sea.

The families back on shore were desperate for information, not knowing if their loved ones were living or dead. The authorities were either powerless, incompetent or unable to care less. Nothing seemed to be done.

Eventually the fishermen had the good fortune to land on an inhabited island far out in the Pacific. They were saved. They found their way back to their homes many months later, to be welcomed joyously by their loved ones. This was not the case with the authorities. They fined them for the illegal fishing. Funny old world, isn't it?

In a second story, poor Mexican fishermen lived a simple existence on a beautiful bay. The only thing stopping the authorities booting them out of their livelihood to build a mega tourist town was the hostility of the local mosquitoes. Only the locals are immune to their toxic charms. Over the generations they have developed tremendously thick skins which resist the 'mosquito kiss', to which all others succumb.

'Thank God for the mosquitoes,' the locals say. It is perhaps the only place in the world where you will hear such a chant.

It was time to move on. Jaqueline and Birch took a flight from La Paz to Mexico City to visit Jaqueline's family: the teeming metropolis for Christmas and the New Year.

To finish, Ian McEwan wrote, 'The actual, not the magical, should be the challenge.' For Birch, the actual and the magical are the issues, because both present the challenges to all of us in the human race. They are separate because we choose that they should be so. Indeed, the magical is ignored or maligned in much of Western culture. In many ancient cultures the two were so interwoven that both were, and are, part of one true reality. As Birch has found in his travels, this combined reality works and possesses a power that is strong and balancing. Unfortunately, materiality has created such a powerful boundary around itself that the magical cannot break through to demonstrate its manifold offerings. Consequently the current partial view of reality has led to the unbalancing of the human psyche, unhappiness, mental instability and the industry of escapism that pervades.

Mexico

Fascinating stories from town and country

The gringo and Jaqueline stood next to the stop sign, waiting for the bus. Maybe we had better point out, once again, what a gringo is. Speakers of Spanish and Portuguese apply the slightly derogatory term to mean Anglophones. At first, Birch and Jaqueline were alone. Gradually Mexicans arrived and formed what could best be described as a scrum behind and around them.

Where is the nice tidy queue that I am used to in England? thought Birch.

The bus arrived and the double doors swung open in front of Birch's face. He prepared to board. Within a second or two he was engulfed by a mass of people fighting to get on. Knees, elbows, bottoms, heads, every part of the body: all were used as battering rams in the mad scramble to get on before others.

Birch stood there, stunned. He realised that he was still standing in the same spot, rooted. Everyone else was on the bus, including Jaqueline, who, by that time, was grinning at him through the window. He must have looked, at the least, slightly ridiculous.

Nonplussed and gathering his English dignity around him, Birch mounted gracefully and rather sniffily. As he joined Jaqueline, he noticed the stares of those that had fought to get on the bus although there had been plenty of room for all. The stares seemed to say, *Crazy gringo. Lose your WASP (White Anglo Saxon Protestant) politeness. This is Mexico.*

Birch didn't have the language, or the inclination, to tell them that he wasn't a Protestant and only the first three elements of this expression had relevance to him. Later he related the story to a friend, who grinned while saying, 'Welcome to Mexico.'

Haines can't resist one of his digressions here. The ancient word for a bus, even before the word omnibus was adopted, even before the widely used charabanc (or chara) from the French, was 'motor diligence': not relevant but a charming titbit.

The niceties of queuing seemed completely lost. The British are world class at queuing. We can queue like no one else. The Americans call it *standing in line.* Their version doesn't seem to have the gentle politeness of the British version. We sometimes even give up our place to someone who needs to complete their business rapidly. We are nice to small children, pregnant women and old folks when in a queue. Our nation has turned it almost into an art form. One day there will be a queue of people presented as an entry for the Turner Art Prize. It may even win. Stranger things have happened.

There is something about Birch and airports. He seems to invite problems and unusual events wherever he goes. Earlier, the two travellers had arrived at Mexico City airport. Jaqueline waited for their baggage next to the appropriate belt. Birch went to find a toilet.

On the way back to baggage claim Birch heard someone call out his name. He turned to see Coti, Jaqueline's sister, a few yards away, waving and smiling. Birch, without thinking, rushed over to hug her and greet her in his extremely limited Spanish. He then turned to return to Jaqueline to help with the baggage.

A security guard refused him permission to return. He'd crossed the line between the airport and the waiting area. Let's get this clear. The only difference between where he had come from and where he was now was a line painted on the floor. The security guard was adamant that, to paraphrase General Foch during the First World War, 'He shall not pass'. Those who have read *So You Think We're Alone?* will recall that Birch has a problem understanding the meaning, the relevance, of these painted lines in airports. Haines flies often, probably every week, and has never once encountered the problem. But, then again, he doesn't step over the lines.

Jaqueline had Birch's passport and air ticket, so he couldn't return the way he'd come. Nor could he return through ticket control. Jaqueline was standing at baggage control with no idea as to Birch's whereabouts and her concern was mounting. She is often paranoid about security around the gringo when in Central America.

Coti and Birch walked up and down trying to find a vantage point close to baggage claim 3, which was where Jaqueline was waiting. They took great care to stand on their side of the blessed line. They couldn't see Jaqueline. Coti started shouting Jaqueline's name at the top of her voice. No one took a blind bit of notice. Imagine this unseemly carry-on at LHR or LGW, but this was Mexico City where noise is endemic, not to say epidemic. In desperation Birch joined in. Fortunately Jaqueline heard the combined yelling, and the top of her head appeared as she pushed a trolley out, struggling with the weight. All of her four feet eleven inches hove into full view. Jaqueline was not a happy bunny and Birch was in the doghouse for the next hour.

Into the maelstrom of Mexico City traffic, four lanes of wall-to-wall vehicles, honking, swerving, shoving, cutting each other up, drivers gesticulating. It made the M25 seem almost sedate. They drove to the apartment of Jaqueline's mother. In this area live a million Latinos. Birch was *el uno* gringo.

From *The Spiritual Practices of the Ninja* by Ross Heaven: 'The challenge for the Magus – the one who truly sees – is to understand and accept that the world is an act of faith, not a 'known fact', and that there are no cut and dried answers or final solutions.'

So when Birch leaves on his travels he is partaking in an act of faith. Good experiences and not so good are expected by him. His vagueness and lack of attentiveness to the administrative systems around him are features of the adventure. His approach to this element of his travels is unlikely to change much.

That evening they all ate together: Jaqueline's mother, Jaqueline, Coti, another sister Olivia, and Birch. He told the family, through interpreter Jaqueline, about his contact with his mother since her death. Two to three months after Birch's mother passed beyond the physical, he was sitting quietly at home when the thought flashed into his head, *call Mum*. When she was alive he would telephone her most days. At that moment Birch made the intuitive leap that his mother was trying to make contact. Without making a logical connection, he formed his thoughts and sent them out into the ether. *Don't worry. Everything is fine here. There is nothing holding you back. Just get on with your journey.*

Birch had no feedback from this contact until two or three weeks later. He then had a dream in which he was driving a silver car. This was significant for him because he has had many dreams in such a vehicle and he had previously been able to make a link between this mode of transport and his lifetime journey. In the dream when he was driving the car, Birch thought, *I must call in and see Mum*. In his dream, Mum was working in a shop in the High Street in Gloucester, an area of the city in which she had lived throughout her earthly incarnation.

Birch drove to the shop and went in. His mother was standing behind the counter, looking in her prime. As Birch entered she said to him, 'Thanks for calling in.'

Birch had his feedback.

In response, Jaqueline's mother spoke of a dream in which her dead husband had appeared and begged her to look out for all six of their children. This was in contradistinction to his lifetime when he gave very little attention to any of his children. Perhaps, in the reality in which he now dwells, he has had the opportunity to review and change his perspectives on his parenting. There is no end point when one passes over, according to Birch. Consciousness continues.

Jaqueline also has had a number of contacts with her dead father. In her dreams he is anxious to communicate with her. Always she says no. Perhaps the memory of his lack of care during his lifetime is too painful to forgive? She is simply not interested. These connections initiated by her dead father continue. He has plainly not given up on having a discourse with his daughter.

After a few days' rest it was decided that the four women and Birch would spend a few days at the coast. The journey began in a Combi from Jaqueline's mother's house on the outskirts of Mexico City to Terminal Sud, the bus station. A Combi is an agonising form of transport. Up to thirteen people cram into a minibus with bench seats around the periphery for up to an hour and a half, trying to rest as they travel. The distances between different parts of the city of approximately 23 million people are so large that these uncomfortable journeys can seem endless.

For a gringo with his long legs, these journeys are at least unpleasant and at worst agonising. The locals tend to keep the windows closed, so during the warm weather the interior heat is intense, not to mention the odours. This is a major form of transport for many Mexico City residents; it's so flexible. Arrangements are made during the journey for passengers to be dropped off at other than the pre-arranged points along the way. There is a relaxed relationship between driver and passengers. By British standards the price of the journeys is extremely low, a few pesos at most.

As the Combi is in motion, the fare is passed to the driver along the seated line of passengers and handed through a square opening. Change is passed back along the line. Arrangements are made between passengers to give the driver manageable or correct amounts of money. It is a co-operative and trusting form of payment. There is also politeness between passengers which is quite often missing outside. As a passenger enters the Combi, invariably he or she will say, '*Buenos dias*' ('good day' in Spanish), and will be greeted likewise by the other passengers. Although there is an interesting sociological picture of life in the Combi, Birch doesn't like it. This discomfort is compounded by the stares of the Mexican passengers who wonder what a gringo is doing in the people's transport. If he never travels in another Combi again, it will be too soon.

Birch was reminded of another painful mode of transport. This was the so-called chicken bus. This mode of transport enjoys near-mythical status in the West, so much so that even the largely Spanish-speaking Central Americans call these vehicles by their English name. We see adverts on the TV where adventurous Westerners explore dusty and distant parts of the planet in a chicken bus.

The romance is lost on Birch. His one journey in a chicken bus in Guatemala was another form of torture by transport. The bumpiness of the ride has to be experienced to be appreciated. Seating is designed to cram in as many short-of-stature Latinos as possible. The bumpiness can be coped with. However, for a six-foot gangling person, the joys of being wedged in for hours, with little opportunity to change position, are to be avoided. The final indignity was the grumpy stare from the person in front. He had to endure Birch's bony knees making indentations in the back of his seat and thus into the back of the unfortunate Latino.

Hot and dishevelled, the party arrived in the Pacific resort of Zihuatanejo. It didn't drop below 21°C, even at night. Next morning Birch arose at 6.30 to make the most of the early-morning cool. He did some tai chi and chi gong on the hotel terrace facing the incoming rollers in the bay; marvellous.

By 9.30 am the party enjoyed a typical Mexican breakfast of eggs, chorizo (spicy sausage), rice, Mexican beans, bread and coffee. While disposing of this wonderful repast, Birch was reminded of his travels in Guatemala. There, breakfast one day consisted of eggs, rice and beans. On a second day it would be rice, eggs and beans, and the third day would be beans, eggs and rice. Breakfast done and the women went shopping.

Birch walked along the line of the breaking surf. A boy was playing with a dead sea-snake washed up overnight. Whether it was venomous or not, who knew? Birch considered the other members of his party who would later be playing in the surf. Should he tell them about this discovery? On reflection he decided not. Positive thinking was the order of the day.

The power of the breakers, and of water generally, was brought home to Birch later in the day when he had an adventure while swimming. The breakers were strong in the afternoon and Birch enjoyed leaping up to meet them as they crashed towards the shore. There seemed to be a routine where three or four really strong breakers were followed by a period of relative calm, then the cycle repeated itself.

After a while of this fun Birch was caught by one wave just as it was breaking, hitting him at its strongest. Birch was flung underwater and he tumbled over and over. He was powerless to do anything, being at the mercy of the power of water. So he relaxed, let it happen and enjoyed the ride.

A few more seconds passed and he suddenly realised that he had become disoriented, not knowing which way was up and which was down. For a moment his thought processes froze. He didn't feel quite so playful any more. The freezing didn't last long and without thinking too much he pushed upwards, although he wasn't sure if his attempt to rise was going up or going down. He was now completely disoriented. Fortunately the power of the breaker eased in its shoreward rush. This phase seemed endless, although it was probably only a few seconds. The thought entered his head, *Is this the end of the Clive Birch experience?* As the thought died away he broke surface, gasping and spluttering for breath. It wasn't the end of Clive Birch in this incarnation. He had his answer. He swam back to shore, red-faced and somewhat shocked, deciding discretion was the better part of valour.

He felt exhilarated when reviewing the incident afterwards. Being in that danger and coming out of it certainly gave an adrenaline rush. Obviously he would not have been so pleased if his difficulties had continued in the one-sided battle with the powerful wave. To paraphrase Emperor Hirohito, the outcome would not necessarily have been in Birch's favour. On balance he decided not to mention it to Jaqueline. The likely response would have been the biggest 'rollicking' he had received for some time because he had placed himself in such danger.

The quote mentioned above comes from the radio broadcast that the emperor made to the Japanese people when announcing the end of World War II. The message was: 'World War II has ended not necessarily in Japan's favour.' One might think that the emperor was a master of understatement. This was the first time that the Japanese people had heard the voice of their emperor. Prior to this he had been awarded near-godlike status in Japanese society.

This part of Mexico is tropical; bananas and coconuts grow wild. It is hot, for a gringo, all the time. This is fine for a holiday, but not so pleasant in summer when the temperature reaches 45°C. Women sell ice creams, and policemen wear big boots and thick clothing as though it is April climate in England. One of the local women suggested that the party come again in the summer. Birch didn't think so.

The diversity of bird life is another feature of this tropical climate. Fish catchers, waders and land birds are there in profusion. On this occasion, there was one small bird that Birch particularly liked. Its plumage was so black that when it preened or spread its wings, the feathers took on a deep purple hue; catching the sunlight, this subtle change of colour was magical. This was coupled with graceful movements of extended neck and beak that enchanted.

The rooms were stifling hot at night as brick and stone released the heat trapped from the sun in daytime. Birch found himself musing on the physics of this process. What determined at which temperature to start absorbing heat, at which temperature to stop and at which temperature to start releasing? No doubt someone with the appropriate technical background may supply the answer and disabuse Birch's musing as fanciful and romantic.

As the party ate their second evening meal, a conversation started with Jaqueline complaining that Americans were buying up all the properties along the coastline. Birch replied that, although he was not the greatest friend of the empire to the north, the economic benefits of US involvement in Mexico were considerable. If the US economy collapsed and its citizens largely withdrew from Mexico, then hundreds of thousands of Mexicans would suffer financially. At the time of writing, Birch's grim prediction is coming to pass. Talk of a possible recession may be a little premature, but there is a clear lack of confidence in the Western world.

Property prices are down, production is down, unemployment is rising and inflation figures make depressing reading.

Birch also points out that if Mexico wishes to limit US involvement in the country, then the government should legislate accordingly. This is extremely unlikely for two reasons. First, the financial cost to the Mexican economy would be unacceptable. Second, the US pressure on the Mexican authorities would be enormous. Big brother to the north would possibly be big bully, and not for the first time as far as Mexico is concerned.

There was a party on the beach outside the hotel. A girl was having a fifteenth birthday party, which in Mexico is equivalent to the celebrations when one reaches eighteen in Britain. In Mexican culture, young people mature much earlier and are expected to become adults accordingly. The downside is that people age quicker, although this may have something to do with the necessity of working hard into old age. So it is for millions of Mexicans.

Day three and Jaqueline heard on the news that flights had been cancelled for the third day at Heathrow, due to fog. The party's main concern was whether they had enough sunscreen on and which restaurant to visit for breakfast. Life can be such a worry.

The time came to return to Mexico City. Birch, hoping to get some shut-eye on the overnight coach, sat next to a girl who was sobbing. As the coach left the station, sobs turned to crying, crying turned to sniffing, sniffing turned to eating, eating turned to bleeping texts. Then the driver put on two rubbish films with raucous soundtracks. No sleep for Birch, then. The ventilation was going full freezing blast.

It was 3 am when the coach stopped. Jaqueline said that the driver was lost. Driver one asked driver two to take over. The latter took thirty minutes to wake up enough to take the wheel. The exhausted party staggered into Terminal Norte bus station at 7 am on Christmas Eve.

Birch mused on the unpleasant and uncomfortable travels during his adventures. It seemed almost a prerequisite that he should suffer through travelling. It was a little like making a pilgrimage, which many say should be difficult. Birch tries to avoid these difficulties, with singular lack of success. Rather uncharitably, Haines views it differently, and says so. Just like his little inconveniences at airports, Haines reckons Birch brings his problems on himself, at least in part. *Thanks for your moral support, Pete.*

Before the uncomfortable coach ride, the party had sat on a wall close to the beach, whiling away the hours. They were to leave their hotel at midday and catch the bus back to Mexico City at 8 pm. An extended Mexican family arrived and parked itself next to Birch's party. Birch chooses the word 'itself' because the group functioned as if it were a single entity. The individual members seemed so comfortable with each other. Obviously the individuals retained their own consciousness and willpower. However, it was as though the underlying rules and modes of behaviour were clearly defined, whether consciously realised or not. In this culture people sometimes need each other in order to survive. Necessity is the mother of invention.

Earlier, Birch had noticed that Jaqueline's mum and sister, along with Jaqueline herself, had formed a tight clique, chattering and straightening each other's clothes, as well as patting each other from time to time. Birch likens it unkindly to monkeys picking the fleas out of each other's fur. For him with his English reserve, it was cloying. They probably thought of him as being cool, if not cold. Birch and the other sister, Olivia, were out of the loop. Birch was not unhappy with this state of affairs. It gave him the space to follow his own trains of thought.

It was interesting for Birch to see the family members switching roles upon return to the family home. On holiday, in the heat, the sisters were in charge, felicitously taking care of the mother's needs as she struggled to cope with her deteriorating health. She became the patient willingly. A complete reversal occurred at her house. As soon as the party entered, the daughters were directed to prepare food, water, flowers, along with performing other domestic duties. Mother was back in her castle, back in charge. Certainly, mutual support mechanisms and co-operation are necessary in Mexico. It has just a rudimentary social service system and a lack of free healthcare. Family networks are vital. Perhaps this family support system has been lost elsewhere in the West, to our detriment.

Birch went to a ladies' hairdresser with Jaqueline. Whole families came in to accompany the one member who was having her hair done. Those not having a coiffure, spouses and children, seemed perfectly happy sitting around chatting, drinking sodas, making it a social event. Most Mexicans that Birch met seemed positively relaxed and stress-free despite the problems of poverty and anger in their society.

Back at mother's house, Birch saw a piece on CNN concerning some sheep in Puebla, an adjacent state and city. The woollies had been savaged by an unknown animal, leaving unidentifiable tooth and bite marks on their flanks. One of the odd things about this creature was that it had what seemed like a technical-type plug fitted to the middle of its lower back. This was verified by local peasants in this report. These creatures had allegedly been sighted in Mexico, Puerto Rico and Peru.

The Peru report claimed that one had been captured by local police. They had transferred it to a military airfield and it had been taken away by gringos in an unmarked aircraft. This had allegedly been confirmed by the local police, who, interviewed by the reporter, had claimed that the gringos were CIA. The report went on to claim that these creatures were being bred underground in South and Central America, and that local sightings and damage to livestock were caused by escaped creatures.

Birch was reminded of attacks by chupacabras, a previously unknown animal. According to a photograph in a book which Birch has since lost, it was black in colour and looked a little like a hairless small bear.

A few days later there was a report on Mexico City news that a person was claiming to sell dried chupacabra bodies. The report briefly flashed a picture of carcasses on the screen too quickly for Birch to examine them closely. However, it was interesting that the TV station should place this report about such a contentious issue in the public domain.

The Wikipedia article on chupacabras gives an artist's depiction of a lizard-like creature. The photograph that Birch saw years ago in his book was different. It was mammalian. Physical depictions of the creature do vary. So, in Birch's view, the most likely explanation is that the 'chupacabra' is in fact a number of previously undiscovered species. The article says that the creatures were first sighted in Puerto Rico in 1990. Subsequent reports claimed sightings as far north as Maine and as far south as Chile. The name 'chupacabra' translates from the Spanish as 'goat sucker' from the creatures' reported habit of attacking and drinking the blood of livestock, especially goats.

The first known attacks occurred in March 1995 in Puerto Rico. Eight sheep were found dead. The bodies had three puncture wounds in the chest, and the poor creatures were completely drained of blood. The first suspects were satanic cults until the killings spread around the island with identical wounds and drained blood. In April 2006, reports of chupacabras emanated from Russia with similar animal blood draining.

One woman, a university teacher in Puerto Rico, met a similar being and, allegedly, had an intelligent conversation. She claimed that the being had glaring red eyes and answered her questions telepathically. It said that, indeed, it was a chupacabra! The woman had settled the beast by saying that she would not harm it. Rest assured you will read all the best stories here!

It was in April 2006 that Michelle O'Donnell of Maine spoke of an 'evil-looking', rodent-like creature with fangs, which was found dead on the side of the road and unidentifiable. In appearance it was unlike any dog or wolf in the area. The carcass was picked clean by vultures before experts could examine it. Photographs were taken, however.

The various creatures in this mystery have been given the pseudo-scientific name Anomalous Biological Entities (ABEs).

Some suggest that ABEs could be the product of sophisticated manipulation. One such suggestion (http://www.princeton.edu/~accion/chupa13.html) goes on to say that a Chinese-Russian (surely he is either Russian or Chinese?) scientist, Dr Tsian Kanchen, has created new species of plant and animal organisms through genetic manipulation. New breeds of ducks and chickens have allegedly been created with physical characteristics of both. If this is the case, Birch wonders if they have the same physical deformities and illnesses that were manifest in Dolly the sheep and other failed attempts at genetic manipulation. Goats and rabbits were also allegedly created as well as corn/wheat, peanut/sunflower and cucumber/watermelon. The website goes on to draw an analogy with the possibility of chupacabras being genetically developed by humans.

Ed Lavendera, a reporter with CNN, says that chupacabras are the 'Bigfoot' of Latino culture and symbolise 'fear of something that doesn't exist'. Not a lot of Latinos in Russia, Ed; probably not that many in Maine, either.

Of course it is fascinating to speculate on the existence, or not, of such exotica. Fascinating, that is, unless you are a poor farmer trying to eke out a living whilst having your livestock destroyed by unknown species, or mange-ridden known ones. No doubt someone will offer tours of chupacabra country before long. There are always opportunities for those of a sharp business perspective to make money from strange phenomena. We suppose it would be too much to hope that some of the profits would be given to the hard-hit farmers.

The mythologies around these creatures seem to be building up as they did around UFOs and aliens in decades past. There are numerous videos of execrable quality on YouTube, at least one of which is a big mickey take. Perhaps the humorous ones are the best?

This is from www.crystalinks.com:

> The chupacabra is generally treated as a product of mass hysteria, though the animal mutilations are sometimes real. Like many cases of such mutilations, however, it has been argued that they are often not as mysterious as they might first appear, and in fact, a series of tests showcased by the

> National Geographic Channel in a show about the chupacabra pointed to the obvious conclusion that every single 'animal mutilation' can be explained by either people killing them or, more likely, other animals eating them. The loss of blood may be explained by insects drinking it.

On the blood loss issue, one investigator claims that chupacabras function as though they are a superior form of insect. His rationale for this is that they trap and consume the bodily fluids of their prey in a way similar to that of a spider. First a drug is injected through a bite which renders the prey unconscious. This is followed by a second injection of acid which liquefies the unfortunate victim's organs. The chupacabra then sucks out the liquids. In this scenario at least the doomed animal is unaware of its bizarre end.

www.crystalinks.com further notes:

> Chupacabras are said to appear in three specific forms:
>
> The first and most common form is a lizard-like being, appearing to have leathery or scaly greenish-gray skin and sharp spines or quills running down its back. This form stands approximately 3 to 4 feet (1 to 1.2 m) high, and stands and hops in a similar fashion to a kangaroo. In at least one sighting, the creature hopped 20 feet (6 m). This variety is said to have a dog or panther-like nose and face, a forked tongue protruding from it, large fangs, and to hiss and screech when alarmed, as well as leave a sulphuric stench behind. When it screeches, some reports note that the chupacabra's eyes glow an unusual red. Subsequently witnesses become nauseous.
>
> The second variety bears a resemblance to a wallaby or dog standing on its hind legs. It stands and hops as a kangaroo, and it has coarse fur with grey facial hair. The head is similar to a dog's, and its mouth has large teeth.
>
> The third form is described as a strange breed of wild dog. This form is mostly hairless, has a pronounced spinal ridge, unusually pronounced eye sockets, teeth, and claws. This animal is said to be the result of interbreeding between several populations of wild dogs, though enthusiasts claim that it might be an example of a dog-like reptile. The account during the year 2001 in Nicaragua of a chupacabra's corpse being found supports the conclusion that it is simply a strange breed of wild dog. The alleged corpse of the animal was found in Tolapa, Nicaragua, and forensically analyzed at UNAN-Leon. Pathologists at the University found that it was just an unusual-looking dog. There are very striking morphological differences between different breeds of dog, which can easily account for the strange characteristics.
>
> http://www.crystalinks.com/chupacabras.html

OK, time for a change. Up until this point, Birch had been separated from any violence in Mexico's crime and aggression ridden society. This was about to change. Birch was reading and relaxing when raised voices penetrated his consciousness. This was not an unusual event, so Birch ignored it. The raised voices developed into screams and bangs. Birch walked swiftly into the next room whence the noises emanated. He saw Jaqueline and her sister, Olivia, fighting. This was no British girlie fight with flapping hands and handbags at ten paces. This was punches being thrown and landing with loud thumps. Each of the fighters was holding onto the other, all the better to land their punches. These punches were being thrown from behind the shoulder, with strength and with the obvious intention of inflicting pain. Or was it so obvious?

It was at this point that Birch made his great mistake. He walked towards the combatants with the attitude of sorting it out. He assumed that was what was required. He laughed at this approach later. He reflected that he had probably looked a little like one of the sons of the British Empire organising the locals in some distant part of the planet. The only thing missing was his pith helmet and a pair of those ridiculous-looking, voluminous shorts that were worn in times past. He remembers saying something like, 'Now, ladies, let's relax and talk about this.' Whoops.

He might just as well have spoken in Martian for all the good that it did. In fact it stimulated a redoubling of the battle. For now there was another target to aim at. Birch found himself in the middle of a maelstrom. He realised, with a sense of surprise, that talking and sensible negotiation were not what the two women were looking for, at all. In fact, Birch realised that the fighters were enjoying the whole thing. At the very least it was therapeutic, allowing old scores to be settled and old frustrations exorcised. The situation was only halted when Coti, aided by Birch, managed to separate the two protagonists with no small difficulty.

As fighters and peacemakers calmed down, Jaqueline's broken glasses, various bumps and bruises and dishevelled clothing were the only harm that had befallen the players in the drama. The next day the whole thing was forgotten.

A few days later, Jaqueline and Birch took buses across the city to see their good friends, Miriam and Jesus. Three buses were necessary in that vast sprawling conurbation. On the last leg of the journey they had to travel through a down-at-heel area. The bus stopped. From the bus parked in front, two nefarious-looking men emerged. As they walked down the outside length of that bus, they banged noisily on the side. *Oh, God*, thought Birch. *I hope that they don't get on our bus.*

It was with a sinking feeling that Birch's hopes were dashed. The two mounted the steps of the bus. One stood by the entrance while the other stood by the exit. Birch realised that they were in trouble from prospective robbers, with both entrance and exit blocked. *What to do now?* Birch and Jaqueline looked at each other knowingly.

The decision was taken out of his hands. Almost immediately, there was an eruption behind him, and the rear-most would-be robber was beating a hasty retreat past Birch. A woman passenger was in hot pursuit. They were at arms' length, fighting. The passenger was giving as good as she got. If this had been a boxing match the points would have been about even. The home judge might even have given the round to the passenger.

The next few seconds were a blur; everybody, passengers, robbers, driver, piled off the bus. Birch saw that he had a cut hand. He had no idea how this had happened. The pair was still fighting, now on the pavement.

A few seconds later, the robber broke off the engagement and ran away from the scene along with his co-conspirator. Why they did this quickly became obvious. Within a few seconds, two policemen ran past Birch, pursuing said robbers. Everyone outside the bus started to calm down. Jaqueline spoke to the plucky passenger, asking her what had happened.

She replied, 'He asked for my gold bracelet. I have had a really bad day. There was no way I was going to give it to him.'

Fortunately, during their brief conversation, the passenger's daughter had spotted the police car parked in front of the leading bus. She had been first out of the bus and had raised the alarm. All the passengers were extremely fortunate, not only because of the bracelet passenger's attitude but also because the robbers had not brandished a gun or a knife, which is only too common in such situations.

Birch has said that the Mexicans are a tough, nuggety people. The country has had many world champion boxers at the lighter weights, probably out of all proportion to the country's population.

As Birch's friend, Jesus, said when the story was recounted to him afterwards, 'Welcome to Mexico.' Funny how people kept saying this to Birch. Jesus and Miriam had been robbed at knifepoint, having their leather jackets stolen.

Birch decided that he wanted to visit Teotihuacan, the pyramid city where 'men became gods', on December 29th. One of his spiritual friends in England had suggested that this was to be a high-energy day. Much information about this magnificent temple of the ancients can be gleaned from our first book, *So You Think We're Alone?*

Five went to Teo. The party comprised Jaqueline, Miriam, Jesus, Jesus' brother and Birch. The party walked out of Miriam and Jesus' house. After roughly half an hour of walking through built-up areas, Birch started to wonder if they were going to walk the twenty miles to the pyramids. They stopped at Miriam's sister's house. Jesus read Birch's unsaid thoughts. 'This is Mexico,' he said, grinning.

Miriam's sister gave the gringo and Jaqueline a tour of the house. 'This is my house, the décor, my furniture, blah, blah, blah.' Twenty minutes later, the party decamped and piled into a car to be driven by Jesus' brother. The car had been loaned by Miriam's brother. Such are the family workings in Mexico.

In Teo, Birch followed the ritualistic pattern and meditations outlined by Miguel Ruiz in his book *Beyond Fear* and explained more fully in *So You Think We're Alone?* To Birch's surprise, everyone followed him in the first eleven meditations. Although Jesus' brother did not speak English, Jesus translated for him. It seemed ironic to Birch that there was a foreigner showing Mexicans their spiritual heritage. Like many others, Miriam, Jesus and his brother had visited the site but had previously seen it as a historic monument rather than the truly initiatory temple that it is. As the party returned to Mexico City, Birch blessed the circumstance that had brought *Beyond Fear* into his possession.

Birch feels that Mexicans are a race exploring emotions through their family relationships, whereas north of the border the US race is exploring the intellect through business and technology. Obviously both explorations are occurring on both sides of the border, but the predominance is as suggested.

The violence that permeates Mexican culture is the shadow side of this exploration of the heart and emotions. Inevitably there needs to be positive and negative in order for there to be creativity at the interaction of the two. One cannot know itself unless confronted with its opposite. This applies both to the two sides of the Mexican heart exploration and to the Mexican–US love/hate relationship. The US abuses Mexico by placing its dirty and polluting industrial factories in Mexico, where employment opportunities are desperately needed. Mexico responds by invading the US with its illegal immigrants, a flow that the US is unable to stop, despite its avowed intentions.

This invasion is an interesting reflection of the US invasion and occupation of the previously Mexican lands of southern California, Arizona, New Mexico and Texas. This could be argued to be a balancing of the historical imperatives of the nineteenth century. Los Angeles is now the third biggest Mexican city by population.

Birch believes that it is time for the heart cultures to have their day; not that Birch is advocating that other countries should adopt the Mexican model, but the head culture is in apparent decline. As one British diplomat said to an American colleague while discussing the issues in Iraq and Afghanistan, 'You don't get it, it's over.' He meant that the ability of the head cultures (as typified by the US) to control events all over the world was finished. Empires, in their dominance, became so arrogant that they were mostly blind to their decline. Birch believes it is no less true of this latest empire. Birch is not anti-American. He is anti-empire. In fact he is very pro-US, the country, and has enjoyed many good and positive experiences with its charming and lively people.

It may be that some citizens reading this book may feel a little like former president Lyndon B Johnson, who remarked dryly, 'If I walked on water across the Potomac River the newspapers would display the banner headlines, "The President Can't Swim".'

After breakfast on the last day of their trip, Jaqueline dragged Birch away from being run over by a car. It must have been Knock Over a Gringo Day. It was time to return to England, to cold, rain, grey skies and certainty in everyday life … maybe.

Travels with 'Crazies' Part 1

Exploring Paris to Brittany. Group energy work

The party gathered at Charles de Gaulle Airport; all seekers of ancient and deep energies from USA, Canada, Germany, England and Australia they came. It was a little like the first day of term at school: new kids meeting for the first time, smiling and talking, extending themselves to mentally feel the personalities of those around them with whom they would spend the next two weeks.

At the regular meditation sessions with Mary and Joan, prior to travel, Mary had received an insight of a family of lions supporting Birch from the spiritual realm. Birch had left Joan's house after this final meditation before travelling, when two crows had flown over adjacent trees: a good luck sign according to Mary. Birch recalled an insight telling him that this trip was the second stage of a journey he had started while working in the Languedoc the previous year.

A forty-five minute wait for Birch's luggage to arrive in baggage claim culminated in him filling out a lost luggage claim form with the assistance of the bored and aggressive clerk, her face set and unsmiling. While they were in the middle of this administration, something persuaded Birch to turn to face the baggage belt. He casually looked round to see his bag, in splendid isolation, gently moving around the belt.

One of Birch's fellow travellers, Sue, the other Brit in the party at this early stage, had the same experience with her luggage. The message for both of them was, *be careful of your thoughts; they can now bring instant action.* Birch's thinking had been defensive and negative as he had waited. The other message was, *patience, patience.*

As Birch sped away from the desk to collect his travel bag, he heard the voice of the clerk in his ears saying, 'Monsieur, you are very fortunate.'

As the party drove to Chartres, Carol, one of Birch's fellow energy seekers, told him the story of Red Elk, a Native American shaman. He would send his consciousness deep into the Earth to communicate with

Satan. Red Elk told Satan that he loved him because he was manifesting the dark side for the Creator. The shaman felt protected by this love. Red Elk said that Satan genuinely felt separated from the Creator, and presumably from the creations of the Creator also. This makes sense if Satan is separated from all the rest of Creation.

This approach conflicts with that of the Christian Church. The pope has ordered bishops to set up exorcism squads to tackle the rise of Satanism. This religion sees Satan as the enemy and separate from God's creation.

As they approached Chartres, Birch felt that this was a group that had been together in Atlantis. Several group members sensed this to be the case. Those that were there and were not part of the Atlantis spiritual connection were connected in some other way. Perhaps members of the group were there to expiate past karma.

The coach was full of chatter as the seekers shared their truths. Sue, an English astrologer, told Birch about Chiron, discovered in 1977, a planet that puzzles astronomers because it doesn't strictly follow Newtonian laws. In astrological terms it has had a function of healing the split between the physical and the metaphysical of humanity from the time of its discovery. It is in people's consciousness enough to assist in bringing about these changes.

As Birch wrote this section he was thinking that it would be nice to have a pen that was thin enough to fit into the top of the pad on which he was writing. Within a few minutes he noticed, caught in the webbing at the back of the seat in front of him, a very appropriate pen of the right size. Was this instant manifestation, or what?

Further to the Atlantis insight, Sue told Birch that at 8 pm French time, the high point of the spring equinox, a perfect hexagram would be formed astrologically and Vesta would be on one of the points of this hexagram. Vesta is a key element of this linking to the temple work that this group performed in Atlantis, Birch feels.

Vesta energy links to focus, purity of intent and manifestation of spirit, and these qualities have been part of humanity's journey since the beginning of time, claims Sue.

Wikipedia has two things to say about Vesta:

> Vesta was the virgin goddess of the hearth, home and family in Roman mythology. She had a large albeit mysterious role in Roman religion long before she appeared in Greece. Vesta's presence was symbolised by the

> sacred fire that burned at her hearth and temples. Vesta's fire was guarded, at her temples, by her priestesses, the Vestales.
>
> Vesta is the second most massive object in the asteroid belt with a mean diameter of about 530 km (around 330 miles) and an estimated mass of 9% of the entire asteroid belt. Vesta lost 1% of its mass in an impact less than one billion years ago. Many fragments of this impact have impacted Earth as meteorites, a rich source of evidence about the asteroid. Vesta is the brightest asteroid ...

Sue possesses another special talent. One day she noticed there was a great stillness in the air; it was palpable and it felt as if time had stopped. A few hours later she woke to her bedroom shaking and trembling. She felt she was being shaken, rattled and rolled. Sue believes that she picked up on the sense that animals have just before a major earth shift. It is a common phenomenon that animals leave an area just before earthquakes and other natural disasters arrive.

It was now 1717 hours: a time of fortunate coincidences. The travellers saw the twin spires of Chartres Cathedral in the distance; exquisite timing. As the old rhyme says, 'No doubt the universe is unfolding as it should.' The French call the spring equinox the Day of Music, during which they mount festivals in many cities.

As the spires grew bigger, Birch's mind returned to the strange events that had brought him on this journey. Towards the end of the previous year, Birch had attempted to join a tour to the most sacred sites of Guatemala: Copán, Quierga, Tikal and Antigua. Set in magical jungles and plains, these were places close to his heart, places where the highest vibrations could be accessed. He was determined to return to these magical centres, from an emotional and intellectual point of view, despite the fact that his guidance had informed him that his spiritual journeying and work was finished in Central America.

Birch emailed the website advertising the tour. Nothing happened, no reply after more than a week. He emailed again. Two more weeks rolled by and no sign of a reply. At the end of this period he saw another ad, this time for a tour of Brittany and Malta being organised with Brenda. It is Brenda who channels the Pleiadians, and her channelling was at the heart of the tour. This rang a chord with Birch. He already knew and was impressed by Brenda's work. He had also completed a month in France the previous year. He emailed the tour organiser. Within twenty-four hours, Chas Smith, the aforesaid tour organiser, had emailed back promising him a place on the tour. He was pleased to accept. Something within his intuitive nature relaxed.

That same day another email arrived, this time from the Guatemala tour, inviting him to join. Now, Birch is a creature who is sensitive to signs and pointers. It was clear to him that his original guidance had indeed been correct, that there was no spiritual need for him to work in Guatemala, but there was some work to be done in France. It was later that his guidance pointed out to Birch that this trip was part two of the work done in the previous year.

Chartres lies on the left bank of the Eure River on a hill overlooked by the UNESCO World Heritage cathedral. The name Chartres derives from 'Carnutes', an ancient people that lived here before the Romans. It was an important town during Roman times. In 1417 it was captured by the English, who were ejected in 1432. In the Franco-Prussian war of 1870 it was captured by the Germans and was an important centre of activity for that conflict. It was heavily bombed during the Second World War.

The town has been a centre of pilgrimage for Christians since the Middle Ages. The poet Charles Péguy, 1873–1914, revived the pilgrimage route between Paris and Chartres before the First World War. There is now an annual sixty-two mile pilgrimage on foot from the Cathedral of Notre Dame de Paris to the Cathedral of Notre Dame de Chartres.

The cathedral is one of the finest examples of Gothic architecture in Europe and built between 1194 and 1260; an extraordinarily quick construction for mediaeval times. It is believed by some that since 876 AD the church preceding the cathedral housed a tunic that was a relic belonging to the Virgin Mary, which certainly stimulated pilgrimage there. Its alleged survival after a fire in the cathedral, which was given miracle status by the Church of Rome, did nothing to restrict the flow of resources in the cathedral-building programme. The relic philosophy of Christian churches holding clothing and artefacts associated with Christian saints is shot through with inconsistencies, alleged frauds and lack of attributable evidence.

Wikipedia says of relics,

> A relic is an object or a personal item of religious significance, carefully preserved with an air of veneration as a tangible memorial. Relics are an important aspect of some forms of Buddhism, Christianity, Hinduism, shamanism, and many other religions.

> In Christianity, relics are the material remains of a deceased saint or martyr and objects closely associated with those remains. Relics can be entire skeletons, but more usually they consist of a part such as a bone, hair or tooth. Pieces of clothing worn by the deceased saint or even an object that has come in contact with a relic is also considered a relic.
>
> Relics have played an important role in Christian ritual since the earliest centuries of the church and were a major part of popular religion in the Middle Ages. Until 1969, relics were placed under the altar stones of all Roman Catholic churches. The veneration of relics was rejected by most of the Protestant Reformers and most Protestants today, but relics continue to play an important part in Catholic and Orthodox Christianity.

From Birch's perspective any material substance emanates a vibration, thus any object or garment that has been infused with the vibrations of an evolved person will continue to radiate that vibration. So there is a deep spiritual truth in the retention of such objects. Whether they should be venerated is another matter. Perhaps if such objects bring one closer to compassion or higher awareness then there is value in them.

All this reminds Birch of the occasion he went to a Catholic church service with his then partner, Brigid. She had been brought up in that culture and was connected to Catholicism. During the service Birch received the illumination that relics were placed under the altar of a newly consecrated church. He was also told by guidance that this religion worked with practices that were close to the mystical rituals of the Rosicrucian Order, AMORC, of which Birch was a member at the time. Birch assumed that these practices were not available to the majority of Catholic adherents.

Touring the cathedral is always one of Birch's great pleasures. This time it was without the companionship of the Temple Study Group and without the profound insights of its co-ordinator, Jacques Rangasamy. It was Friday, so the chairs in the nave had been removed, allowing the maze, in all its glory, to be revealed and for pilgrims to walk it. As on the previous visit, Birch walked the maze performing the Pilgrims' Walk as demonstrated to him by a German pilgrim several years before. The walk consists of taking two steps forward and one back with a rocking of the heel and toes between both sequences. This is a wonderful paradigm for life itself. Life is a series of progressions and apparent reversals. In addition, the rhythm of the walk can take one into a meditative state assisted by the wonderful vibrations of this harmonious temple. Every time Birch performs this walk in Chartres, he feels as though he is a dweller in two worlds, which, by the way, is the way he feels about his current existence.

As far as the walk in Chartres is concerned, it is necessary to be in this three-dimensional consciousness as well as in an exalted state, for the Pilgrims' Walk takes some time to complete. On this occasion it took an hour. Others not working with this walk wished to overtake. As before, he could usually sense the vibration of the person immediately behind him, so Birch stepped aside, smiled and waved the person through before continuing with his own perambulation.

The other obstacle to complete atunement with Pilgrims' Walk is the passing of often annoyed Christian worshippers who walk along the nave on their way to mass being performed further up the cathedral near the altar, and also on their return. Their annoyance may be based on the premise that the mystics shouldn't be there, in the view of the Christians. Birch reached this impression as he watched the Christians stomp across the maze with muttered comments and set faces. The fact that the maze-walkers all behaved in a sacred manner, although from a mystical rather than a Christian perspective, didn't wash with many of them.

The group toured the lower level guided by one of the official cathedral guides. They toned together in front of the Black Madonna for peace and for the invocation of healing energies. Toning is the process of singing or chanting a particular note or notes on the harmonic scale. Sometimes a word or vowel sound is incorporated, sometimes not. It is considered particularly efficacious if toning is done in a group and at a spiritual location. Sometimes toning can be done with a particular spiritual purpose in mind.

The group stared into the depths of the druidic well and were reminded that this had been a sacred site for thousands of years. Indeed there is a story that water was deliberately funnelled through the greatest depths under the site in order for the power of the water energy to increase the already powerful energies.

As the toning was being performed, Birch and the Brenda group were stared at in bemusement by other groups, probably more conventionally minded, who were walking through wondering what the devil (oops!) was going on.

At dinner that evening, one of the group told a story of how the people of Peru employed a burying technique that retained potatoes in an eatable state for twenty years. Birch supposed that this was used as storage against possible future famines. The person telling the story said that she had eaten one and couldn't tell the difference between that and a fresh one. This person talked to many of the others in the group. Birch felt that she was assisting in focussing the group energy and also stimulating others. In the Atlantean group, Birch sensed, she had performed the same role, focussing group energy and practices.

It is very interesting how personal contact can bring up communications from the past. Birch felt that there had been a dissonance of energy between Brenda and him in the far distant, Atlantean times. His guidance said that the two had each 'fronted up' different priesthood groups and consequently fell out with each other in a big way. Birch's issue had been ego; Brenda's had been power. This clash had destroyed them both in the long term, although Brenda had been victorious in the short term. There is certainly no problem between the two now; quite the reverse. Birch likes her very strong energy.

On the coach from Chartres to Brittany, it rained very heavily; the water element was attempting to cleanse the Earth of pollutants, while also showing humanity that to ignore the elements was a perilous path. Around 25th June, Saturn is opposite Neptune in the astrological chart, manifesting water. What did the group get? Rain every day. Birch wondered if man's manipulation of the climate was also having an impact.

Chas, the trip organiser, explained the so-called chemtrail interference with the weather where aircraft traverse the sky in a grid pattern, laying a clearly visible trail. Sometimes a gooey substance falls to earth after such a performance, covering car windscreens. He claims that one person of his acquaintance developed a fearful rash after some of this substance fell on his arm. One person in the States gathered some of this material and sent it by post to a laboratory to be analysed. They were taken to a court of law and fined for sending a harmful substance through the post. Birch has seen these grid-like patterns over Cheltenham a couple of times. One claim was that after these trails had been laid, clear skies turned dull and appeared polluted.

Haines is reminded of something he witnessed back in 2003, or maybe it was 2004. On a bright, cloudless day, he was in his back garden in Gloucestershire, England. The sight of commercial aircraft and their contrails was by no means unusual. But this time it was different. An aircraft must have passed by, for Haines could see the contrail running from west to east. This was no ordinary contrail. Every so often, at regular intervals, the trail was punctuated by a doughnut-shaped ring, as if there were a regular pulse. Some months later, he watched a programme on TV which discussed this very effect. From memory, Haines thinks the programme was implying a new and secret form of propulsion. Authorities denied that any such propulsion existed. That, of course, is what they must do with secret projects. Fast forward to 2008 and we now know of the existence of pulse detonation wave engines. Might this have been what Haines saw?

Saturday arrived and a diversion seemed reasonable. The group played the game of writing a message or word that comes from the inner-self, passing it on and then taking a message written by someone else. Birch wrote the word 'release'. Whether that was for himself as well as the person to whom he passed it is in some doubt.

Les Alignements de Carnac is one of the very ancient wonders of the world. Miles and miles of stones, laid out in perfect alignment, attest to a great intelligence and engineering ability. Huge dolmens are sprinkled throughout the complex. Indeed, dolmens are very well represented in this area.

Archaeologists say that the Alignements were erected 6,000 years ago. Many legends have grown and been discarded over the centuries. Mythical figures were said to move around the stones and to appear as fairies or dwarves. Another story said that the site was Caesar's army turned to stone.

The stones at the first site the party visited, the Le Ménec Carnac alignments, were laid out in perfectly straight lines, terminating in a working centre. The largest stones were nearest the working centre; the smallest were furthest away. Birch walked down as far as he could to the small stones. Paradoxically he received the strongest energies from these. He walked in a purposeful but open, energetic stride towards the working centre, tiling the largest end stones. Birch's buddy, Sheena, saw him as a druid shaman in this place. Birch certainly felt at home there.

Many archaeologists have hypothesised about the purpose of these alignments. No one knows for sure. For Birch they are places that focus great energies which could be manipulated and used by the ancient shamans. The consciousness of the ancients interwove with and manipulated their environment to a far greater extent than ours today. They saw themselves as being part of the panoply of nature rather than the controllers. The consciousness of separation between humanity today and the environment is exemplified by the perception of nature bringing positive benefits or negative results, and humans being the passive receivers. This appears to be a common way of understanding the relationship.

At the second site, Chas explained that successive stones had alternating straight and curved sides. On learning this, Birch immediately saw the energy moving up the lines of stones in a spiral fashion to be focussed at the ends of the lines. The spiralling energy moved around the curved surface, the relative positive one. The flat surface on the other side was the relative negative or passive side. The energy was then worked for social, fertility and human benefits.

Carnac is of the heart. Before the group reached the second site, Birch's heart became constricted. As he stood there he could feel his heart relaxing and releasing. Birch felt his asthma cause his lungs to constrict briefly and then release. As he stood with his back to one of the large stones, it was as though his heart were being worked on by forces, or beings, unseen.

The whole group toned at a large straight stone at the end of the site.

A third site was entirely different. The stones were straight and tall. The energy was going vertically with very little coming out to be accessed from the sides. The vertical energy was connected to inter-dimensional and extra-terrestrial dimension. Group member Maureen sensed that the interaction of the stones was creating energy vertically up into the cosmic realms and also down into the Earth.

So this was Birch's experience in Carnac. The scale of the plan and the layout over many square miles indicates a strategy that was vast in scope. Birch has visited many much smaller sites which have incredibly powerful energy patterns and purposes. The work performed at Carnac and its purpose must have been truly important for the ancients.

'There were giants in those times', one reads of myths from the past. These myths may be closer to the truth than we are prepared to admit today. It is alleged that humanoid skeletons have been found of thirteen, twenty-two, fifty feet in height and that the discovery of these remains has been suppressed. The story of David and Goliath may have more to it than merely being an interesting myth.

Certainly this incredible place, Carnac, would have been to scale for a race of beings that towered over the landscape. In addition, it seems to Birch that Carnac is a place that functions in a number of realities. If you like, it is a temple complex that functions in this three-dimensional world of humans and also in other realms of existence with which humanity struggles to communicate, but which are nevertheless real in the multiverse.

Some years ago Birch had an experience at a much smaller circle of stones: the Rollright Stones in England. Immediately after leaving the site, he was taken by his inner senses to another version of this temple in stone. There he saw the energies circling, akin to a child's spinning top, but this top was spinning on many planes of reality. Carnac is another of these places which will realise its extended potential for those sensitive souls that are sufficiently in tune with it. As we, as a race, progress toward greater contact with inner forces, Birch looks forward to the secrets being revealed. He looks forward to humanity being able to work with the released energies and secrets.

Birch was jolted back to conditions in England when Jaqueline rang the hotel one evening. She said that the river behind their flat had reached the top of its banks due to the excessive rain and was in danger of overflowing. Birch asked the group to work on the problem. Brenda suggested that the group move the rain clouds away from the home. It worked. The rain stopped and the river subsided.

Phil, who called himself an unbeliever and was only in the group to support his wife, had nevertheless an energetically empathetic role to play in this group, Birch sensed. First he played the role of the watcher. This is a profoundly mystical principle that requires much inner work to tease out its full implications. There is a theory in a number of circles that says that simply watching something changes the nature of the energy or object. Scientists say that if a person watches an experiment, then that changes the nature and result of the experiment. In chi gong, the gaze of the person performing the movements is considered very important in focussing and directing energy. Birch had the subsequent insight that the watcher adds his or her energy to that which is being watched. The watcher may not be aware that they are contributing. Awareness increases the influence of the watcher on the watched.

During chi gong and meditation, Birch and his two friends, Hazel and Audrey, have experienced a being, the Silent Master (as he calls himself), standing close by and watching. Birch points out that the chi gong practitioners need to be particularly sensitive in order to be aware of his presence in another realm, while they are in the third dimension.

So this was the role Birch saw Phil performing. He was an understanding soul. His watching energy was contributing in a way that was difficult to explain but was, nevertheless, very powerful.

Phil's second role was that of the trickster. This archetype persuades us through jokes, humour and unexpected interventions to look at reality and our understanding of it in a way other than that of the past. The trickster will make its presence felt when there are lessons to be learned that we are not absorbing by other, more conventional means. It can shock us into a mode of thinking or understanding that is for our highest good.

Phil had such a great sense of humour which relaxed, took members of the group out of an over-serious approach, and assisted in allowing the energies of understanding to enter.

He told Birch a story of how he and Mamie, his wife, went to a new age weekend some years before with a couple of friends. The other woman in the little party was a pot smoker. One evening, when the four were together, the pot smoker pulled out a very large and long joint. Phil and Mamie had no previous experience of this particular addiction. Phil was not a smoker, so after taking a little puff and initially feeling no effects, he was admonished by Pot Smoker to take long deep draughts into his lungs. The joint was passed around, all four partaking of the happy weed.

Mamie became morose under the influence. Phil, on the other hand, taking deep gasps of the smoke, became more and more light-hearted. He caught the eye of Pot Smoker, who was similarly afflicted, and they both broke out into sustained and uncontrollable laughter. They laughed until their eyes ran with tears. They laughed until Phil was struggling and gasping to take enough air into his lungs to breathe and send out explosive shouts of hilarity. Their laughter went on and on. People in neighbouring rooms banged on the walls and complained that they couldn't sleep for the incredible din. By this time it was midnight, and everybody had to be up for morning meditation at 5 am. Eventually the four staggered to bed and into a drug-fuelled slumber.

The next day, Phil and the others attended an esoteric discourse at the end of which questions were solicited from the audience. Mamie kicked Phil's foot hard. 'Don't you dare put your hand up,' she hissed in his ear.

Phil was still under the influence of the previous night's inhalations and the response to Mamie's attempted control was, of course, predictable. Phil raised his hand and immediately went into a flow of verbiage to the whole group. He didn't have a clue what he was saying. His mind was a blank, but the opening and shutting of his mouth and the emanating sounds continued for some time.

At the end of the session, as Phil and Mamie left the room, a number of the other participants came up to him. As they approached, he felt the worst was about to be heaped on his head. Instead, to Phil's jaw-dropping surprise, he was told by admiring commenters, 'What you said was so profound and inspiring.' To this day Phil doesn't have a clue what he said at this seminar.

There is an old saying, 'out of the mouths of babes and sucklings', which is an indicator of wisdom spoken by the innocent. Perhaps this could be amended to 'out of the mouths of babes, sucklings and those under the influence.'

Diane, yet another member of the group, told Birch the story of sitting next to Laura Bush's publicist, who said that the first lady was going to Mali, a poor African desert kingdom, in order to check on projects being funded by the mighty US dollar. Diane was puzzled, as was Birch, as to the reason why Mrs Bush was going there. There had to be some other reason, Birch hypothesised. A public official used to the way in which money was spent effectively would have seemed a better bet to oversee these projects.

The Morbihan region of Brittany has a unique collection of megaliths. The Gavrinis cairn lies at the heart of the region, on a small island in the gulf. Archaeologists claim that the structure was completed between 4500 and 2000 BC. Some of the stones seem to have come from even older monuments.

The word megalith comes from the Greek words *mega*, meaning large, and *lithos*, a stone. Megalithism is a worldwide phenomenon wherein large blocks of stone are used for cultural, religious and spiritual reasons. A cairn, from the Gaelic word *carn*, describes an architectural structure made of dry stone covering a space that archaeologists call a grave. Those of an alternative persuasion doubt that these were graves. Originally, the inner space could have been sealed by the stones.

Lying at the southernmost tip of the island of Gavrinis is the cairn, a dolmen covered by a pile of stones. It is an example of Stone Age architecture making use of dry stone building techniques.

There were amazing energies inside this dolmen. When Birch closed his eyes he was immediately taken into another conscious space. He perceived that one purpose of this structure was to project individuals into another dimension of consciousness. The individual would be prepared outside and then he or she would lie down in the chamber within the dolmen. A priest would then strike the prone person's third eye, externally identified as the space between the eyebrows, with a tuning fork-type metal rod. This would project the lying person's consciousness into another dimension for the purpose of illumination, knowledge and adventure.

Energy patterns also ran around the outside of the structure. In this dolmen, selected deceased people would be placed to assist them in moving to other realms. The patterns of swirls on the walls inside the chamber acted as trigger points for sensory deprivation in the consciousness work. The carvings on the walls could also be used as visual stimuli to tune into certain energies. Some in the group saw this place as a spiritual womb. It was perceived that women would give birth just outside the chamber.

Later, Birch had a further insight detailing ceremonies that were performed there. The aspirant would undergo an intensive period of preparation before the ceremony. A period of severe meditation and fasting was necessary to begin the process of gently separating the aspirant from three-dimensional, everyday consciousness. Closer to the planned ceremony, the aspirant's body would be washed in purified water and smeared with unguents. Special clothing would be worn by the aspirant, priests and priestesses. This would further raise the vibrations of all concerned in the ceremony. The day of the ceremony would have been pre-selected by priests, cosmically inspired or convinced by the propitious times. These propitious times could include quarter days, solar and lunar eclipses and full moon.

A select gathering of priests, priestesses and aspirants would gather outside the sacred cave. The aspirant would enter and lie down. A period of chanting and the burning of sacred plants inside would take the aspirant into an ecstatic state. When the appropriate level of consciousness was reached, the chief priest or priestess would strike the aspirant for the first time on the third eye with the specially prepared tuning fork. The arms of this tuning fork were quite long in order to create the required vibratory conditions. After the first strike, the chief priest would wait to see if the aspirant was fully out-of-body or not. This was a psychic condition for priest and aspirant. If it was felt necessary to raise the vibrations still further, there were opportunities to strike the third eye twice more. If the required out-of-body state had not been reached, then the ceremony would be abandoned and the aspirant gently returned to three-dimensional consciousness.

If the ceremony was successfully performed, the consciousness of the aspirant would move out of the body and into an extra-dimensional reality. There, he or she would be guided through various experiences by angels and spiritual guides. The soul, or higher consciousness, would function in this extra-dimensional reality but would remain connected to the body through the silver cord joined to the solar plexus chakra. The physical body of the aspirant would remain in the cavern throughout the extra-dimensional experience, being cared for until normal consciousness returned. The priests and priestesses would be made aware of the return by a change in breathing pattern and would begin a gentle process of returning the aspirant to everyday consciousness. This was a very delicate procedure. If it was not performed properly, then the psychic shock could kill the aspirant.

There would be occasions when the consciousness of the aspirant would not return to the physical body. The decision would have been taken by the aspirant and the higher forces for the aspirant to remain in the higher dimension. The priest in the cavern would become aware of this psychically as the silver cord connection would disintegrate and disappear. In this case, the body of the aspirant would go through the normal death process. There would then be a period of rejoicing and feasting to celebrate the aspirant moving to a higher level of consciousness. Not for them the doom and gloom of a religious funeral.

The priestess would have the responsibility of holding the enhanced vibration around the cavern in order to allow the process to be completed successfully. It was recognised in this culture that the female had access to the highest possible consciousness and vibration.

Drunvalo Melchizedek says this in *The Ancient Secret of the Flower of Life* vol. 1:

> This photo [of an ancient Egyptian wall mural] shows the tools and symbols of resurrection the Egyptians used. The object … is a shortened form of a rod that's usually about four feet long and has a little tuning fork on one end … This was used at the back of the head to transfer vibrations into the body.

So this tool was definitely used in ancient times. Birch's insight demonstrates its probable commonality among initiatory cultures. The difference in use of the tuning fork was that, in the above example, the aspirant was struck on the back of the head. In Birch's vision, the strike was on the third eye between the eyebrows.

Birch was told by Sue about a book called *The Gentle Art of Blessing* by Pierre Pradervand. Birch was so impressed with the highlights recounted to him that he bought a copy on his return home. Pradervand had been forced to resign from his job by partners. He was full of rage for the next three years. His anger was so intense that it made him ill. His life was on hold. This was until he read a book by an American doctor who had been with the troops in World War II.

The American told of his time in the army when he had been involved with the liberation of a concentration camp near Wuppertal. In the camp he came across a Polish Jewish lawyer who was apparently completely unaffected by the starvation and deprivation around him. In fact, the man exhibited vibrant health. The American initially assumed that the man had been in the camp for a short time. Not so; he'd been there for six years. The Polish Jew spoke numerous languages and acted as translator for the Americans. He was popular with all ethnic groups in the camp despite the fact that many of the groups loathed each other. He worked up to sixteen hours a day showing no signs of tiredness. The American asked him for the secret of his success. He replied that he had seen his wife and children shot in front of him by the Germans. The Germans had also been about to shoot him until they had discovered that he spoke German. So the assumption had been that he may be useful to the Germans in the future. While all this horror was going on he had had an illumination. He had decided that every day, for the remainder of his life, he would love everybody with whom he came in contact. So this was the way that he lived his life, and the result was clear to see.

So Pradervand started to work with this idea. It took him several years to become proficient, finding it especially difficult to bless his business enemies. When he felt that he had succeeded, he started to travel and to teach the techniques. Birch felt that there was something here for him.

The fairies play a large role in megalithic legends. La Roche-aux-Fées, or the Rock of the Fairies, is the most famous. The closest deposit of red shale, of which the dolmen is constructed, is 2.5 miles away, in the Theil forest. It was, of course, the fairies who transported the blocks in their aprons, according to legend. Les Roches is situated in Bretagne; Ille-et-Vilaine is sixty-two miles north of Nantes. The site has been known for centuries, but only recently made presentable. The local community cleared the area in the last couple of decades. Originally it would have been covered by a tumulus, which has now disappeared. A tumulus is a mound of earth and stones raised over a sub-surface space.

The group stood in the enormous cavern and toned. As they did so they tuned into the vibrations of the place. Birch suddenly dropped out of three-dimensional consciousness and into a surprising and unexpected vision. In his vision, the circle of humans was surrounded by another circle of beings, the difference being that this second circle consisted not of humans but of pixies, living in another realm of existence. They had been attracted to the sacred place by the toning and inner approach of humility and sensitivity. Birch saw their green jackets and red hats as they watched and communed with the energies that the group was invoking and transmitting. The vision lasted for seconds only.

Birch's visions make up a considerable and daily part of his life and reality. In his consciousness he has a foot in the camps of both three-dimensionality and more subtle realms. If Birch were confused by such realities and went to a doctor for a cure, no doubt Prozac would be prescribed.

As told in *So You Think We're Alone?*, Birch was in San Francisco on one occasion. As he walked down the street, there was a man in the gutter begging. He held up a sign written on cardboard. It said, 'Prozac did this to me'.

26th June and back to La Roche-aux-Fées; it was Birch's birthday. As a treat Brenda suggested that he stand in the middle of the group, which slowly circled him. The group toned as before. The toning vibrated around the dolmen, although there was no identifiable change in Birch's consciousness. One of the group members saw Birch moving in and out of physical manifestation and reality.

There was a really ancient oak tree next to the dolmen. The tree was connected to the pixies, in Birch's intuitive sense. It was at this point that he shared his vision with the others of them working together in Atlantis. There was another ritual performed at this oak tree, and that was a more party-oriented celebration of Birch's birthday. Food, drink, party hats and streamers created a birthday celebration. It was organised by Sheena and will live in Birch's memory for years to come.

Brenda told the story of a doctor in the US who had found cures for some forms of cancer by researching and applying ancient remedies. He was hounded out of practice by the FDA in the United States and sent to prison for eighteen months. His wife was told not to protest, otherwise their children would be taken away from her and she would never see them again. When he leaves prison the doctor will emigrate from the US to Ecuador.

Mont St Michel is a rocky island at the mouth of the Couesnon River in Normandy, roughly 0.62 miles from the north coast of France. The inhabitants of this island are called Montois. Mont St Michel was previously connected to the mainland by a narrow strip of land which was covered at high tide and exposed at low. In 1879 the land bridge was converted into a causeway which has allowed the passage of motorised traffic in most recent times. This status of sometimes being an island and at other times part of the land provides Mont St Michel with a powerfully energetic influence. Perhaps this is heightened by the imposing view as one drives toward it, and a powerful feeling of loss as one leaves. This latter influence was exemplified to Birch as the party left by coach. He found a continual emotional need to look back toward the disappearing island.

Legend says that the Archangel Michael appeared to the local bishop in 708 AD and instructed him to build a church on the rocky island. Angels and archangels were clearly bossier in those ancient times. The island is commemorated in the Bayeux Tapestry, which is dedicated to the 1066 Norman conquest of England. There is a further legend that Jesus visited it as part of his travels, according to *Anna, Grandmother of Jesus* by Claire Heartsong.

Constructed in the eleventh century, the Romanesque church on the island was converted to a prison after the French Revolution (1789–1799). The vibrations from that time would give opportunity for healing. The prison was closed in 1863 and declared a historic monument in 1874. It is also a UNESCO World Heritage Site. This trip seemed to be a tour of such affiliated sites. There remain a small number of monks still in residence.

A tour of the monastery during the evening, without the press of other tourists, was a blessing. It gave the group opportunity to explore at leisure and to tone at selected points, despite the presence of a guide.

Checkerboard symbology was evident on the floor of some chapels. This patterning is allegedly used by those manipulating three-dimensional reality in order to access other realms. The cross points between the squares are junction points for these connections. Sue told of standing on a similar floor and, when talking to another person standing on the same floor, realising that the quality of the sound in their conversation had changed. She felt somehow separated from the reality outside the squared floor. This occurred before she became interested in other realities and was absorbed by three-dimensional awareness in all aspects of conscious life.

The checkerboard symbology in one chapel was of three colours: black, white, and red. Brenda said that the red indicated that those working magically there were working with the allegedly sacred bloodlines. It was clear to those present that this place of high energy was being used for other than Christian ideals.

The tour reached a refectory, a long room with windows recessed and angled so when one looked down its length the windows were not visible. The group did several rounds of toning. After the first set was complete, Birch sensed that a tear had been made in the Christian skin over the suppressed energy which was attempting to well up. After the second round of toning it felt as though the skin had been ripped away. Birch also felt that healing for the prison environment had taken place.

A couple of the group were unhappy with the energies in the monastery. Perhaps it was caused by the manipulation of energies in the chapel, or perhaps an energetic contribution came from the time when it had been a prison.

At the time of this visit Birch was reading *Demons of the Inner World* by Alfred Ribi. He says:

> The saints (Christian) needed their demons in order to become saints, and the demons owed their existence to the one-sidedness of saints …
>
> If those ascetics had lived like other people around them, they would not have become more conscious. Their one-sided instinct resisting life violated the natural man in them and artificially invoked all the demons they needed to prove themselves in their struggle.

In this place of the Christian faith, the above seemed extraordinarily apposite.

Around six o'clock the following morning, a man entered Birch's consciousness. He was wearing a light-coloured coat buttoned all the way up the front, without collar and with alternating light and dark-hooped sleeves. He called himself Laurent. His role was as master of ceremonies in the rituals performed at the monastery. Kings, princes, queens and princesses of the alleged higher bloodlines and those that thought they were, Laurent added dryly, would come there when the women were heavily pregnant.

These kings and princes called and still call themselves cognoscenti: the knowers. They don't like the word 'illuminati', which is used in some quarters. The cognoscenti consider themselves a special group within the so-called bloodline families.

Laurent performed this work in the 1400s when in physical body, and is now part of the work that goes on at the monastery from his non-physical realm. The ancient ceremonies are still performed there by the cognoscenti families. The purpose of the ceremonies with which Laurent is involved is to imprint the unborn child with certain patterns of consciousness. Thus, when the child is born, it will be able to carry the consciousness of the bloodline forward. Without the continuation of these ancient ceremonies that go back to Atlantean times and before, the consciousness and effectiveness of the bloodlines tend to break down.

The reason for the abusive practices of certain other groups, Laurent explained, was that they didn't, or couldn't, replicate the Mont St Michel practices properly. As a result, they invoked the most appalling energetic forces in order to obtain similar effects. In addition, their own energetic signatures became extremely weak as they separated themselves from practices of the light.

These other elements did not have access to the purest bloodlines; they did not possess the essence of the cognoscenti ceremonies. The so-called illuminati realised that their practices became less and less effective as the astrological alignments changed over time. There are many cycles within cycles that are due to terminate at the winter equinox in 2012. Some are vast in time. 26,000 years, the Maya calendar cycle, is not the only Mayan calendar or even the longest cycle. All the cycles will finish on the winter equinox 2012. These changes are having profound effects on the cognoscenti and rival group energy practices. All these groups are extremely worried that their power is dying. They are looking for ways out and alternatives.

Let's return to the ceremony of impending birth: a term coined by Laurent. The kings and queens would come to this place and perform a movement ceremony at astrologically propitious times in order to invoke the best conditions for the babies to be imbued with codes of consciousness. Laurent wouldn't give Birch the astrological alignments because he, Birch, knew nothing about the art. He said that Birch should ask someone who knew about astrology to tune in to him. Birch discussed this with Sue, the astrologer on the trip. This was what she said:

> The planetary energies most linked to conception and birth are Moon, Venus, Chiron and Pluto, but the soul/essence of the child chooses the moment in time. The mother and father bring together the polarity energies and the spark of light is infused into the next incarnational journey. I have noticed that both Pluto and Chiron are key components in the timing of birth, and Venus is the diffusing, projecting, focussing planet of love at this frequency. The Moon in its cycle is not only intimately interconnected with the female hormonal cycle, but is equally responsible for breaking the waters at the time of birth.
>
> Fields within fields, our solar system linking into the galactic system, our galactic system linking into the universal system and so on and so on. The children that are being born now and in the future are conduit connections not just to this solar system but also out into deepest space. (As are many on the planet already. Indeed all are; it is just that many are unconscious of this reality.) As to the ritual that you spoke of, I do not have any recognition of the exact method used, but probably an invocation on the theme of the pentagram (the five-pointed star) would have been used in those times. However, we are now in a period when our intent and consciousness create the present and the future [and re-create the so-called past, says Birch] and our ability to create is directly proportional to our connections to source.

It was important that the king or prince take a role in the ceremony as the watcher and the presenter of the queen or princess and the soon-to-be-born baby. This ceremony was, and is, conducted by priests who were not Catholic. We would call them magicians today. They were of an ancient and powerful lineage. They were involved in the church and used it as a cover. Often the pope would have a dual role of pope and magician and would see both roles as equally important.

The second ceremony was (and is) performed in the bowels of the Earth, in a cave. In this ceremony there would be invocations to the deep powers of the Black Madonna cult, which is much more ancient than Christianity, in order to drive the codes of consciousness deeper into the blood and DNA of the unborn. This enhanced blood would then assist in the continuation of the superiority aspects, enabling the cognoscenti to continue to rule the roost on Earth as they saw fit. They see themselves as the true inheritors of alien consciousness and the other groups as repugnant usurpers.

Laurent said that he had contacted Birch because he was interested in the work that the group was doing. He said that, from his perspective, the group was doing two things. First, speeding up the final breakdown of the Christian element of consciousness. This was a prop for the work outlined above and the final ceremony which was to follow. Second, creating a template for the new that would be born there and brought through by others.

Laurent wished to be part of the new work and continue what he was doing. Birch did point out to him that he was part of the old, which might exclude him. Laurent replied that he had access to the greatest secrets, which would be useful to a future process. There is a third ceremony, called the Egyptian Rite, which is sexual in nature but not abusive. This is designed to bring conscious energy into the unborn through the ecstasy of the mother, re-enforcing and overlaying previous inputs of consciousness.

Laurent then moved to a different but related topic. He said that the meeting between HM Queen Elizabeth II and George W Bush that had just taken place (this was in 2007) had been cover for the different factions of cognoscenti and others to come together in order to re-establish their power. Laurent felt that this attempt would end in failure because no one in the various groups trusted those in the other groups. They cobbled together an agreement that would fail when tested. Centuries ago, one of the other groups had attempted to violently force the cognoscenti to give their secrets up. They had done so but had left certain elements out, thus reducing the potential power available. This was one of the reasons for the lack of trust.

With the above, Laurent withdrew, leaving Birch to ponder on their exchange. From Birch's point of view, many individuals were working so that the days of manipulative control groups over the lives of the remainder of humanity could be over. Thus he couldn't go along with the idea that one secret society would be replaced by another.

Birch sought some feedback from the meditation group friends at their monthly meeting at Hazel's house. Apart from Judith, the group was universal in feeling that this entity had used Birch for its own ends as he had been so open on the visit. Judith was of the view that there was some karmic issue. This would tie in with Maureen's view that Laurent was an aspect of Birch's own consciousness. This would certainly explain the ease of communication between the two. Birch subsequently felt that he had been given an opportunity to heal this aspect of his being.

In the future it is important that psychic power and energy be available to a much wider constituency. Every person on the planet has psychic abilities. The future is about assisting people to develop these abilities rather than ridiculing those who put their heads above the parapet. There should not be a future that retains these powers for the benefit of a self-appointed elite.

Prince Charles, the heir apparent to the British throne, once asked, 'What is wrong with elites?' If he would like to spare five or six hours, Birch would love to tell him.

Brenda made the point later that those in the know arrange the birth of the offspring at certain astrologically advantageous moments from a bloodline point of view.

An interesting insight that Birch received at Mont St Michel concerned the group's trusty tour organiser, Chas, and his wife Karen. In his vision Birch saw Chas as a monk in the Middle Ages and in contact with Karen even then. Karen was a man in that lifetime. He was arrogant, imperious, a representative of the local lord and a horse rider. He was on his high horse giving Chas instructions, orders from the lord. Even in those days Chas dealt with it in his diplomatic way while still holding onto his power. Chas did not resonate with this vision. Karen was more interested.

To Paris, and a tour hosted by Chas sharing his perspective of the alignments created by those who knew how to use the energies. There were black and white checkerboard squares at many road intersections: the 1 and 0 symbology which is linked to the checkerboard and which, of course, is the base of computer software structure. We will comment further on this symbology in the next chapter.

As a number of the group walked around a park near the hotel, they came across a most extraordinary sight. There, in the middle of the park, they happened upon an Ethiopian dressed in a bright yellow silk suit with a small black Chinese hat on his head. He was performing chi gong style movements but, incredibly at the same time, standing on a half-inch-wide metal ledge which ran around the grass area. The subtle movements would normally be performed with feet flat on terra firma to give a solid base to the performer. This man was in such an elevated state of physical balance that he could work in this extraordinary way. Birch, Maureen, and Sue were impressed.

The Ethiopian saw the trio watching and invited them over. After a brief mutual introduction, he demonstrated a trick of grabbing their hands before they could grab his. This was from a start position of backs of their hands together, his against theirs, back to back. He competed against the trio, one at a time. He won every time. He was so adept that he could beat the visitors even when he looked away from them. He subsequently explained that he started from a point of complete relaxation and concentration in which he could feel their energies. He was such a happy soul. The only sign of stress that he demonstrated occurred when a gendarme approached. This broke up the meeting. The three and the Ethiopian went their separate ways.

The way that this man appeared to Birch, Maureen and Sue in his highly coloured outfit, and his personality, indicated the work of the trickster we have discussed before. Birch took this as a cue to look deeper into movement systems. He had recently given up teaching chi gong. He'd reached a plateau with the techniques that had been learned and practised over several years. Clearly there was now more for him to work with to develop his techniques.

This signalled the end of the France and Brittany leg of the tour; time to move on.

Travels with 'Crazies' Part 2

Fantastic temples and insights – Malta and Gozo

Before we go further accompanying Clive Birch on his adventures, Haines points out that, contrary to his better judgement, Birch continues to refer to himself as 'a crazy' and those with whom he works as 'the crazies'. Perhaps one day we will all learn the truth about whether or not he is crazy?

From www.visitmalta.com, one can find that the Maltese Islands are steeped in 7,000 years of history. The islands were a centre of much activity in Neolithic times, leaving remains of mysterious megalithic temples allegedly dedicated to the goddess of fertility. The Phoenicians, Carthaginians, Romans and Byzantines all left their marks on the islands.

St Paul was shipwrecked there in 60 AD while on his way to Rome. Christianity had arrived. The Arabs were dominant from 870 AD and are best remembered for their impact on the Maltese language. Until 1530, Sicily dominated Malta. The Military Order of St John ruled from 1530 to 1798 (now the Sovereign Military and Hospitaller Order of Saint-John of Jerusalem, Rhodes and Malta or Sovereign Military Order of Malta, whose present constitution dates from 24th June 1961). This was a golden age as the island was a key element in the culture of seventeenth and eighteenth-century Europe. Caravaggio, Mattia Preti and Favray were commissioned by the knights to beautify churches and palaces.

Bonaparte conquered Malta in 1798 and held it until the British took over in 1800. Independence came in 1964. It converted to a republic in 1974 and has been a member of the EU since 2004.

The Republic of Malta comprises seven islands, the largest two of which are Malta and Gozo. Found there are prehistoric megalithic temples and underground chambers which are perplexing to archaeologists. They have no answers to how and why they were built. They offer theories. Birch has no answers either, but does offer some insights.

The party arrived in Gozo, the second island in the Republic, after a flight from Paris. The most notable element of the flight was Birch having his prized jam and honey, purchased in France, confiscated as he was carrying them in hand luggage. Birch's protests were met with a comment that he should have put them in his case. Apart from the potential mess that would have been caused if the jars had broken when the luggage was handled at either airport, it escaped Birch how, if he were bringing a lethal substance, it would be any less lethal in his case compared to hand luggage. It will occur to the reader, sooner or later, that Clive Birch and air travel go together like peaches and creosote. In the not too distant future, Haines and Birch will be flying to Albania, where Haines has business interests. Haines has vowed not to leave Birch's side for a moment at Gatwick and especially not at Tirana's Mother Teresa Airport. Haines says that the Albanians are some of the friendliest and most charming people in the world, but he fears that Birch will try even their patience as he stumbles around the airport arguing with the staff.

The Ġgantija temple complex consists of two temples surrounded by a massive boundary wall. The enormous dimensions of the megaliths have helped to create stories of construction by giants. The name of the temple is derived from the Maltese for 'giant'. It is claimed to be one of the oldest temple complexes in the world, as old as the pyramids, allegedly.

Birch felt nauseous after visiting what looked like temple walls behind the hotel. He had stood on the walls, sending out healing to the place. It felt as though it were needed. As the party drove in the coach towards Ġgantija, Birch processed the energy up through his body and out through the crown chakra, cascading the energy through his aura, allowing and asking the higher-self to deal with it. After about ten minutes he felt much better.

Ġgantija is a temple to a goddess and was built on principles similar to New Grange in Ireland, according to group member and builder Tony. The outer back walls, built in a semi-circle, exhibited the 1 and 0 alternating pattern. Sue told Birch that this pattern unlocked the energy pattern of the mind. The ancients, by building these patterns into their temples, had linked this energy to nature. Present humanity has lost that connection. Our computer language, also based on 1 and 0, has separated us from nature.

Karen explained that some of the stones were coloured red, indicating that, possibly, menstrual blood had been used in ritual. Birch has talked before about the use of menstrual blood for psychic and control purposes. Women in Mexico have used it, mixing it with food to control their partners. They need to take care with this technique, for too much of the blood could turn their partners into near-automatons. Birch believes that this could be the case only if the partners were unconscious in psychic and spiritual terms. A spiritual awareness would counteract this manipulation in his view.

Some paternalistic religious groups show their terror of the power of menstruation by, for example, banning sexual intercourse during the menstrual cycle and separating women from normal family activity, branding them as unclean.

Birch stood at the back middle of the temple with the end walls curving away from him. He felt a great, powerful energy flow. At one point, Maureen stood in front of him to take a photo. Immediately the energy changed. The energy was modified as it went through Maureen, and then Birch felt a softer, gentler energy moving through him. In that moment, the two were playing out an ancient ritual of moving the energies through their bodies in tandem. They had worked together in a similar mode eons before, Birch sensed intuitively.

Maureen told Birch of a visit that she had made on another Brenda tour which had included an audience with the pope. There had been all of 10,000 people in the massive audience room. The pope had been so far away from them, in the vast building, that he had looked like a tiny figure. The ribbing of the ceiling had been interesting, orientated in straight lines from the back of the room to the front. This would have facilitated the movement of energy forward. Normally, ribbing of ceilings is crossways. Behind the Pontifex Maximus had been a large statue, very odd in design. It had almost looked like a devil in its curious weaving shape. Thus the energy projected forward could have been concentrated into this figure and into the pope.

The group had managed to become part of this Christian ritual and energy projection by saying that they were members of a church attended by one of the group, Birch believes. The Pleiadians had told Brenda to go and see the pope. At the audience, the group had waved checkerboard flags to show that they were there to play the game. Brenda had followed this up with a letter to the pope, asking him to reveal the secrets of the past.

The harvesting of group-generated energy by religions, gurus, life-style consultants, celebrities, politicians, so-called royal families, whether it be consciously or not, is a practice we might best put behind us. We need to reclaim our power, Birch believes. Many people are doing this in their march towards wholeness. This leads to an awareness of those mechanisms which seek to separate us from that wholeness.

The Catholic religion is very important in Maltese life. Enormous churches have been built in small towns and villages. The churches are built out of limestone quarried on the island. Because it is a soft material and easy to work, sculptors, architects and builders have used it to create complex sculptures, inside and out.

Ta' Pinu church is situated in a remote location away from other buildings. It was built after a woman heard the voice of the Virgin Mary in an old chapel. Many miracles are claimed to have been witnessed there. A number of the group were impressed with the energy inside the church. It was certainly powerful. Birch's main interest was outside, where many statues had been erected. They stretched from the road to the church, and then on the other side up a slope to a flattened piece of land which now had Christian crosses on it.

Birch sensed that this high piece of land had been used as a pre-Christian place of worship. The Christian constructs had, very cleverly, incorporated the place of worship into the Christian energy pattern by the judicious use of the road up to the site and of the statues along the way. Birch also sensed that the statues were another way of absorbing energy from the church worshippers as well as blanketing the Christian energy onto the ancient spiritual land.

Birch sat on a low wall in the temple complex of Ħaġar Qim, and relaxed into meditation. As he tuned in he received, through intuition, some of its past uses. One use was as a place for dimensional travel. Beings could leave from this place; others could arrive from other realms of existence or other places on the planet. Another use was as a holographic imaging centre. The group that used this could project their consciousness and thus view scenes of other realms or places in third-dimensional reality. In this state of consciousness, events and environments could be viewed, but not influenced or interacted with. Other beings, too strange and different to function on the Earth plane, could use the place as a communication device.

Mnajdra Temple is just a few hundred yards from Ħaġar Qim, which would suggest that there was a connection of energy work between the two. It is positioned on Malta's southern coast, near the Isle of Fifla. The latter helped create a triangle of forces, the two temples and the island. The concave walls of the temple indicate a roof was possibly in place in the past.

The lower temple has an astronomical alignment. At summer solstice, the rays of the sun light up the edge of a megalith to the left of the doorway connecting the first pair of chambers to the inner chambers. At the winter solstice, the same effect can be viewed on the corresponding megalith on the right-hand side. At the spring and autumn equinoxes, the rays of the sun pass directly through the temple's main doorway and light up the main axis.

Birch stood in one corner of the field that enclosed the temple. He relaxed into a comfortable chi gong stance, facing what appeared to be the opening to the temple. The relaxation deepened and realisation grew that a lemniscate (a figure-of-8 shape, horizontally placed to the plane of the Earth) loop of energy was being created. One loop of the lemniscate, the larger, moved around the temple; the smaller looped around Birch's body. The energy flowed around the boundary of the lemniscate, and he entered a deeper state as the work progressed. Birch was held for some time as though in a vice of transformation, conscious and unwilling to break the spell by moving. Sometimes he moved involuntarily as energy leaked from the lemniscate. One part of Birch attempted to plug the leakage. Eventually he felt that this part of the work had been done.

Birch moved to the opposite side of the temple, on slightly raised ground. This seemed to be the relatively negative end of the looping power. The first location in which he had stood had been the relatively positive. Here Birch refers to changes in energy vibratory rate.

The insides of the temples were roped off, preventing the public from entering. Thus it was only possible to traverse around the outside. A guard explained that this was to prevent vandalism. However, priestesses in the group penetrated the interiors of both temples.

Sheena entered Ħaġar Qim as Birch sat and watched from the low wall. Immediately, from behind, a guard popped up. He was exquisitely polite in telling her to come back behind the rope. However, the guard was unprepared for Sheena's range of persuasive skills. She walked over him.

'May I enter if I remove my shoes?' Sheena's charm offensive had started.

'No, madam,' said the guard.

'There is no one else around; can I slip inside while it is so quiet?' Sheena continued determinedly.

'I'm afraid no, madam.'

'How about if I slip inside the temple while there is no one else around, and I take off my shoes?'

This exchange continued for several minutes. Eventually Sheena's persistence and persuasive powers won the day and into the temple she went.

Sue entered Mnajdra Temple using one of her particular talents: the psychic. She found herself inside the temple when no one else was around. After being there a little while, she turned to go back outside. To her surprise, she came up against a rope barrier. Yet there had been no rope when she'd entered. The extra dimension of the temple had opened to her. She was there to do the work of the spirit and had moved through in an altered state. So the temple had invited the priestesses in to do their work in two different ways, using the talents of both.

Birch was convinced that in the past Mnajdra had been a repository of, and would have been lit by, the sacred fire. This was not fire as we know it, but the brilliant fire of the ancients: bright, shining, but not consuming or heating. This was the fire that illuminated across the dimensions, that lit every dark corner, the symbol of the finest spiritual light. This was the fire that illuminated all possibilities.

There was one more psychic experience to be had. As the party left Gozo to return to Malta, once again Birch felt a little nauseous. Once on the ferry he sought out a quiet corner and went into meditation. It came to him that this was, truly, the land of the giants. Once, there had been no sea where they were now sailing. The sea level had been much lower in the past.

Then the giants and Birch played with each other's energies in ecstatic union, they in their dimension, Birch in his, but each had a foot in the other's realms. They all tumbled and moved with grace and harmony. For the whole trip they played. There were no words to describe in detail what was being experienced; it was ecstasy in the moment.

'Have you anything to tell me?' Birch asked.

'When you return home we will speak with you.'

The ferry docked and Birch returned to three-dimensional consciousness. There was still the connection between the giants and him.

A small bottle of water disappeared from Birch's backpack. He had been carrying it for several days. Other people were losing more personal things. When individuals and groups work in sacred sites, they leave things which contain their vibration, or those things are taken without their conscious intervention. This phenomenon has happened to Birch throughout his journeys in sacred places.

Archaeologists say that the complex Tarxien temple site was used extensively for ritual. It consists of four megalithic structures. It is claimed that the site is of great interest because it suggests how the temples might have been constructed. Stone rollers left outside the south temple were probably used for transporting the megaliths.

'Have they tried to replicate their theory?' Birch asked. He was reminded of the Japanese attempt to build a half-scale version of the Great Pyramid of Giza, a few years ago. Using the latest crane technology, they failed.

There was a gentle constriction that gathered in the throat chakra here, not for blockage reasons but for speaking one's truth. The ancients would go to the temple to access the gentle energy to facilitate speaking their truth. They departed with this ability enhanced.

Much of the Hypogeum complex is underground. It was discovered accidentally in 1902 by a stonemason laying foundations for some houses. It consists of chambers and passages dug out of the rock. The deepest room is thirty-five feet under the road surface. http://www.heritage-malta.org says of the site, 'Curvilinear and spiral paintings in red ochre are still visible in some areas.' This sounds very similar to the designs that are found elsewhere in the megalithic sites such as Cairn de Gavrinis.

To ensure its conservation, the site's microclimate is strictly regulated. Temperature, relative humidity and carbon dioxide levels are constantly monitored to ensure the Hypogeum's survival for future generations.

Birch saw and felt it as an initiation chamber. There were three levels and, in his insight, he saw the availability of progressing to a deeper level after having satisfied the initiatory requirements. The third and deepest level was available to the highest initiates.

The group toned, much to the amazement of the guard who showed them around. He said that he had never heard anything so amazing. Birch told him that it was now down to him to keep the vibrations up by continuing what the group had started.

Bones had been found in the deepest level. Birch felt that they had been deposited as part of ritual ceremonies by later people, long after the unique initiatory nature of this place had been forgotten and abandoned. The remains of giants had been deposited as the original sacred purpose had started to wane in popularity and knowledge, in Birch's view.

Thus the party ended its work in the temples of Brittany and Malta and the sacred temple of temples, Chartres.

So the trip came to an end: a great trip of sharing and companionship. As he looks back on it, Birch feels a special gratitude to Sue. It was she who showed him to look beyond threats (from those behind the scenes who are attempting to create mayhem) and negativity in his work. Sue persuaded him to concentrate on the positive and beauty.

A Final Look at Mexico

Shamanistic, magical and mysterious stories

Birch chose this title as this will be the last time he writes on this country for the books written with Pete Haines. Well, that's what he says now.

There is an interesting twist in approach when one attempts to make improvements in one's character in these enhanced energetic times. The twist is that one's decision will be tested quickly. On what he describes as his high moral horse, Birch had convinced himself that he would work on reducing (certainly) and eliminating (possibly) his tendency to judge others negatively.

Haines is confused by Birch's view. He claims Birch is one of the least judgmental people he has met. Checking Birch's diaries and notes, Haines can find little evidence of this claimed tendency to judge unkindly. In fact, Haines suggests that the only person Birch judges harshly is himself. Haines will wait for future evidence to support Birch's view of himself before he revises his opinion.

As the two, Jaqueline and Birch, walked towards the aircraft that would take them from Gatwick to Houston, they were slowed by a woman hauling a considerable load of carry-ons. She dropped her bits and pieces several times before reaching the aircraft. She was holding up the boarding, yet seemed oblivious to the delay she was causing. Birch felt there was the potential for annoyance here. He does like his journeys to run smoothly, since he doesn't consider them to be part of his adventure. They are merely a necessity to enable him to get to his intended destination.

Once on the aircraft, it was Baggage Lady who shared the duo's triple bank of seating. Oh, deep joy. Yet another less-than-perfect journey for our intrepid traveller. Out of the hundreds of people in the tin beast, Baggage Lady was the person with whom they were to be in close contact for the next ten hours. This should have told Birch something.

As Jaqueline and Birch waited to get into their seats, their travelling companion couldn't decide how to place her baggage in the overhead storage lockers. Thus more delay, until a male voice behind Birch blurted, 'For God's sake help the woman.'

Birch, and another person, duly did so. Again, Baggage Lady seemed oblivious to the disruption around her. The disarray continued on the long flight to Houston. The woman sat in the window seat, and ten or twelve times in the flight she got out of her seat to wander around the aircraft. It mattered nothing that Jaqueline and Birch were attempting to sleep. 'Socially unaware' is how Birch describes her. Any mild attempts to remonstrate were met with an uncomprehending stare. One issue of this test was that Birch managed not to become annoyed.

It was intended that Jaqueline would spend some time with her family, mother and sister specifically, who live in Ixtapaluca, a feeder town of Mexico City. This is really a city in its own right, similar to the physical relationship between London and Watford. There is no break in the conurbation between the two. The only appreciable difference is the civil administration.

Birch had no work to do, as far as he was aware. He was there to support his wife. However, interesting events came his way, as is so often the case. The day after the pair's thirty-hour trek, door to door, Cheltenham to Ixtapaluca, Birch was stricken by a strong migraine. He failed to clear it with his own healing. Jaqueline's mother took a raw egg and rubbed the shell over Birch's head, forehead, chest and arms. After this rather strange massage, she cracked the egg and emptied the contents into a glass, which she presented to Birch. There, among the yolk and the raw clear liquid, floated a curious white film. Mother explained that the negative vibrations had been absorbed by the egg, and it was these that caused the white film. She also explained that someone had sent Birch negative thoughts. These had penetrated Birch's natural defences, weakened by the long journey. The migraine quickly disappeared.

Was the migraine a result of some physical cause, or the projection of powerful energies? Did Birch heal himself through suggestion, or were the negative energies absorbed by the egg? It is not easy to reach a logical conclusion. Nevertheless it was an interesting experience of healing.

Soon after arriving, Birch had a powerful dream. Freud said, 'Everybody in your dream is really you.' The dream put Birch in a situation in which he finished a relationship with a girlfriend. The reason for the break-up was his realisation that the emotional life between the two of them had disappeared. The ex-girlfriend was full of resentment, yet contact between the two continued. Despite her resentment, Birch continued to try to hang on to a semblance of emotional contact with her.

The final scene of their dream was one where Birch was driving in a stream of traffic. As he approached a junction, there was a terrible accident. Two other cars in the stream of traffic were badly damaged, one somersaulting several times. The two damaged cars, along with Birch's own undamaged one, ended up on an open grass area opposite the junction. The ex-girlfriend was there, attempting to separate herself from Birch physically. Birch was still trying to create an emotional contact between the two of them. One of the drivers of the damaged cars attempted to blame Birch for his accident. He felt that this blame was unwarranted.

The last point in the final act of the dream had Birch driving a big car which had an extension at the back, similar to that of a bendy bus. And so the dream ended.

He asked his inner-self for guidance. Immediately a flash of inspiration said that one aspect was connected to his resentment of people and of issues that he came across in his daily life. He concluded that it was, therefore, time to eliminate resentments in waking life. This was one step on his journey towards clarity.

An interesting, or maybe significant, feature that was different from other dreams was the nature of the car that he had been driving. For years he had driven a silver saloon in dreams. He had always believed this vehicle was a symbol of his spiritual journey. This latest dream had seen him driving a large estate car similar to the one that he had recently purchased in waking life. In the dream there had been the added element of the bendy bus extension. Could this mean that the nature of his journey, physical and spiritual, was about to change? Time would no doubt tell. Perhaps the decision to change his car in waking life was a portent of these potential changes?

This pointed finger of blame led Birch to wonder if it might be forewarning that he would be unjustly blamed in his waking life, whereas the ex-girlfriend appeared to be a reflection of the old attitudes from which he was attempting to escape. This experience reinforced the importance of working with dreams and the guidance they can give. This is as important to our inner work as meditation, visualisation and healing. The higher-self communicates to us those things that will be of importance for our development.

Birch, with the entire family in tow, visited the spa town of Chignahuapan to experience the healing sulphur-loaded hot waters that pour out of the ground. The smell is not overpowering and one quickly becomes acclimatised to it. After a swim in the pool, all the travellers experienced head, neck and shoulder massages. During Jaqueline's massage, the masseuse told her a story.

The masseuse had been born in Chignahuapan but, as a young woman, went to Mexico City in order to seek a metropolitan future. There she met a man whom she married. Two children were the result of their union. The husband became a drug addict. As he descended into his personal hell and chaos, he beat the wife and terrified the young children. Unable to cope further, one morning the woman woke up, packed her bag, roused the children and left. With no other practical option, she returned to the town of her birth. The children were put into the local school and they started to resume a normal life. Children can adjust so quickly. Unfortunately, the woman continued to live the emotional trauma of the past. Unable to cope, she was hardly able to dress the children for school. A doctor prescribed diazepam, a Valium derivative. It didn't help. Her pain and suffering continued.

In desperation, she changed her doctor. The new one became a lifeline and a gatekeeper into a new life. The new doctor told the woman to flush the medication away and prescribed massage. Immediately the woman's spirits lifted and the trauma began to subside. She felt better, more relaxed, and she was able to reach a balanced perspective of her experiences. So impressed was she with the dramatic turnaround in her life that she trained and became the masseuse at the spa. She was renewed; almost reborn.

Every person has their story. Sometimes, telling a stranger an inspirational personal tale of those twin imposters, triumph and disaster, can inspire others to overcome their difficulties.

This is from *The Placebo Response* by Howard Broady:

> 'I would like you to remember only this one thing,' said Badger. 'The stories people tell have a way of taking care of them. If stories come to you, care for them. And learn to give them away where they are needed. Sometimes a person needs a story more than food to stay alive.'
>
> Barry Lopez, 1993

Further to the use of salt as a psychic protection, the masseuse told Jaqueline of the use of salt as a protection against envy. For best results, she advised placing salt in a small bag. Place the bag next to the heart. The bag is thus carried throughout the day. At the end of the day, the bag is emptied into a container of water which is then poured away for Mother Earth to deal with. The water will hold the negative vibrations that the envious person has been directing. Care should be taken in ensuring the mouth of the bag faces away from the person when opened. This is to ensure the negative vibrations do not escape and attach to the person's aura.

It was Sunday afternoon in the Alameda Park, Mexico City. People danced in the fresh open air. Others ambled while lovers canoodled among the trees. Horse-mounted police in traditional dress, sombreros on their heads for the benefit of the tourists, moved slowly through the park. No one else in Mexico's daily life wears a sombrero. It is a symbol of the past, so often lampooned in Hollywood movies.

Birch, Jaqueline and two friends, Miriam and Jesus, sat on a bench watching the world go by. Jesus told Birch that this very park had been the location for the gruesome tortures carried out by the Inquisition, and the burnings of so-called witches. Birch wondered if this organisation and its umbrella leadership realised the karma of these acts. Probably not at all. He also wondered if those who were involved then, and those involved now by being part of the present-day organisations, knew and know that they were and are attempting to suppress the power of the feminine.

Birch explained to Jesus the concept of different time periods functioning concurrently in cosmic terms. In this way, the Inquisition was creating its pain and suffering at the same time as the quartet of friends was enjoying the early-evening balmy temperature, innocent pursuits and relaxed environment. Birch continued by asking, 'What can we do with this knowledge?' He answered himself, 'We can send healing to the past, which will ameliorate what is happening in that reality. Also this healing will bleed through to the present, creating a healthier now.'

As they returned to mother's house, Birch was hit by rampant diahorrea which, in a perverse sense, complemented the heavy cold from which he was suffering. He thanked the cosmic that this affliction had waited to erupt on his return, eliminating extreme embarrassment on the subway or in the Combi. Birch felt that this illness was a clearing. As he worked on judgment and resentment, as well as his occasional aggression and ego issues, there was a lot going on internally. The proximity of the powerful energies of Teotihuacán could have been a factor in this spontaneous clearing, also.

Birch and family found themselves on the coast in Huatulco, Oaxaca State. They all ate delicious fish in the market, caught in the local sea; a treat after a hard day on the beach and shopping. They were approached by a small and very thin boy. 'I haven't eaten all day. Could you give me something to take away?' he asked plaintively, but not in a begging manner. Jaqueline believed that he wished to take food away to share with someone. Birch bought food for him from the restaurant in which they were eating. The boy departed with a smile and a 'Gracias'. Jaqueline said that it must be hard to be so poor in a tourist area, with so much money around. But these experiences are not confined to Central America. They can be encountered much nearer to home.

Haines spends much of his time in Albania, where he has a number of business interests. Albania is a country he has come to love, along with its people, whose welcome and generosity are legendary. But it is not without its discomforts, being one of Europe's poorest nations. He often feels uncomfortable there, just like Birch on other continents. He has so comparatively much while his hosts have so little.

Just like those in Mexico, visitors to Albania can be besieged by beggars. Following Foreign & Commonwealth Office guidelines, Haines rarely gives to beggars. Yet when he is alone, so often he softens and gives beggars a few leke.

Earlier this year, Haines was in Tirana with a colleague from Dubai who was on his first visit to Albania. They had enjoyed dinner in one of the top restaurants in Tirana; the finest fresh food, great wine and service which would match (and surpass) anything in France. The bill was around £25 for three.

As they left the restaurant, Haines's colleague, six foot four, very well nourished, designer suit and Grenson brogues, was approached by a beggar, all of ten years old. The mite grabbed his trousers at around knee level and tugged. At the same time he held out his free hand, hopefully. Not knowing what to do, the colleague looked at Haines for guidance. Haines grimaced and shook his head. But the colleague, Christian and kindly, ignored the advice and succumbed to the big brown eyes that were looking up at him. The visitor gave the lad 100 leke (around 80p). Haines braced himself, and with good reason.

Within two seconds, and apparently from nowhere, the Dubai visitor was surrounded by at least twenty more street urchins. All laughed, shouted and clamoured while all the time tugging at his trousers. A forest of optimistic hands was held out. In panic, the visitor looked at Haines for salvation. None came. Haines was too busy laughing at his plight: helpful, no; amusing, yes. The expression of fear, bemusement and confusion on the visitor's face was a picture. His original generosity cost Haines another £5 so they could escape from what Sherlock Holmes would no doubt have called the Baker Street Irregulars. Clutching their gains, the kids ran away, cheerfully smiling and shouting with joy. Had Haines not paid out more leke, he reckons it would have been no easy matter to extricate themselves from the urchins.

On the whole, this was not an unpleasant experience for Haines, although it was for his business colleague. The kids were charming, joyful and, despite what might have been thought, not very threatening. A couple of weeks previously, an experience with a beggar had been of a very different complexion. Haines was returning to his apartment in downtown Tirana. He came across a young woman of about twenty. She held a young child in her arms. Neither mother, if that was what she was, nor child was clean, each being caked in mud and grime. Seeing the suited Westerner walking down the pavement, she approached, holding out her hand. Haines foolishly gave her some loose change. He watched her enter a shop and buy some bottled water which she did not share with the child.

The next morning Haines was drinking excellent Albanian coffee with his lawyer at a pavement café. The same beggar appeared, talking in rapid Albanian and placing her hand on Haines's shoulder. She was after more money. Haines, not speaking Albanian, could only lamely say no in English, while his Albanian lawyer and friend told the beggar to leave in her native tongue. That was when it started to get unpleasant. There was an abrupt and harsh exchange. Then a male waiter arrived to rescue his customers. Very gently, he tried to steer the beggar off the premises. Rather than leaving, the woman thought it might be a good idea to fight the waiter, whilst still holding the child in one arm. It wasn't a good idea.

These stories serve to highlight the dangers of giving to beggars. Haines has every sympathy with Birch, and with the struggle Birch has with his conscience when faced with, *should I give or should I not?* On balance, Haines suspects giving is not the better choice, yet it is so difficult to pass some beggars by. Birch says he has never been placed in an uncomfortable situation by beggars in Mexico.

One of Birch's objectives on this visit was to persuade Jaqueline's mother, Victoria Robles, to tell some of her stories. He knew that she had had an adventurous life. With the encouragement of Jaqueline and Coti, mother opened enough to tell titbits from her supply of adventures. Birch knew that there was much more, but he decided it was advisable not to push her too hard.

Once upon a time, when Victoria was a child, her uncle, a gentle man and a worker in the church, was psychically attacked. From his bed in which he was recovering from the assault, he said, 'They have come for me now.' The priest was called and he started praying in the room. Suddenly, something fell into the room that had not been there before. There on the floor lay a corn tamale, a local food delicacy. Wrapped inside it were human bones. The priest told those present not to touch the object and he took it away. A week later the priest died suddenly. Because the uncle was such a pleasant man, it was assumed that a curse had been placed on his wife, Romana. Later it was discovered that Romana had a lover and that it was the wife of the lover who had invoked the curse.

A man in Victoria's village became very frightened on one occasion, so much so that he locked and barred himself in his windowless house. Thus he was totally cut off from the rest of the village. The only movement around the house was the sound of a cat miaowing. Some time later, local people broke into the house to find the man dead. There was no sign of violence. Soon after, a man made a presentation to the village: a pot filled with blood. He said that this was the blood of the dead man.

When Victoria was about nine years old, her mother went to collect water from a local well. Victoria's brother, Guadalupe, was very sick and Victoria was told by her mother that on no account should she leave her sick brother alone. After the mother left, Guadalupe said to Victoria, 'Can you go and collect quelites for me, little sister?' (Quelites are various wild greens.) Victoria did as her brother asked. When the mother returned from the water collection, she found a lot of blood around an avocado tree that was next to the house. The mother scolded Victoria for leaving her brother. Victoria lied vehemently, saying she hadn't left her brother alone. Within a week, Guadalupe was dead.

Victoria and her mother regularly saw little people dancing near the village, or when they were travelling in the nearby mountains. (By 'little people' we are left to wonder if this describes fairy-like or leprechaun-like little people.) One day, Victoria and a friend were sent to clean the schoolhouse. Their journey took them past a depression in the ground where villagers would throw the clothes of dead people. The two children glanced into the hole as they passed. To their surprise and consternation, there was one of the little people searching through the clothes. When he saw the children, the little person started to throw stones at them. The two quickened their pace away from the hole, only to be followed by the little person, who continued to throw stones at them. In fear, the girls ran to the school and barred the door. The little person, who had been wearing a hat made of palm fronds and a poncho down to the floor so the girls could not see his legs, had disappeared.

Victoria would go to school from 0900 to 1300 and from 1500 to 1800. In the break she was required to go to the mountains to take food to workers employed by her father. She would often return to school late due to the length of the journey. Because of the authority of her father in the community, Victoria was never chastised on her return to class. This was much to the chagrin of the classmates who did not possess such parental clout.

Another brother of Victoria's, Fortino, at four or five years old, was sent alone to the mountains to tie a bull that had broken loose. He would have been away more than a day, as the mountainous land was some distance off. So no consideration was given to the fact that the young boy would be alone in the dark. Despite the toughness of everyday life, at least this poor society was not afflicted with the abuse scenarios in our 'civilised' communities. The father of the young boy gave no consideration to whether the boy was frightened or not. It was expected, in that rough rural farming village, that children grow up quickly. Victoria and Fortino's mother was regularly pregnant. Only Victoria and Fortino survived into adulthood. Medical care was rudimentary if it existed at all in this community.

We continue with more strange tales from magical Oaxaca State. A few years ago, Jaqueline and Coti travelled to Oaxaca State to attempt to resolve a dispute over the ownership of land with local relatives. They slept in a room sparsely furnished with only a bed. In the middle of the night, the pair was awakened by a tremendous crash inside the room.

Fearing that the roof had fallen in, the two women leapt out of bed, only to find nothing. The room was sparse and tranquil, just as it had been upon their retirement. The two were so frightened they slept not a wink for the rest of the night. Jaqueline believes that the local relatives had sought magical help to frighten the two women away from the property. Thus the property would then fall into the hands of the locals, and Jaqueline and Coti would leave. The two hardy females recovered the land after many legal battles.

One day when Jaqueline's aunt, the wife of Fortino, was pregnant, a neighbour came to their home to borrow money.

'I am sorry,' said the wife, 'we don't have enough money for ourselves right now.'

'You will be sorry,' was the neighbour's ominous response as she left.

Almost immediately, the wife experienced a blockage in her abdomen such that she became constipated and, more disastrously, she could not give birth to her child. She died.

We are aware of the power of suggestion in our comfortable Western, materialistic lives. People in these remote places, however, are masters at invoking extremely potent energies. These principles have been practised and honed for hundreds, if not thousands, of years.

The next story concerns a distant relative of Victoria's whose Oaxaca home was visited by other relatives. This relative was so poor that it was necessary for the visitors to sleep on the floor, as there was a lack of bedding.

During the night, the floor sleepers were woken by the relative stepping over them and going outside. As soon as she was outside, there was a caterwauling noise which subsided into silence for a while. The wailing repeated and then stopped again, then the relative re-entered the house. The floor sleepers had seen no signs of any cats in the area. Was the relative a shape shifter, or were the visitors the victims of over-excited imaginations?

These communities are extremely conservative and traditional in their beliefs. The linear, logical thinking of Western societies is not their way. Therefore minds are focussed more towards nature, the magical and mystical. In this atmosphere, the magic works partly because people believe that it will, for good or ill.

Victoria's father was a man of standing and substance in their village. He would loan money so that borrowers could buy a cow, or he would lend corn or beans. One day, the father experienced great pain in one knee. A *curandae*, or magician, was called. The magician instructed Victoria's mother to perform certain magical incantations in one corner of the room and over the affected knee. In this manner, and with the assistance of the magician, a piece of glass was removed from the knee by a process akin to psychic surgery. This reversed the insertion of the glass which, it was claimed, had been done by black magic.

The Day of the Dead is an annual festival in Mexico on 1st and 2nd November, in honour of the dead. Food is prepared and left in homes and graveyards for the dead to approach and appreciate it. For people who passed over when they were older, tequila and tobacco is the preferred offering. It is believed that the dead can appreciate the food through smell. They can take the odour through their subtle bodies. In the case of fruit, it is believed that, after the visit of the dead, the produce completely loses its flavour. In Jaqueline's mother's house, candles are left to light the journey of the departed loved ones and friends who return to their old, familiar environments. Many people don't celebrate the festival in these more secular times. Or perhaps the rising cost of produce has an impact? This reminds Birch of Mothers' Day in Britain when the price of flowers rises considerably in preparation for the dubious, imported occasion. The strength, both subtle and overt, of the Mexican practice can be gauged by Jaqueline commencing the celebration of the Day of the Dead, for the first time, after nine years living in materialist England.

Food prepared in Victoria's village includes tamales made from corn. Hot peppers and chicken are commonly used as food gifts together with mole, a spicy sauce, yellow in colour and served with prawns. Black mole with turkey, tamales with beans, consommé with turkey, piles of tortillas with dried fish and beef, all complement the offering. Chayote, a local vegetable, is included with bread specially made in the village and from Oaxaca City. After the celebration, eatable food is consumed by the householders or given away.

One local story tells of a man who became sick and died. For the Day of the Dead, the widow prepared tamales. However, in a fit of pique for his death, she placed stones inside them. On the Day of the Dead, the spectre of the dead husband appeared to a neighbour. The ghost said that he was going to take his wife. He also asked the neighbour to prepare tamales, and to include the stones just as the widow had done. The wife died unexpectedly after the neighbour had prepared the stone-filled tamales.

In another incident, a man was living with his mother. The mother said that she was going to the mountains to work. The man, left to his own devices, was visited by a woman, and the almost inevitable happened between the two. The Day of the Dead approached and the man moved out to live with the woman. They took basic cooking utensils with them. The mother returned to find that she did not have the utensils necessary to cook the food for the dead. She fell on her knees apologising for her inabilities and cursing the son for his selfish and thoughtless action. The son developed a severe infection in one knee which caused him to need the use of a crutch for the rest of his life. Victoria's brother, farmer Fortino, took pity on the man and would give him work when he needed extra hands.

This last story concerns Victoria's father who, one year, prepared a special local drink as part of the gift for the Day of the Dead. The non-alcoholic atole (mainly made from corn, although it can also be made from rice powder) was duly made. The father sat and contemplated taking the drink for himself, then preparing another one later for the Day of the Dead. As soon as the thought passed through his head, a large cooking pan lifted from the table next to him and fell to the floor with a loud crash, shaking the father with shock. 'Perhaps I won't take this drink after all,' said the father out loud to ensure that the message reached the required sources.

Jaqueline and Birch, on their way to the Zócalo, the heart of Mexico City, passed a large plaque commemorating the site of the meeting between Montezuma (Moctezuma in Spanish) and Hernán Cortés, the leader of the Spanish invasion force. The meeting took place in the sixteenth century. Montezuma thought that he could buy off the Spanish with gold; the more gold that was given by the Aztec leader, the more the Spanish greed increased. This culminated in the defeat and the slaughter of the Aztec army and people. Mexico was changed for ever. Birch leaves it to the learned to explore this in depth. Nevertheless, he remains convinced that this was abuse on an industrial scale.

The two walked through the Zócalo. There was a small demonstration and collection of signatures. The demonstration was against a Catholic priest who had sexually abused a child. The priest had also infected the child with a sexually transmitted disease. In contrast to the annihilation of the Aztecs, this was abuse on an individual scale.

The protesters were collecting the signatures in order to bring the case to the notice of the International Conference for Children.

'They are not sending the protest to the Vatican?' questioned Birch.

'No, indeed,' replied Jaqueline.

A few yards further on and the pair came across an enormous flag in the middle of the Zócalo. It flew from a hundred-foot-tall metal pole.

'The people's symbol,' piped Jaqueline; 'of no practical use, but a focus for the people.'

'Mmm,' replied Birch, 'a flag is a lot cheaper than a royal family. Did you know that the Nepalese are scrapping their royal family?'

'Why start one in the first place?' came the reply from the arch republican. 'When I worked for the British police,' she continued, warming to her theme, 'I was working on the computer in the office during the Queen Mother's funeral broadcast. As I typed away there was absolute still during the two-minute silence, except for me keying on the computer. One of the others in the office almost spat at my alleged disrespect to the departed royal. Later they showed a photo of a tiara with a diamond as big as an egg on it. I told the others in the office that this monstrosity would buy a meal for most of the poor in the world. There was silence from the royalists.'

As they waited for the Combi to take them back to mum's house, they watched some animal antics. A mouse scratched around on the pavement, oblivious to the line of people four feet away. Enthusiastically it foraged for scraps of food as children chased it away time after time. Each time it returned, apparently possessing little fear of people. The mouse retained enough awareness to avoid the dangers around it. For the remainder of the time, its awareness was devoted to foraging. This downward and inward-looking focus on obtaining the basics of life is so typical of the lives of many Mexicans. Birch wondered if the people around saw the analogy.

Before leaving Central America it is worth retelling the story of Alice and Maria. The sensitive will find it distressing, sad, even shocking, but it provides a microcosm, an illustration of this unfamiliar culture which is so alien to ours.

The knock on the door was loud and insistent. Victoria moved towards it, wondering who could be calling at this time. She opened the door only to see no one at eye level. Her gaze travelled downward to reveal two pairs of large open eyes staring back at her. Standing there were two young girls. Victoria estimated their ages to be approximately seven and four. The older girl spoke.

'We are your new neighbours. We don't have a grandma and we were wondering if you would be ours.'

Victoria, a grandmother a number of times over, was much amused by this approach and invited the pair into her house. Over the following weeks and months the trio became firm friends, particularly Victoria and the elder girl, whom we will call Alice. Perhaps just as significantly, Victoria became involved with their family dynamics. The father of the girls was a chef, and the mother a housewife. It was fairly clear from the start that the younger girl, we will call her Maria, was the favourite with the mother. Maria was the one who seemed to receive all the hugs and affection, the best presents and parental praise. Alice was treated very much as second class, with very few positive strokes.

Maria had cottoned on to this unequal treatment by the parents. Thus, when Alice complained about her sister breaking her toys and possessions, she was not believed and received little support in these disputes. Maria had said to Alice, 'I am the one child that was wanted. You were an accident.'

One can imagine the hurt and sadness that was building up in the sensitive psyche of the elder daughter. There was little that Victoria could do overtly about the situation. She gave Alice support whenever she could. It was necessary for her to be careful about this, as there was danger in upsetting the girls' mother. The mother could withdraw support for the girls, particularly Alice, visiting their proxy grandmother. This withdrawal had been practised a number of times on a temporary basis. There were times when Alice visited when she said that she was hungry, having not been fed by her mother. She also claimed that Maria did receive food on these occasions. Jaqueline's mum fed Alice when it was possible, without other eyes watching.

So, Birch and Jaqueline arrived in Victoria's house for their annual visit, bearing gifts for Jaqueline's family and the two 'nieces', as Jaqueline called them. The gifts were suitable but attractive clothes for young girls of their age.

During Jaqueline and Birch's first evening, there was a loud knock on the door and in walked the two girls. Birch noticed that Alice was tall for her age, pretty, with a sensitive face. Birch sensed a fineness about her that distinguished her from her peers. The other girl was an average kid with nothing remarkable about her. She was somewhat pudding-faced, and wouldn't have been picked out in a crowd. Alice went to each person in the room, shaking their hands and giving kisses on cheeks. The other girl didn't bother.

The giving of the presents began, followed by the girls trying on their new clothes. Coti had previously set aside some of the clothes which had been purchased for the younger girl, in order to give them to a friend's daughter. This meant that there were more clothes for Alice. Birch was concerned about this, as it meant possible retribution against Alice for the apparent favouritism. Alice had great fun trying on her new clothes. Maria needed to be cajoled to do likewise.

A little while later, the girls' mother arrived. As Birch shook her hand he sensed an exterior hardness of character. The mother sat and talked to Victoria, Coti and Jaqueline, and she gradually relaxed. With Birch's practically non-existent Spanish he was able to sit back and sense the dynamic of the situation washing over him without too obviously watching proceedings.

It appeared that Alice was emotionally isolated from her mother. It was the younger girl who received the warm looks and gentle fondling. Our trusty traveller also sensed that the mother, although carrying a hard exterior, was internally weak and insecure. He felt that the mother was jealous of Alice because of the older daughter's aliveness, personality and balanced character. These attractive elements appeared to be absent in the mother's personality and character.

The mother's insecurity was demonstrated by her insistence that she did not like her daughters to be in the company of their father if she, the mother, was not there. The mother needed to be the only person close to the man of the house.

Birch felt that it was appropriate to give Alice some extra support and did so with a meditation to help bring strength in coping with the situation into which she had decided to be born.

It is Birch's belief that we decide the parents and family into which we are to be born. We decide this before birth. This is to ensure that the soul has maximum opportunity to experience the lessons that we need to work on in regard to our character and soul development. This is a very difficult concept to accept given the horrendous early years that many young people experience. Nevertheless, for Birch, this is entirely harmonious with his personal cosmic view of life.

When we are born we forget these decisions, and all that has gone before, so that a clean-slate start can be made. In addition, our higher-self presents those experiences that are needed for our progress, comfortable or uncomfortable. This forgetting is also important as we live in a free-will universe, so we always have the choice to follow our pre-birth path or not. There is no rush to achieve enlightenment. No one is setting us targets apart from ourselves. We have all eternity.

Perhaps a couple of quotes from *The Spiritual Practices of the Ninja* by Ross Heaven might be helpful.

> *You also have a responsibility and a duty of care to the people you have allowed into your life so far. You just cannot become someone else overnight. You still have to be there for them. You are now between a rock and a hard place. Welcome. Pull up a chair.*
>
> *It takes intention, focus and concentration not to get caught up and distracted by the drama around us and to keep focussing our vision. The key is to see, hear, feel, smell and taste the life you want to have and the world you want to live in as if it is happening now.*

Birch, Jaqueline and family decided to visit the coast for a few days. Victoria asked Alice's mum if the older girl could join the party. The first response was not negative. Later, the girl returned to say that permission was not now forthcoming because 'Mother has already paid for a children's party'. Alice left in tears. There was also a problem with the allocation of new clothes, the younger making a fuss over receiving less than 50% of the total.

On another visit by mother and the two nieces, Alice asked her mother, in front of everybody, why the younger girl received most of the presents and attention. There was no reply from mother. Everyone else in the room stayed silent, which caused a most interesting moment of absolute stillness. Birch wondered, in the moment, if the older girl were deliberately raising this issue with an audience. He hasn't ruled out the possibility that Alice was not always telling the truth about her personal difficulties, although certainly she has much cause for complaint. Birch hoped that the mother, sooner rather than later, would relate Jaqueline's family's preference for Alice to her own preference for Maria. Perhaps this would assist her to come to a more balanced perspective concerning her parenting. Will the penny drop? One hopes so.

Another Alice story relates to her excellent student record. In Alice's school, money was given to students for success. Of course this would not happen in England, but we are in a different culture here. Alice frequently received financial rewards. She saved the money to buy presents. Her mother would sometimes borrow this money and not pay it back. When Alice complained, she was chastised for being selfish. This became such a frustration for the girl that eventually she refused the money offered in school.

After the return from the coast, the mother and Alice turned up on Victoria's doorstep with a big bowl of flowers. Sometimes Victoria would pick up the children from school. Either the flowers were for that service or perhaps there was a guilty feeling concerning the withdrawal of permission for Alice to join the holiday party. On this occasion the mother showed some sign of affection for Alice. This was the first time Victoria had seen this.

The following quote is from *Afterwards, You're a Genius* by Chip Brown.

> She illustrated the distinctions using the commandment 'honour thy father and mother' ... that is honour teachers and mentors who have served you in the role of father and mother ... credit those who opposed you, whose resistance or refusals resulted in valuable lessons.
>
> An idea most eloquently echoed in the Native American tradition of the 'good enemy' who teaches you what you need to know ... the tasks of parents was not to nurture and protect children per se, but to inflict the 'sacred wound' that would shape and organise the children's lives – the wounds that the child's soul required for its development and for which its parents had been selected precisely because they were equipped to deliver it.

There is one element missing from this story so far: the psychic. One day, just before a visit from Alice's mother, Victoria told Birch that it was important that the gringo's name not be revealed. It was also important not to give the mother or child anything with Birch's vibration on it. When asked why, Victoria replied that this information could be used to get at Birch by means of black magic. It transpired that Alice's grandmother was a serious practitioner of black magic, and Victoria suspected that Alice's mother was using such techniques also.

Every time Alice's mother entered Victoria's house, there was a psychic visitation of an unpleasant energy at Coti's bedside during the night. Later, this black magic activity was proved, at least in the eyes of Victoria and daughter Coti. Coti started to suffer from a nervous illness: Bell's palsy. Victoria and Coti believed this to be a psychic attack. This happened twice. Birch had the insight that if Victoria and Coti sprinkled salt outside the house and threw it around themselves, this would protect them and their house.

The use of salt as a remedy or protection comes to our attention again. Birch's friend, Bryan, claims that salt contains some of the highest psychic vibration on the planet. When Bryan paints his house he always sprinkles a few pinches of salt into the paint. He says that this has a positive impact on the energy of the room. He also says that if a few pinches are placed in the corner of the room, this will raise the vibration still further. An additional benefit for those who are unhappy with creepy-crawlies in their home is that it will keep spiders away. So household tips, as well as psychic stories, are included in this book.

As the situation became more difficult, Victoria tried to keep all three out of her house. Sadly, Alice suffered most from this step, but Victoria felt it was the only viable decision available to her.

There are those who will laugh at the prospect of being affected by black magic. In response, Birch will point out how Aboriginal shamans in Australia pointed a stick at intended victims. These unfortunates would often sicken and die in days. This became such a problem that an Australian government enacted a law which banned pointing a stick as a serious criminal offence.

So, do we need to be frightened by such a phenomenon? Most certainly not. Remember we are empowered beings. Our health and wellbeing are in our own hands. First, have confidence in yourself. Do not allow fear into your mind. If it arrives, simply banish it. We cannot be influenced by such attacks if we choose not to be. Many people are physically attacked a number of times. There may be something in their thinking that is victim-based. Attackers will pick up these subtle signals. Many criminals are very psychic. Second, to give yourself an extra ring of protection, simply surround yourself with a ball of light. Remember, all this is in your own hands. Alternatively, if you follow a religion or specific spiritual practice, speak some sacred words or verses from that practice. This will protect also.

The apparent last word on this story is that the family have now moved away. The father has taken up new employment in Cancún. Perhaps this is the last that will be seen of the two girls and the family. For some reason, Birch is not convinced this is the end. Most certainly it is a relief to Victoria and Coti that this pressure has now been removed.

So much, then, for Mexico. Birch remains grateful for the wife, insights and rich cerebral bounties this fascinating country has bestowed on him. He is happy to be able to present a different face of Mexico from the one most tourists experience: sun, sand and high-rise hotels. For him, this vast and colourful country, its equally colourful people and its unique identity have left a lasting and rich legacy.

And now a somewhat baffling and strange story from the Internet as a final offering from chaotic, magnetic, colourful, dangerous, attractive Mexico. If anything it demonstrates how differently the Latin and Western thinking manifests.

The *Times of India* reports that researchers at the University of Nuevo León near Monterrey in Mexico have found that when the Mexican spirit tequila is heated under pressure it produces diamond structures, which are able to conduct electricity. The crystals, used to make diamond film, have previously been made from a number of different chemicals, often including nitrogen. However, this experimental attempt is believed to be the first time that researchers have proven that any type of alcohol can be used to produce synthetic diamond. Diamond film is tougher than silicon, so it could be useful for devices that must operate at high temperatures or under other harsh conditions. However, diamond films are expensive and difficult to make. Now, researchers from Mexico have shown that the crystals can be created by heating the country's national drink. For the experiment, the researchers heated 80 proof tequila blanco, which has a short aging process and is bottled soon after distillation, in a low-pressure chamber. The drink formed into crystals which tests later confirmed had a diamond structure and were able to conduct electricity.

Then again, of course, it could be a joke!

Shall I ascend right now? Maybe later! Birch in British Museum

Statue of Sekhmet British Museum

The Dolmen Languedoe

Birch and Friend. Clive is the one without the teeth, Zihuateneco, Mexico

The Saint and Other Adventures

Exploring the work of a saintly person

The coach weaved its way through the sodden English countryside. The passenger manifest showed that the travellers comprised thirty grey tops and a few younger people in their early and mid twenties. Mary, Joan and Birch were among them. Good manners prevent categorising them as grey tops or twenty-somethings. This looked a typical complement for such a journey in the world of modestly priced travel. So much rain had fallen that some towns were cut off from the outside. England in July!

The small party was on its way to London for an audience with the saint. The weather and the forecast over the next twenty-four hours had been so dubious that they had debated whether to make the trip or not. Mary and Birch had asked their respective guidance whether to travel or not. Neither of them had received any information from their sources. The decision was down to them. It seemed, from the deafening internal silence, that the journey was not vital for their spiritual development or wellbeing. Therefore, all three went for personal interest, entertainment and, for Birch, an opportunity for stimulation outside Cheltenham.

The previous year in Greece, Joan had been told by Hera, the goddess, that the waters were coming; they certainly had. More than one month's rain had fallen in a few hours. Sandbags were piled against front doors. The River Chelt stopped rising a foot below the sandbags in front of Birch's flat. Perhaps Birch's pleas to the water element had had some influence. As the water rose inexorably throughout the sheeting downpour, his [expletives deleted] didn't have the slightest impact on the rising water, but they did serve to relieve his increasing tensions. Sadly many people were presented with the agony of being flooded, including Haines and his family. Thankfully, Haines and his wife were at their home in France at the time, 20th July 2007, while their youngest son, Harry, was in Vancouver.

There was one positive that came out of the problem. The local water treatment plant was flooded, bizarrely drying up fresh water from the tap. Water bowsers were installed at the bottom of roads. Thus people needed to get out of their cars, leave their homes and involve themselves in the rudimentary social activity of drawing water from a common local area. People started talking to each other. At their communal bowser, Birch spoke with a woman who lived in his road but with whom he had never conversed in fifteen years. Now every time they see each other they say 'hello'. It is an ill wind.

As the coach wound through the grey and overcast countryside, Birch looked around at the people close to where he was sitting. An older man to his right, smartly grey suited and wearing an inscrutable expression behind thick spectacles, sat impassively with arms folded. *What is going on in your head, Mr Greysuit? Something? Nothing? Are you planning the next Great Train Robbery?* Birch wondered. *Probably not if you're travelling on cheapie transport with the coffin dodgers' discount.*

Behind Mr Greysuit, a younger man wearing short trousers slept open-mouthed, head thrown back, oblivious to Birch's interest in him. Humans can look so unattractive sometimes. *OK, sad man,* Birch asked himself, *what else can you find for entertainment on this coach trip?*

Haines feels that Birch should not have been quite so hard on himself. People watching is a compelling and harmless pastime.

First stop in London was the British Museum, Egyptian section.

The story had begun some months before. As with other spiritual insights in the past, after an apparent fallow period, a series of insights and visions had presented themselves to Birch. One day he was given an insight into an energy flow that needed to be developed or assisted into manifestation, linking the three sacred energetic sites of Callanish in Scotland's Isle of Lewis, Carnac in Brittany and Karnak in Egypt. The energy flow that he was asked to work on was of the nature of a closed system around the outside of each site, much like a figure of 8 expanded to circulate three rather than two locations. Thus each site received a flow of energy around it. This is the lemniscate again.

Birch worked on this in meditation every day. As he did so, his inner-self informed him that the energy was being focussed and co-ordinated by higher forces. These then stepped back, leaving the physical manifestation and grounding to humans. The spiritual beings responsible set the whole scenario up, then passed it down for humans to work with through visualisation and working physically at the sites themselves. This work was then done as opportunities presented themselves. Significantly, the energies could not work until humans took on the projects and carried out the tasks.

Birch was told that the three centres of Callanish, Carnac and Karnak were connected by a grid through which energy flowed, one centre feeding another. This is part of a worldwide grid that will be used to hold a higher energy reality in place on the Earth in the times ahead.

Visiting and working in these sites is an important element in the energising process. When the three energy centres are fully activated, they will link with the worldwide grid. The cosmic energies enter each centre individually, then the co-ordinating energies are activated by the work carried out by humanity, after which the linkage to the worldwide grid will take place.

There is only so much energy that one person can hold and transmit, so working on the whole project needed groups of committed people to speed success. So Birch's friends, Mary and Joan, became involved and a further dimension was thereby added. At one of the trio's joint meditations, the two ladies saw the involvement of Sekhmet. Sekhmet is one of the oldest versions of the destructive aspect of the mother goddess. She is the ancient Egyptian equivalent of Kali. The destruction is necessary to clear a way for the upsurge of the new.

Birch's first vision of the three sacred sites was of what he would describe as a kink, or disruption, in the energy flow between the three. Birch also involved another friend, Hazel, in this work. Initially she saw Callanish in a higher aspect of energy and cleared a blockage before moving her awareness to the other two sites. The energy was not connecting and it took several attempts before a clear energy flow was accomplished.

Sekhmet spoke to Hazel, saying, 'Look at me and be aware of the animal and lower human energies that need clearing.' As she said this, Hazel could feel the energies flowing smoothly and regularly. Energy in the shape of a unicorn horn had been psychically inserted at Carnac by darker forces in order to disrupt the energy.

A further insight that Birch received was that the energy flow was a complete unit for all three sites. Each of the three sites had a different vibration frequency with all three contributing to the overall whole, which then melded into a group frequency. This was a little like a choir of different voices all contributing to the whole. The total unit was akin to a meridian in the Chinese energy system of the human body. See Figure 1 (on page 142) for a pictorial representation of the three centre energy flows.

Soon after all this work was completed, Birch received another visitation. Anyone visiting the statues of Sekhmet in the British Museum will see a circle of stone surrounding a leonine head. Similarly, the being that visited Birch had a very large head with two round protuberances, one on each side of the top of the skull. The skin of the face was so pale it was perceived as the colour of ivory. It looked much as one might imagine an alien. Birch calls the being a he because he was wearing, quite bizarrely, a business suit with a white shirt and tie. Birch realised later that the reason for this was to impress on him the seriousness of the visit. The being did not look at Birch, but down towards the floor, which indicated that he was telling the human something rather than engaging in a debate. The only movement came from the being's right hand moving on the arm outstretched towards Birch. The hand was making a downward waving movement as though urging Birch to stop doing something.

Later, Birch felt that he was being told to stop the energy work with the three centres. The work was complete and anything further was unnecessary. The energy in the three centres was now flowing sufficiently. Further interference from all those involved on Earth would detract from the progress. So this completed the energy work with Callanish, Carnac and Karnak, at least for the time being. Visits will follow to work on site, but that is for later and maybe for a later publication.

In a subsequent meditation performed by Birch, Faye and Audrey, Audrey saw Sekhmet as the consort of the lion king, and the guardianship of humanity as part of her remit. She saw this great being of energy as the great predator, but also the great sustainer.

'When humankind releases me from my predator guise, then the disasters of the world will be seen. Individuals need to work with me in my sustaining role and call on me for assistance,' Sekhmet said to Audrey.

Faye sees Sekhmet as the masculine element of the feminine energy, the pro-active righter of wrongs of the big cats. For Birch, Sekhmet presents herself as a benign form, similar to the British Museum statue, with the addition of a luminous aura indicating life and energy. She indicated to Birch that her benign appearance was because the trio were working in alignment with her purpose. Sekhmet also urged humanity to utilise her creativity for healing trauma and building new appropriate structures in the third dimension.

This image was immediately followed by the figure of a Hathor being: one of the alleged beings living in another dimension and adopted by the ancient Egyptians as one of their gods. This being said that it would be guiding the trio in their upcoming visit to Egypt in March 2008. But that's for the future. Now back to the British Museum.

As Mary, Joan and Birch stood in front of the four figures of Sekhmet on the ground floor of the museum, Birch asked Sekhmet if there was a message for him. *We are here, you are here. That is all that is necessary now*, was her message. Mary was told to calm down as she had become so excited being there.

Wall-to-wall people, from every corner of the globe, roamed the many rooms of the museum. The many languages, faces and dress styles suggested as much. The three visited Venus in the Greek and Roman section. As far as Birch was concerned, this topped up and balanced his connection to the female vibration.

Mary, Joan and Birch said their goodbyes to Sekhmet and left. It was time to visit the saint. There had been little apparent insight while in the museum, but that was not unusual. As Sekhmet had said, being there was enough.

There were a thousand people crammed into the town hall, people of all ages and cultures, Sikhs, monks, mostly white people of the thinking and sensitive classes, or so it seemed. On a raised section at the front of the hall sat the saint, a diminutive figure in a sari with a red spot painted in the middle of her forehead. She was flanked to left and right about eight feet away by two minders. On her left was a severe-looking, middle-aged woman wearing a deep red, assertive-looking sari. A strong-looking, muscular man stood to her right. His role was to position those at the front of the queue seeking darshan, or blessing, with the saint so that there was no delay between each individual receiving the blessing.

The role of minders around saints and spiritual leaders is an interesting one. Birch remembers Don Alejandro's priestly minder in Guatemala. He had a psychic as well as a physical protective role. Any attacks of a psychic nature against Don Alejandro would be intercepted and dealt with by the minder.

Birch had gone to this darshan, as the bestowing of a blessing to each person is called, pretty much with an open mind. The two organisers of his most recent trip to France were devotees and obviously enthusiastic about the saint. Another person on the trip, Tony, a down-to-earth builder, had previously attended a darshan, but he had not been impressed with the rigid organisation and behaviour pattern that had been imposed. He had been so uncomfortable that he had left before receiving his personal darshan. Thus Birch had two alternative perspectives on the ethos and process of the event.

The routine was the same for each person. Each one would kneel in front of the saint with head bowed, touching her feet. At the same time, the saint would place her hands on the person's head; for Birch it was on his temples. When the saint removed her hands, the kneeling person would straighten up and each would look directly into the eyes of the other. When the saint lowered her gaze, this was the signal for the end of that person's darshan. The so blessed would rise and exit, making the space available for the next person. This process went on for hours. There were a thousand people in the hall and each one received at least three quarters of a minute.

There were many of the saint's adherents directing the movement of people. Initially those present sat quietly. A stream of people moved from the chairs at the back of the hall to the central passageway, then up the middle of the room towards the saint. This phase was conducted kneeling or cross-legged, depending on the individual's comfort. Those in the central corridor moved slowly as those in the front of the phalanx were picked off and directed to the stage. Those still seated gradually moved to the back of the hall. Although the event was carefully managed, Birch didn't detect the rigid behaviour that Tony had complained of at his darshan. It was quite a logistical exercise to make sure everybody received their darshan whilst at the same time maintaining order. On the stage at any one time there were four or five kneeling people gradually inching closer to the saint as she went through the routine with each one.

As Birch sat in the body of the hall, he first watched the process and then relaxed into a meditation. He found the atmosphere conducive to a successful attunement with the cosmic. A thousand people quietly waiting, with a central focus and positive intent, contributed to an environment rich for the meditator. Birch sat, observed, meditated for maybe an hour and a half. It came to his logical mind to compare his experience with the saint's. Immediately his intuition jumped in and gave him this message: *This person is several levels above you in spiritual attainment. Don't get ahead or too confident in yourself.* So that was telling Birch to seek a little more humility.

Birch began to realise that, with the numbers present and the time factor for receiving darshan, he was in danger of missing his coach back home unless he jumped the queue. He spoke with one of the saint's organisers and joined the central line moving inexorably forward behind brown, white and saffron-robed monks and nuns with shaven heads. They all looked so slim and healthy. Birch had no idea to which religion or sect they belonged. It didn't matter who was a Sikh, who a be-robed monk, who a Westerner. They were all there to experience freedom from religion and dogmatic interference.

It was Birch's turn for darshan with the saint. He kneeled, placing his hands on her feet, feeling her hands strongly on his temples. In that moment he sensed a circulation of energy between the two of them. The acupuncture points in Birch's hands were open, as were those in his temples, so this allowed the circulation of energy from the saint into, and around, his body. Then he sat up as the saint's hands released his temples and they held each other's gaze. Birch found her energy very gentle, not over-strong. A controlling guru would have been tempted to attempt either to drain his energy or to overpower him with his or her stronger power. This didn't happen. Birch felt a very benign and loving energy. It was at this moment that he realised the saint was the real deal in terms of spiritual attainment and intent.

When the saint lowered her gaze, Birch rose, left the room and found his friends. As the three walked back towards the underground, they talked of their experiences in the hall. Joan had a little difficulty bending down to kneel, so as she had struggled she had felt the saint take hold of her hands and perform the darshan in that position. She may have been the only person not to have gone through the standard routine.

Mary spoke of a previous visit she had made to the saint. A physically large and egotistic friend who had gone with another group had proclaimed loudly after her darshan, 'I towered over her, gave *her* darshan.' Mary had kept her mouth firmly shut, deciding that discretion was the better part of valour.

Mary also said that the saint can see glitches in each person's karma. She can untangle or clear elements, giving them knowledge and some release. ('Karma' means 'knowledge'.)

Bryan tells the story of a visit he made to the saint, along with a friend, Alan. Alan is a hard-bitten, tough business man who runs a lap dancing club. Alan is not the sort of person one would normally associate with welcoming a blessing from a sainted person; quite the reverse. On this occasion he had been persuaded by Bryan to try it. Alan went through the process of darshan. When he came out from darshan to rejoin Bryan, he was grasping and clutching his chest. With eyes bulging he slumped into a chair.

'I'm having a heart attack,' he choked.

'Sit down, breathe normally and relax,' soothed Bryan.

Alan recovered. Bryan told him that what he was having was an opportunity and the actuality of his heart opening, long closed in his normal business and personal life.

Birch reflected on his experience further. He was impressed by this woman performing this routine of blessing with so many people. The visitors would bring their hang-ups, their attached discarnate entities, their psychological splits in the psyche, all their baggage. Birch knew from previous experience how easy it was for attachments to cling on to one's own aura when one was dealing personally, psychically and psychologically with other people, even one at a time. Yet here was this woman offering the spiritual gift to perhaps 3,000 people over three days. Birch was as sure as he could be that she had been unaffected by all this energy which she willingly circulated through her body and being. No doubt a few of those receiving darshan would attempt to dump their various issues on the saint. Birch is sure that she has her own cleansing and protection routine. Nevertheless, what she is doing is a monumental psychic and spiritual practice, in his view. She is truly an enlightened being.

The saint's website tells:

> An avatar is an incarnation of the divine and comes to Earth whenever there is a need to uplift and protect humanity.
>
> In this time of crisis [the Saint] offers a direct transmission of light that dissolves all barriers and changes the entire being. She asks no special allegiance and offers her transformative powers to all.
>
> Thousands of people from all over the world come to receive her darshan, her silent bestowal of grace and light through her gaze and touch.

Birch will here make a final comment on gurus. He is reminded of the time when a well-known guru came into his consciousness. Birch's first reaction was one of slight suspicion and concern. He felt that his defences were being subtly breached.

'What do you want?' Birch asked.

'We will do some work together,' the guru replied.

'I don't think so. Goodbye.'

Birch felt that this particular guru was an energy vampire. They do exist in all walks of life. They may be conscious or otherwise of their damaging influence. The saint was in a different class of being: purer and non-demanding.

One final story now, to demonstrate an attachment to the psychic body. Jaqueline brought a book from Mexico into their Cheltenham home. It was by a well-known writer on dark mysteries. Birch was unhappy with this book, not because he had read this author but because he sensed a dark energy around the book.

One night, a couple of weeks later, Birch was woken by Jaqueline's screams. She was very frightened. She said that she had woken to sense a threatening figure next to her bed. Birch sensed nothing but performed a short protective meditation. They both returned to sleep and forgot the whole incident.

Some days later, Birch woke in the middle of the night, screaming. He sensed and saw a vile energetic form attempting to break into his aura. Birch's natural defences were sufficient to keep the entity at bay. Awake, he banished the form. Sleep was elusive that night.

The following morning, Birch reviewed the previous night's psychic attack. He came to the conclusion that this was linked to Jaqueline's experience and that both were linked to the presence of the unpleasant book. After conversation with Jaqueline, the book was destroyed. To Birch's mind, this incident demonstrated that entity possession can occur not only within a person's body, as outlined in *So You Think We're Alone?*, but also by attaching to mundane three-dimensional objects, if the energy is of a sufficiently powerful vibration.

FIGURE 1

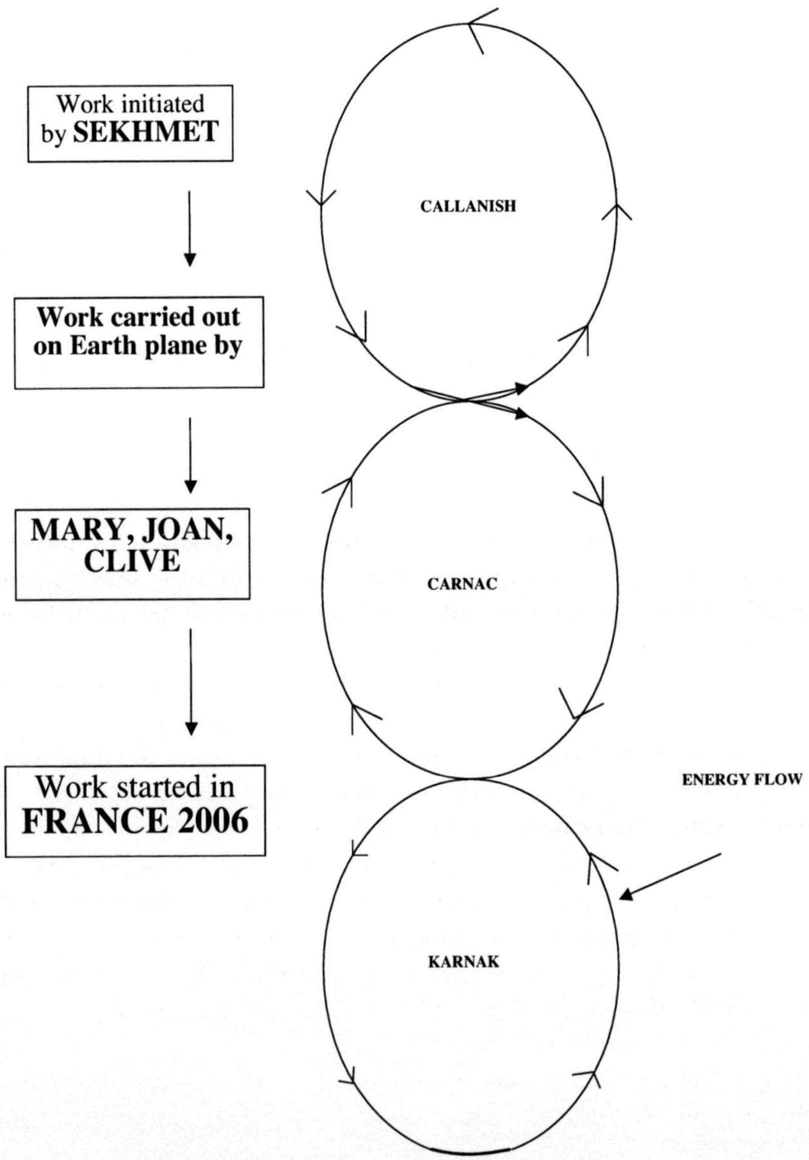
Work initiated
by SEKHMET
Work carried out
on Earth plane by
MARY, JOAN,
CLIVE
Work started in
FRANCE 2006
CALLANISH
CARNAC
KARNAK
ENERGY FLOW

So You Think This is Easy?

Intuitive insights of a mystic

Haines emailed Birch a novel that had been written by a third party. It contained material concerning reincarnation and its part in current lifetimes, connections with disincarnate entities and battles with negative forces. All these are subjects for *So You Think We're Alone?* Birch started to read the book with eager anticipation.

Sadly his hopes were dashed as the book was a very disappointing read. The plot was laboured and Birch struggled to get into it to enjoy. The subject matter was certainly as advised; however, the hang-ups of the main character overwhelmed the story development and, Birch's intuition told him, the personal issues were a projection from the author. All the while, the hero of the story was interacting with spiritual entities of various positive and negative persuasions. The sexual hang-ups, and personal relationship issues seemed to hang over and depress the mood of the book. Birch gave up at page 127 and returned to his own writings.

Reflecting on this reading experience, Birch remembered how much clearing of his own baggage has been necessary over the last thirty-five years in which he has been engaged in his work. This has been necessary to enable him to cope with the accelerating spiritual energies and the entities, incarnate and discarnate, embedded therein. In order to work with spiritual energies it is necessary to be very clear about oneself. Psychically and energetically, the process of becoming involved with these energies without long periods of preparation is akin to giving a child a hand grenade with the pin pulled out.

Birch remembers being in meditation in a Rosicrucian meeting. At the start, a powerful aura of high energies had been invoked to assist the group members in attaining a deep state. For two successive meetings, Birch became nauseous and it was necessary for him to leave. He was puzzled that it was on these occasions that he became ill. A light meditation, with a request to his higher-self for enlightenment, resulted in his becoming aware that he had not forgiven or dealt with some painful issues from his past. Birch sought counselling over a considerable number of weeks, temporarily abandoning the deep meditations. His existing spiritual background helped his awareness to respond fairly rapidly to the counselling opportunities for healing, and Birch was thus able to heal and forgive sufficiently to put the childhood traumas behind him. Thereafter, Birch successfully resumed his meditation practice.

A subsequent book, recommended by a friend and read by Birch, generated an interesting series of events. The book claimed to be an exposé of the events that would occur on Earth after winter solstice (21st December) 2012. This is a subject much beloved by those with an alternative perspective of reality. The book was a slim volume, probably half the size of this one. This is not necessarily a criticism. Quality will outlast quantity. However, quality was not the keynote of this book, in Birch's view. It highlighted a number of features that it considered key for the 21st December, 2012 event. There would be major Earth changes due to cataclysmic volcanic activity and rising sea levels engulfing large swathes of land. These dramatic events would cause major disruptions to food and energy supplies, as well as destroying cities and killing large numbers of people. The book proposed that new communities of skilled people, living off the land in a modest way without the benefits of lost technologies and fuel supplies, should be set up post haste. The author went on to claim that this information had been given to him by ascended master beings (beings who no longer need to be incarnated on the Earth because they have learned all the lessons of humanity).

As Birch read further, his brow furrowed deeper and deeper. This was not because of the nature of the argument but because of the dubious nature of this book. The alleged master beings' sources must have been behind the times, because Birch had read all these arguments a number of times before in other books. Some of these original sources were over a decade old. There was a paragraph that Birch was convinced he had read elsewhere, in almost exactly the same wording as that this book had reproduced. So the book, to Birch, was a cut and paste affair: stolen information purporting to be a work of originality. Birch was angered by the sheer effrontery of a writer plagiarising others and passing it off as his own work. Worse, he, the writer, was claiming a superior spiritual source for his theft of ideas. The few ideas that the writer did discuss were reproduced over and over again with slightly changed order in an attempt to give a patina of originality. Birch did read all the way through, just in case there was a thread of true originality somewhere. There wasn't. The whole thing could have been written in three pages, or, better still, not written at all, leaving the field to the original writers who at least produced interesting stories and information with the proposed ideas concerning 2012.

So why does Birch highlight this story? The reason is to encourage those interested in alternative ideas to become discerning of the material presented to them. If in doubt, reject it. It is important not to lose one's natural filtering of good and bad material when one is presented with new and exciting ideas.

There is a corollary to this. The writer listed a whole series of 'ascended masters' who had allegedly provided the material. One of the names appeared to attach itself to Birch's consciousness. Over the next twenty-four hours, this name regularly popped up in Birch's awareness. Puzzled, Birch meditated on this alleged master being, attempting to make psychic contact. There was nothing. It was as though this name were attached to an energetic husk, empty. Birch thought that the lack of connection was due to him, although given the nature of the book he was not entirely sure.

He then spoke to his own spiritual guidance. 'Does the book have value?' he asked.

'If you think so then it does,' came back the unsatisfactory reply.

'That isn't what I asked,' said Birch.

'Let's put it another way. Did it have value for you?'

'No,' replied Birch.

'Then you have your answer,' was the final comment from guidance.

There are those who claim that certain ascended masters are 'looking after' humanity. Others say that it is a big con and these alleged ascended masters are psychic leeches sucking energy from humanity for their own selfish benefit. This could be one explanation for the 'psychic husk' of the alleged master being mentioned above. From Birch's perspective, it is vital to trust and work with one's own common sense and intuition. We are totally responsible for our own development. There may be discarnate beings assisting us. However, it is not wise to lean on such ideas. Be your own spiritual advisor and empowered being.

The path of the mystic is not an easy one. A good analogy is the journey up a mountain as a metaphor for human development. Those who are not on a mystical or spiritual path take the long route from the base, circling many times and slowly rising. The mystical path is much shorter, but steep and rocky. So those taking the latter path have many difficulties, but also many rewards. There are hindrances, barriers and frustrations to be faced and overcome. They tend to come thicker and faster for the mystic, but this is not always the case.

Listening to the promptings of one's inner voice and intuition will guide one along this rocky path. Once having taken the decision to become a mystic operating primarily from one's spiritual centre, not listening can have very difficult outcomes for the aspirant.

One friend of Birch's was flung from a ladder by her higher-self. Her leg was broken as a result of ignoring the inner promptings. It can be that serious. We are talking of commitment to a most powerful way of being. Those not on a mystical path would point this event out as an accident. The mystic knows that there are no accidents, no chance, there is no good or bad luck. Every situation that presents itself has been attracted to the individual by a psychically magnetic process.

Another friend was flung through the windscreen of his car in an 'accident' and very seriously injured. In a car behind was a doctor who was able to give life-saving treatment on the spot. Was this another accident? The accident was so serious that a helicopter was called to airlift Birch's friend to hospital. Fortunately (or was it?) the 'accident' was next to a field on which the helicopter could land, and the friend's rapid transfer to hospital saved his life. He recovered completely. Was the nearby presence of the doctor also an indicator that the whole situation was being set up by the friend's higher-self? Birch says that it was. In this way, the lesson can be learned, coupled with the survival of the physical. The friend's comment on the accident was that he would not have missed it for the world. It shook him out of a dead end of awareness into which he had allowed himself to slip.

By the way, the first friend also recovered completely.

So our higher-self, once alerted to a decision to enter a higher consciousness, will guide us, prompt us, advise us, but also shake us out of backsliding.

There are occasions when energies not of the highest vibration are attracted to the work that we do. For some time, two friends of Birch's, Jay and Mona, sensed they were being attacked psychically. The source of the attack was identified as a supposed friend of the couple. The friend was always charming in outer personality. This person was being used by negative discarnate energies as a vehicle for attack, and subsequently attempted disruption of the spiritual work being conducted by Jay and Mona. Invariably, over a period of some weeks, this person would telephone Jay during meditation with a social excuse for the call. Always the calls were made during meditations. One time, Birch, Jay and Mona were in deep meditation when they were shocked back into three-dimensional consciousness by the front door bell ringing insistently. They struggled back into this world. The door bell was answered. There was the supposed friend bearing a gift for Jay. Any excuse to break the positive energy pattern, it appeared to the three. She had already made one of her telephone calls less than half an hour before. This 'friend' was quickly ushered back out of the house after delivering her gift, and the trio was able to resume its meditation successfully. At the end of this session, Birch received the intuitive message that this small group should doubly protect itself from this unwarranted intrusion. It was believed that this person was being used by negative energies, whilst she herself was unbalanced and needed much healing. It was felt that the three could not perform this work of healing, as this person was infected by very powerful energies.

Negative energies will be attracted to the work of the positive. This positive energy will be extremely uncomfortable for them. A few days later, Jay and Mona were entertaining friends when Mona suddenly felt ill for no apparent reason. When the visitors had left, Jay admitted she felt ill also. Further discussion brought the odd news that both ladies had succumbed to the sick feeling at precisely the same moment. This was most puzzling to both.

Later Birch arrived for the weekly meditation and visualisation session. He was asked by his two companions to look into the problem during the meditation. In a deep state of concentration, Birch saw the supposed friend as the source of the sickness. She had been sending negative jealous thoughts to the pair. Birch saw her, metaphorically, stuck in mud and in a deep trench. There was no way that she could raise herself energetically and spiritually, hence the jealousy and black projected thoughts. Subconsciously, she saw Jay and Mona as being happy and fulfilled in their home and personal lives. In a subsequent discussion reviewing the meditative insight, Birch suggested two things. The first was that Jay and Mona see the supposed friend as little as possible, as Birch sensed she was attaching psychic hooks of energy into the pair during their meetings to accentuate the attacks. The second suggestion was to create a psychic bubble of energy around the supposed friend's home with mirrors facing inward so that all negative projected thoughts would be reflected back.

A little while after the 'mirror facing inward' meditation was completed, an acquaintance of the supposed friend, who had been in the thrall of the latter, suddenly broke away. She said that she never wanted to see the supposed friend again. This staggered Birch's two friends, who had watched with some sadness the plight of this unbalanced relationship. Birch and friends put this breakdown to an unplanned result of the 'mirror facing inward' meditation. Still later the supposed friend visited Jay. As she sat on the settee drinking tea she was observed and stared at by Opal, one of Birch's friends' psychic cats. After staring for some time, Opal jumped on the arm of the settee immediately to the right of the supposed friend, stared again, then walked straight across the seated person to the left-hand side. The psychic animal then sat with her back to the somewhat unwelcome visitor until said visitor left. Birch sensed later that Opal, by her staring and perambulations, had created a barrier around this person. This was so that the unwelcome vibrations would stay inside the barrier and would not leak out towards Jay.

In our previous book we explored the battle between the forces of light and dark in this third-dimensional reality. More recently Birch has been asked, with others in a meditation group, to visualise counteracting one aspect of negative energy that is working against the best interests of humanity. Birch was, at that time, concerned about this approach for two reasons. The first reason concerned the question of the security of the meditation group members. He had had an experience of similar work in the past which had been counteracted by a negative energy so strong that it had caused him considerable discomfort. The second reason for his concern was based on the premise that virtually all of his previous visualisation work had been connected to building the light and accentuating the positive rather than counteracting the negative. Nevertheless he agreed to this work.

Before starting the negative blocking meditation, the members of the group were supported by the information that their guidance would support the work by cloaking their activity psychically. This was further supported, for Birch, by a dream a few days later. In the dream he was a prison officer who was charged with the task of guarding two dangerous criminals. He had to take them to another prison in a van driven by a woman prison guard. He was nervous about this task as he felt insufficiently trained for it. (It is interesting and powerful that he experienced emotions in the dream. This does not happen very often.) Birch sought assistance from a senior officer, asking for a gun for protection. The senior pointed to a gun rack on the wall of the prison and suggested that he take the largest shotgun that was there. Birch removed the gun, broke it open at the breech and saw a shell already positioned in the barrel. Much heartened (more emotion), he continued with the task. Suffice to say the transport of the prisoners was completed satisfactorily.

When Birch woke in the morning he tuned in to guidance for advice on his dream's meaning. He was informed intuitively that this had been a demonstration of the protection that he had received in connection with the negative energy blocking visualisation.

There was a possible postscript to the above. A little later, Birch suddenly went into another reality to find himself confronted by another being. He could not tell if this being was human or not. The being shot a ball of negative energy in the direction of Birch's throat. The ball was diverted by an unknown force. Whether there was connection to the blocking visualisation he could not tell. However, the experience demonstrated the necessity of always creating a safe psychic space in which to do one's work. There was a further issue that may or may not have been connected to the ball of negative energy issue. A few days after this event, Birch developed a debilitating cough and cold that was centred in his throat. The negative ball throwing and the cold were connected, Birch believes.

Some potential wake-up calls need not necessarily be traumatic. They may even be slightly humorous. Birch was resting on his bed one day, quietly musing, when what felt like a tremendous kick or blow to the middle of his spine lifted and arched his back a good foot into the air, up and away from the mattress. All around him was completely calm apart from this single apparent blow. There was no after-effect, shock or pain associated with the event. Birch was mystified, having no explanation. Later he shared the experience with Ian, a mystical friend with a mischievous sense of humour. With a twinkle in his eye he said to Birch, 'The spiritual forces couldn't reach to give you a kick up the backside.'

Birch later had a car accident in which no one was hurt apart from his pride. This accident focussed Birch's mind on some issues that he had been avoiding. Perhaps this accident was the next stage in pushing Birch to address that which he needed to do. If he had been able to sort these issues out after the friendly knock in the back, perhaps the car accident would not have been necessary.

Now for two stories concerning the flow of psychic energies.

Before Birch went to the US for the first time in 1998, he decided to destroy all the Rosicrucian literature that he had accumulated over twenty years. There were over 1,000 monographs, as well as many books. As wonderful as the contents of the material were, he was no longer a member of the Order and therefore no longer studied the material. He sat down, ripped up all the monographs and deposited the small pieces in bin liners, then put them out for rubbish collection. The result of this disposal the next day was most extraordinary. The energy in the room where the material had been stored started to flow with an ease that he had been unaware of before the disposal. There was a change in the degree of flow, although he had not sensed a blockage before the disposal. He had become accustomed to the previous energy. Now, with the monographs gone, there was a new energy flow that was fresh and invigorating.

The second story concerns Birch's library. He was proud and content to gradually accumulate book after book and he enjoyed owning them. After a time, a friend spoke to him of the joy and pleasure when she lent and gave away books. This precipitated a twinge of regret in Birch. Was he being selfish hanging onto his library? So he started to do the same as his friend. As soon as the loaning and gifting began, other people started to do the same, giving and loaning books back to Birch. He realised that it was no longer necessary to buy so many books, because many were coming into his possession without effort. The second realisation was that, as in the story above, he had uncorked a blockage of energy. Now, with his changed approach, thinking of his collection as a lending and giving library rather than a possession library, he had allowed or created a circulation of energy.

These two events were valuable lessons, teaching Birch the energetic limitations of possessing anything that he was not prepared to pass on. Birch does not advocate giving away that which sustains one's life or the lives of loved ones. He does propose, however, that we do pass on that which we can without self-denial. In this way, we attract to ourselves the beneficence of the universe.

The next story is a variation on the theme of the above two. Birch had the sad duty of being the executor of his mother's will. At the end of the bequests and other requests that were completed, a residue of money was left which was willed to Birch. When the whole process was finalised, the residue funds were placed in Birch's bank account. Within a couple of days of this final transaction, he received an insistent message in his consciousness. This message was so strong it was as though someone had approached close to his ear and spoken loudly into it. The message said, *Give Matthew the money*. At the time, Birch's son, Matthew, was attempting to set up his own business and was, consequently, sorely in need of capital. Birch was taken aback at the strength of the message that he'd received, but was impressed by it. Immediately he made arrangements for the money to be transferred to Matthew. Two years later, Matthew has developed a successful and growing business. He has done this with energy, skill and a fine sense of honesty. Birch is immensely proud of him.

Birch cannot be sure of the source of the message. Perhaps it was his mother, the original source of the funds, speaking to him; perhaps it was Birch's own intuitive sense. Could it have been Matthew's need crying out for assistance? As with many such situations, the source is not the most important factor. Listening to the inner voice and allowing the flow of energy (after all, money is energy) is the most important element.

This is from *Anna, Grandmother of Jesus* by Claire Heartsong:

> This is a new model of coherency dynamics based on the science of quantum mechanics and chaos theory. In your day there is research being done that indicates that a person's well-being and actual state of health is enhanced when his or her mind, emotions and body are in harmonious relationship with one another – a coherent energy field.
>
> Those involved in this research have found that the most coherent field is subjectively called love and appreciation. When discordant, limiting time-space perception shifts into quantum, holistic awareness (spacious, embracing love and appreciation) there is healing, or re-established order, balance and wholeness. Another way to look at this is to see crucifixion, resurrection and ascension as those processes that return incoherence to coherency.

Some Native American nations used to train their children to sit for hours on end, alone and in silence, to listen to the music of nature. This simple, and seemingly idle, exercise is a wonderful and effective way of developing contact with the inner-being, for strengthening concentration and attuning with the curative forces of nature.

The Feel-good Factor – A Different View

An alternative view of nutrition and nutrients

Birch has recently turned his attention to the utilisation of energies to supplement the food and drink requirement of the human body. Much of Birch's previous work has been organised around healing modalities, maintaining fitness and health levels, combating and slowing the ageing process. He loves this work, believing it is essential in these times of great physical and mental stress, corrupted food, water and air supplies and the overuse of unnatural, chemical foods in our bodies. The work assists in the enhancement of the feel-good factor. He believes that our natural condition should be one of joy and happiness. This links into, and is part of, his spiritual and psychic work.

His interest leads him to alternative ways of supplementing our daily nutritional needs with remedies that are freely available to all who choose to explore them. Birch is not advocating that people remove anything from their current diets; in fact he urges that we change nothing.

Deepak Chopra, a qualified medical practitioner as well as an alternative healer and thinker, says that our bodies, when properly maintained, are the most powerful generators of chemicals and antibodies. They are able to supply all our needs. This is subject to having an appropriate, pollution-free environment. The trick is to harness the effective creation, distribution and functional use of naturally produced chemicals and antibodies.

Combining these ideas with the ancient Chinese perspective that we are surrounded by useful and useable, indeed essential, cosmic energy, it struck Birch that there must be ways of incorporating such energies into our wonderfully creative bodies in order to supplement our daily human energy needs. Food and drink are compressed potential energies. They are converted by the body into useable forms. In Birch's view, there are potentially other sources to provide that useable energy and thus to *supplement* our food and drink intake. Note *supplement* and not replace; as stated later, it is vital that no sudden changes be made to dietary patterns. From that premise we'll go to an extreme form of satisfying that need, returning later to somewhere in the middle for a more appropriate approach. Bear with Birch; there is method in his madness. In recent times, Birch has come across two sources who claim to have met and interviewed individuals who sustain themselves without eating any food and, in some cases, without drinking any liquids, sometimes for years, decades even. Birch respects their work.

Bob Frissell, in his book *Something in This Book Is True*, comments on this phenomenon, as fantastic as it may seem. He starts by saying that in the West more people die from over-eating than under-eating. Frissell tells us:

> A common denominator among the five immortals in the Bible (Jesus, Moses, Enoch, Elijah and Melchizedek) is that they each fasted for forty days with no food or water ... Leonard met a woman in Kathmandu, Nepal, who looked like she was in her thirties, yet she had fasted with no food or water for twenty years. If that sounds too advanced for you, maybe it is well to consider the possibility of short, frequent fasts. They can teach you more than long infrequent ones ... I will refer you to an excellent book on this subject, *Diet for a New America* by John Robbins. If you have read this book, you will see how diet plays an essential role in living in harmony and disharmony with the Earth.

For those who wish to explore fasting further, you may be able to purchase a copy of this fascinating book on the Internet. There are books published in the UK on this subject. It is vital to study it in depth before attempting any of the techniques and to make sure that one is in good health. It is as well to consult one's doctor before embarking on this particular journey.

Paramahansa Yogananda, in his *Autobiography of a Yogi*, recounts the story of Giri Bala who was investigated due to claims that she neither ate nor drank. She agreed to be tested and was locked up for three periods of two months, twenty days and fifteen days. During these sessions she was subject to rigorous scrutiny. Her investigators became convinced that she didn't eat or drink.

Her brother claimed that she had never eaten a morsel in five decades, and that she had never sought solitude for her yoga practices. She had lived her entire life surrounded by family and friends in a simple Indian village. Yogananda visited her in her home village. The following are extracts of his story about her.

> The little saint seated herself cross-legged on the verandah. Though bearing the scars of age, she was not emaciated; her olive coloured skin had remained clear and healthy in tone …
>
> 'Tell me mother, from your own lips, do you live without food?'
>
> 'That is true. From the age of twelve years four months down to my present age of sixty-eight – a period of over fifty-six years – I have not eaten food or taken liquids.'
>
> 'Are you never tempted to eat?'
>
> 'If I felt a craving for food, I would have to eat.'
>
> 'But you do eat something. Your nourishment derives from the finer energies of the air and sunlight, and from the cosmic power which recharges your body through the medulla oblongata.'

Giri Bala then recounted the background to this fantastic transformation from apparently ordinary person with a very healthy appetite to her present condition. After being married at twelve years of age, living with a difficult mother-in-law and tendencies to overeat, she sought a way out.

> In a secluded spot I sought my heavenly father. Lord, I prayed incessantly, please send me a Guru, one who can teach me to live by the light and not by food. A divine ecstasy fell over me.

Led by a beatific spell, she set out for the River Ganges. After she had immersed herself in the sacred water, her master materialised before her. He surrounded them both with an aura of light.

> He initiated me into a Kriya [yoga] technique which frees the body from dependence on the gross food of mortals. The technique includes the use of a certain mantra and a breathing exercise more difficult than the average person could perform. No medicine or magic is involved, nothing beyond the Kriya …
>
> I sleep very little, as sleep and waking are the same to me. I meditate at night, attending to my domestic duties in the daytime. I slightly feel the change in climate from season to season. I have never been sick or experienced any disease. I feel only slight pain when accidentally injured. I have no bodily excretions. I can control my heart and breathing.
>
> 'Mother,' I asked, 'why don't you teach others the method of living without food?'

'No.' She shook her head. 'I was strictly commanded by my guru not to divulge the secret. It is not my wish to tamper with God's drama of creation.'

'Mother,' I said slowly, 'what is the use of your having been singled out to live without eating?'

'To prove that man is spirit.' Her face lit with wisdom. 'To demonstrate that by divine advancement he can gradually learn to live by the eternal light and not by food.'

There we will leave the story. As fascinating as it is, there is no way that the above could be recommended for us in the West. This woman was a one-off, it seems to Birch, even in the highly spiritually charged environment of India. Her example does, however, open the debate on how we can supplement our normal food intake with energies that will complement our diet in a positive way.

Here is another aspect of this debate from *Life from Light* by Michael Werner and Thomas Stöckli.

> ... biophysicists today confirm that electro-magnetic radiation accounts for three-quarters supplied and given off in humans and that quantitatively the acquisition of energy via food plays only a small part. We have known, at the latest, since the development of quantum theory that light and matter are different states of the same thing. And we have known since the discovery of photosynthesis that sunlight can produce starch, that is solid matter of foodstuffs, out of CO_2 and H_2O, though to this day the process is still not scientifically understood in every detail.
>
> ... If the possibility of living on light depends on one's own conscious attitude, would it not be necessary for consciousness to have the character of light and for light to have consciousness or some kinship with the content of thoughts?
>
> He [Steiner] concluded his deliberations by describing how we only eat so that exertion of digestion can stimulate the body to take in something from the etheric sphere, that is from the environment, from the general life forces around us which can then be transformed into the substances that maintain and build up our body.
>
> ... In other words our bodies gain structure and substance by taking in light, or light forces, and condensing them.
>
> I am convinced that the process of being nourished by light is a gift from the spiritual world which is all around and within us, an endeavour to break through the materialism that is having such a devastating effect just now.

Birch's guidance on this matter suggests that when a sufficient consciousness is reached, then each individual cell in the body is able to harness such energy directly. This energy is infinitely available from cosmic sources and is always around us. When this advanced level of consciousness is attained, through mystical development or indeed through any vehicle, then the following occurs. This cosmic energy is constantly being absorbed by our electro-magnetic aura. Further, it is taken into the body by the action of the chakra vortices sucking the forces inward. The enhanced cell activity then converts the electro-magnetic energy into usable energy for the body. There need be no objective consciousness involvement. The process is automatically organised by the unconscious.

Birch has an exercise he has found to be extremely beneficial in developing his daily energy requirement further. The exercise works with certain extra-planetary energies which are available to all of us. In order to enable ourselves to access them, we attune with them using meditative and visualisation techniques. Possibly the amount of detail in the exercise is irksome. If so, feel free to create your own version which works for you. Perhaps you could simplify it. Then, if you find the exercise useful, gradually extend it to incorporate more.

Daily practice or, failing that, as often as you can manage will be greatly beneficial. Treat the exercise with respect. It is not a toy to be played with. It requires commitment and focus. Approach each performance of this exercise with enthusiasm. If you are tired or in a negative frame of mind, don't do it. When doing this work, approach it with love in your heart and compassion for all creation. Without love the work is merely magical practice which should be of the past in these accelerated energy times.

So here we go with Birch's **Energy Exercise**.

Stage One. Relax in quiet comfort. Close your eyes. Visualise the sun in all its energetic glory and warmth and, at the same time, be aware of your own body. Next, draw a figure of 8 such that the sun sits in one loop and you sit in the other. Be aware of a continuous energy flow around the perimeter of the 8, which is thus encompassing you and the sun. Work with that until you are comfortable with it and are ready to move on. See and feel the energy moving continuously around the figure. Make it live.

Now we will work with a greater interaction. As the energy moves continuously around, feel some of it sloughing off and being attracted inside both circles. Feel your body being energised. Every cell in your body resonates with the influx of this new energy. Work with this for a while.

In this final phase we work with the above and add another element. We become aware again of the circulating energy around the periphery of the figure 8. As we concentrate on it, we become aware that not only is it releasing energy to be absorbed by the sun and our bodies, but it is also picking up energies from inside the circles. As the flow around the 8 moves your consciousness away from your loop and towards the loop containing the sun, it is carrying your energies to be absorbed by the sun. As the flow moves towards your circle, the sun's energy is available to be absorbed by your body.

The movement continues. The sun is absorbing your released energies and you are absorbing the sun's released energies. Work with this idea. See and feel the flow, see and feel the absorption of both. Continue to work with this as long as you feel comfortable.

When you feel that you have done enough with the sun, Birch suggests that you progress through the stages below in order to further develop the exercise.

Stage Two. Repeat Stage One, but place the moon in the circle previously occupied by the sun.

Stage Three. Replace the moon with the stars and cosmic bodies, then repeat the exercise.

Stage Four. Replace the stars with the energy of the cosmic spaces and repeat the exercise.

Stage Five. At the completion of this part of the meditation, allow the figure of 8 to gently sink back into the cosmic realms and finish with the thought that any remaining energy will be used for the benefit of the Earth and all creation.

Become aware of two energy points in the centre of the bottom of your feet. These are acupuncture points called 'bubbling well' by the Chinese. Become aware of the tip of your coccyx. There is an energy centre here called the base chakra. Feel these three centres opening to allow the Earth's loving and positive energy to enter your body and, as in the above, feel your cells vibrating to this wonderful energy. Continue to absorb the energy for as long as you feel comfortable.

When you have done enough, you will have completed the energy exercise. Allow the final energy within the visualisation to disintegrate into the cosmic realms.

Become aware of your body again. Feel your feet on the floor, feel your limbs. Become aware of the clothes on your body. Do some deep breathing. Feel your lungs inhaling and exhaling. After a few of these, re-establish your connectivity with the material world around you.

When you are ready, rise and continue with your day.

One final remark about this exercise: the figure 8 is the mathematical symbol for infinity. See Figure 2 for a pictorial representation of this exercise.

In his book *DNA Pirates of the Sacred Spiral*, Dr Leonard Horowitz touches on the comparison of food, water and oxygen.

> In one hour, the average adult inhales more than two pounds of oxygen. Daily, he or she consumes nearly two pounds of water, four pounds of food, and almost six pounds of oxygen. It is interesting to note that you process nearly the same weight of oxygen as you do food and water combined.

So it is an imperative that we consider our oxygen intake as part of this re-evaluation of our daily energy intake. As we age, the tendency is to breathe shallower and shallower. If you watch a baby breathe you will see that he or she starts to breathe from the abdomen and then engages the lungs from the bottom to the top. This is the way to most effectively use the energies of the air. Stress and the demands of life encourage us to forget to breathe consciously. Over the years and decades we pay less and less attention to our breathing pattern, and the inevitable happens. We abandon the involvement of the abdomen. We breathe further and further up the lungs, less and less into the back of the lungs. So let us consider a breathing pattern that will help us to reverse this trend. Be careful with this exercise if you suffer from a lung or heart disorder. Consult your physician if you are so afflicted before working with it. It is important that all who practise this exercise start slowly, treating it with respect.

Now try something else: the **Breathing Exercise.** Stand or sit comfortably in a relaxed manner. Your head, neck and back should be straight to release the abdomen and lungs from stress. Place both hands on your abdomen, one hand over the other. Start with a few conscious breaths. The object of this is to bring your awareness into your breathing pattern.

Now start to breathe deeply. Begin by breathing into your abdomen, and then fill your lungs afterwards. You are now working from the bottom to the top. As you breathe in, regularly and without stress, feel your abdomen expanding and pushing your hands out. At maximum breath, hold briefly, and then allow the air to escape from your lungs in a relaxed and calm way. As the escape continues, allow the hands to follow the contracting abdomen. This relaxation is important in avoiding stress in the body. Continue with this exercise as long as you feel comfortable.

You can do this exercise any time of the day to suit your schedule. In addition, from time to time, become aware of your breathing becoming deeper and, in a relaxed manner, engaging the whole of the lungs. In the bus queue, traffic jam, supermarket queue and while sitting quietly at home, work with your breathing. It will pay dividends.

N.B. TAKE CARE WITH THESE EXERCISES. THEY ARE POWERFUL TECHNIQUES. IF YOU ARE HEALTHY THEY WILL BE OF GREAT BENEFIT. DO NOT CHANGE ANY OF YOUR CURRENT DIET WHEN STARTING THESE EXERCISES.

The following is an exercise for all. In the centre of each palm is an acupuncture point which is putting out energy all the time that you are alive. We will use that energy in the following exercise to strengthen the recuperative powers of the liquid.

And so to the **Water Exercise.** Sit comfortably with a glass of water in your hands. Wrap your hands around the glass so that your palms (and thus the acupuncture points) are pressed against the glass. Relax and focus your attention into the palms of your hands. If it helps, close your eyes. Feel the glass against your palms. Allow the energy to pass through the glass into the water. Spend some time working with this energy flow.

When you feel that you have done this enough, relax for a couple of minutes, still holding the glass but emptying your mind. Finally drink the water, which will be greatly energised. A maximum of twenty minutes performing this exercise each day will be extremely beneficial: the feel-good factor.

Now let's take a look at another way of working with cosmic energies.

Birch was told a true story that came from Jaqueline's family in Mexico. A psychic woman had used her powers to help many people in authority, including senior policemen and politicians. One day, she visited a woman and found her dead; murdered, most likely.

The dead woman's husband was a drug dealer who had an interest in separating himself from his wife. He had acquired a girlfriend. The drug dealer accused the psychic of the murder, together with her two sons. The woman was arrested on flimsy, not to say non-existent, evidence. She had merely discovered the body. She turned to those she had helped in the past. They all turned their back on her, perhaps through fear of the drug trafficker.

The psychic's husband went to a lawyer who asked for 30,000 pesos (£1,500). This was an enormous sum for a poor family. By selling possessions and borrowing from friends and family, the husband succeeded in raising the required amount. The money was handed over to the lawyer. He promptly disappeared. The husband called at the lawyer's house on numerous occasions, even cycling there at 2 am. The lawyer and the money had disappeared into thin air.

The husband, in desperation, went to a well-known psychic and asked for help. The psychic said, 'Yes, I can help you. It will cost you 20,000 pesos.' By this time the husband was so destitute he didn't even have the money to pay for the Combi to visit his wife in prison. Jaqueline's mum and sister gave him some money and food to keep him going. The two women, along with the husband, visited the women in prison.

On a previous visit, the husband had brought a chicken and beans to supplement the very poor prison fare. The woman was losing a lot of weight. The chicken never reached her and she had to make do with the beans. 'Don't bring me anything else other than beans in future,' she told her husband.

At the time of writing, the woman is awaiting sentence.

There is a mystery surrounding the gold chain and locket that she has worn since her internment. Everything else that she took in with her has been stolen, except for this pure gold item. Why has this most valuable item been ignored by her fellow inmates? Odd, we might think. The reason lies in the locket itself. It is a figure of the Saint of the Dead highlighted in an earlier chapter. It seems that the imagined, or perhaps real, power of the saint through the medium of the locket is such that there is a potent fear of retribution from beyond the physical world.

The couple's son, a seventeen-year-old, has been convicted of the murder and sentenced to five years' imprisonment in a jail that is run internally by the Mafia. The family cannot visit him because it is assumed that such visitors have money and they will thus need to pay protection.

Birch was appalled by this story and determined to take it to his meditation and healing group to seek advice and help. The members of the group went into meditation after Birch had recounted the details. Birch worked with the lemniscate, described in previous chapters, and enclosed the woman and her son in its circulating energy. The energy was extremely powerful on this occasion. Birch felt that much protection was carried out for the two languishing in prison. Mary Earle, another member of the group, saw protective energy flowing from Michael to the suffering family; this being is known as St Michael to Christians. This was significant, for this angel is the highest being of protection for mystics.

Paul Hover saw a skull which had had its teeth removed. He later felt this represented the hierarchy involved in this miscarriage of justice having had their power removed. Paul also felt that the woman was being used by higher forces to demonstrate the extent of the abuse of the legal system. Maybe media attention would bring the situation into the public arena?

The day approached when Birch and his friends heard that the woman was about to be sentenced, outrageous as that was. Birch, in his righteous indignation, could not allow the event to pass without further energy work on behalf of the woman. He constructed a medicine wheel. This is a Native American spiritual symbol consisting of a circle of materials constructed on the ground. It has a cross inside it. Birch has found this a most powerful energy focussing and generating agent. When the wheel was constructed, Birch used crystals and stones for this purpose. A ceremony was performed. During the course of this ritual, Birch's consciousness was connected to three Native Americans with whom he had been working on another project. These three beings live in another realm of reality, or dimension. At the end of the ceremony, Birch felt good work had been done and, by the presence of the four, was relieved that other support had been given.

Energy has been sent psychically to help. Birch and members of his family are helping in a more material sense. And there we have to leave this story for now. When Birch hears stories such as this, it makes him realise how lucky he is to be living in the UK.

Another case that was discussed at a meditation meeting concerned a woman in an industrialised country. Over twelve years she had developed a new variety of foxglove. The seeds were stolen by the company with which she was attempting to negotiate its production and sale. When the woman protested, she was threatened. A lawyer to whom she went for legal help was bought off, presumably by the thieves.

This time, the group did not go into deep meditation but discussed the matter between themselves. It was Paul's opinion that those responsible would be likely to suffer karmic retribution as a result of their action. Birch had a flash of inspiration that 'seeds of disharmony' would be sown within the organisation.

So there are plenty of things to work on if you want to make a contribution to the human condition. Two quotes seem apposite here.

'Seek and ye shall find. Knock and the door shall be opened.'

'It is better to light a candle than curse the darkness.'

FIGURE 2

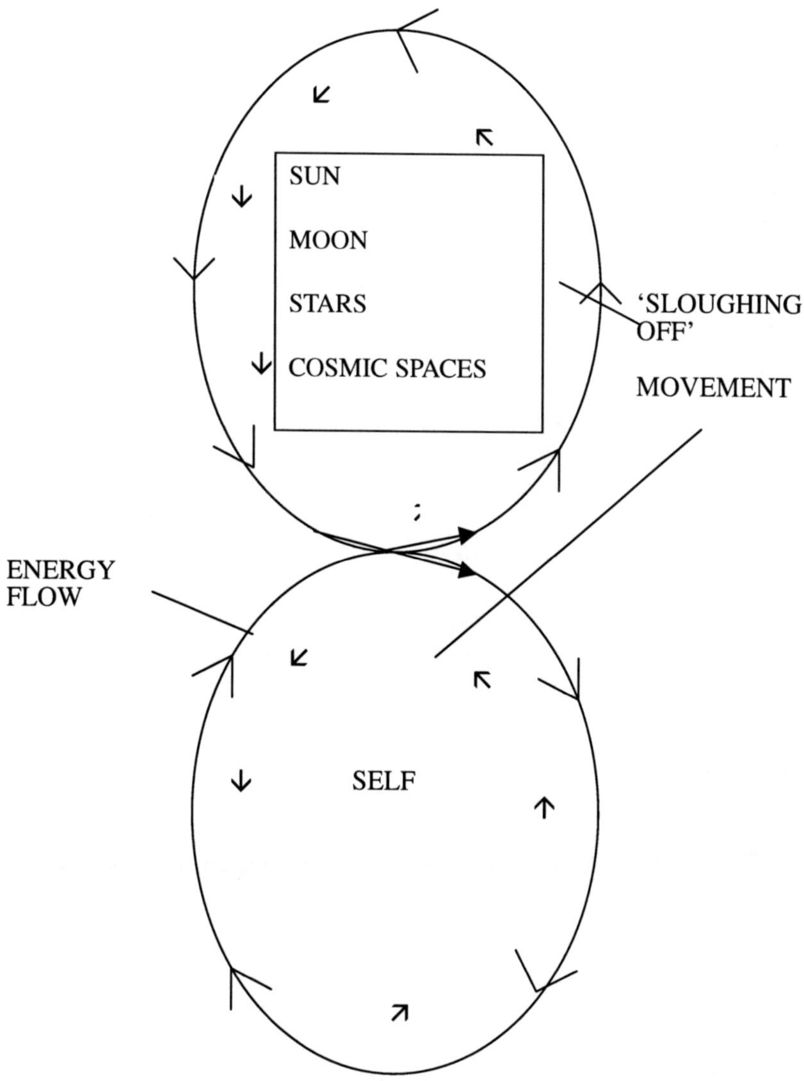
SUN
MOON
STARS
COSMIC SPACES
'SLOUGHING OFF'
MOVEMENT
ENERGY FLOW
SELF

Ghosts and Ghost Sensitives

Embracing another reality

Wikipedia has the following to say on ghosts:

> [A ghost is] the apparition of a deceased person, frequently similar in appearance to that person, and usually encountered in places she or he frequented, or in association with the person's former belongings. The word 'ghost' may also refer to spirit or soul of a deceased person. Ghosts are often associated with hauntings …
>
> Ghosts are controversial anomalous phenomena. According to a poll conducted in 2005 by the Gallup Organisation, about 32% of Americans believe in the existence of ghosts …
>
> In many historical accounts, ghosts were thought to be deceased people looking for vengeance, or imprisoned on earth for bad things they did during life.
>
> Critics of 'eyewitness ghost sightings' suggest that limitations of human perception and ordinary physical explanations can account for such sightings, for example, air pressure changes in a home causing doors to slam, or lights from a passing car reflected through a window at night.

Bryan, whom we first me in *So You Think We're Alone?*, has a very interesting talent. He sees negative, ghost-like energies as dark brown or black clouds attached to domestic objects such as curtains, furniture, animals or people. These energies, which seem to Birch to be thought forms, can be disturbing, debilitating and depressing to people living in houses infested with these things. People are affected by them but do not necessarily see them.

If those affected are fortunate enough to be able to attract Bryan's ghost-busting services, then the negative energies will be cleared using a very simple process. His intuition has told him to use salt, or salty water, to cleanse the negative energies. By washing objects, humans or animals, one can cause the energies to dissipate. Bryan particularly recommends washing in the sea. Yet again, the salt connection comes to our attention.

On one occasion during his ghost busting, Bryan saw many of these repulsive forms attached to the back of the home's old dog. The way that these things attach themselves is by hooking the energies to objects in the material world. He says that they feed on fear, so another way of clearing these energies is to laugh. Now, this seems like good advice in general to raise our spirits (so to speak).

Birch reinforces Bryan's view that negative energies attach themselves to physical objects, particularly dirty or neglected items. Matthew, Birch's son, asked his dad to perform a clearing ritual in his pub. Matthew, although not interested much in the spiritual world, nevertheless recognises the value of an alternative perspective on physical energies. Matthew had become increasingly unhappy with the feel in his establishment. He was of the view that the thoughts and actions of certain members of staff and customers were lowering the atmosphere of the place. Birch did as he was asked and performed a clearing ceremony. There were some abandoned rooms above the premises which contained old clothes, rubbish and peeling décor. The atmosphere there was awful, Birch sensed. After the ceremony was over, Birch appealed to Matthew to clear out the upstairs rooms, for it was clear that negative energies were attached to the things dumped there and were contributing to the general unease that Matthew was feeling about his pub. The pub has become a pub-restaurant and is a thriving business.

Bryan has contact with another ghost buster, a woman with wild hair and a broad Bristol-Gloucestershire accent. This woman must have quite a reputation. She was called by the Ministry of Defence and invited to do some ghost busting in an old aircraft hangar. She replied, 'That's fine, old dear. It will cost you foive 'undred pounds.' The MoD accepted the quotation. The deal done, Wild Hair went to the underground hangar. Security personnel and other staff were terrified to enter due to the constant banging of doors, including banging on the hangar doors. This was often when no live person was around. There was also a constant cold, spooky atmosphere.

Once in the hangar, Wild Hair waved away the security officers 'Off you go, me dears. I don' need ye, go on, clear off.' She was pretty bossy. As she entered she had ascertained immediately what the problem was. Up in one high corner of the hangar, psychically she saw hundreds of ghosts. It transpired later that they were the spectres of dead people.

So, true to personality, she stood facing them, hands on hips. 'Right, me dears, I want yew to go. Go on now, off yew go now. Yew are not welcome here.'

And off they duly went, the whole pack of them. The last sight she had of the assembled spirits was them flying away towards the spiritual light. The hangar became quiet and subdued. The MoD staff could relax and Wild Hair pocketed her 'foive 'undred pounds' for a minute's work. Everybody was happy. As she left, Wild Hair was told that the hangar had been used as a temporary store for body bags containing US servicemen killed in Vietnam. They had been flown in from Asia, stored and then transferred to the United States.

Haines also has a talent related to discarnate entities. He sees ghosts of people all the time. In the street, in buildings, in his own home, he sees hundreds of them. In his world, the number of ghosts that are visible is huge. One time he was sitting in a café; through the window he idly watched the world go by. He saw a man crossing the road accompanied by a dog. *Mmm...* he thought. *That dog looks like a ghost to me. I wonder if that chap knows he has a dog walking by his side?* No sooner had the thought formed than both man and dog disappeared. So Haines had been half right; both had been ghosts.

Not so long ago, Haines was required to fulfil a commitment at a secure establishment in a remote part of the UK. He was collected from his home by a car driven by one of those silent types. His silence was made up for by Haines's co-passenger, whom we shall call James. On the journey, James was explaining that there was a guest flat on the unit or a cottage outside the perimeter fence. Haines was given the choice of billet. It seemed reasonable that he choose the cottage off site. James said he used to bring his dog to the cottage, but had had to take it back to his parents in Liverpool. When left alone to its own devices, the dog used to trash the cottage. Apparently this was uncharacteristic for this normally well-behaved canine. Haines thought no more about it.

It transpired that James was formerly of 2 Para (The Second Battalion, The Parachute Regiment), having served in the Falklands War of 1982. He had also studied martial arts in Japan. With his background, James was down-to-earth and not given to flights of fancy, less still liable to be spooked.

So it was that Haines spent his first night in the guest cottage. Pretty soon he realised he wasn't alone. Intense cold would come, and when

Haines said aloud, 'Step back, please. You're too close and making me cold,' the warm comfort would return instantly.

This ghost definitely had a sense of humour. When Haines made one of his countless cups of tea, he would place the teabag in the mug and leave it for several minutes. Now, Birch attests to the fact that Haines cannot tolerate weak tea. His yardstick to determine if the tea is brewed is that a mouse must be able to walk across the surface. Nothing less will do. Well, the ghost had other ideas. She (Haines had immediately determined it was female) insisted on removing the tea bag. Each time Haines returned to the kitchen to collect his tea, he would find the tea bag steaming away in the bin.

Haines enjoyed the antics, having no fear of his invisible companion. He felt only benevolence and wellbeing when she was around. Each night Haines's immaculately shined shoes and boots would be on the floor at the foot of his bed, and it amused him that each morning the laces would be tied in perfect bows. Significantly for Haines, he never once saw this ghost. Each day the ghost would announce her presence by a new manifestation of her abilities, all of which Haines continued to enjoy. There was one small exception. He was always aware that when he was in the loo or the shower he could sense her presence, much too close for comfort.

The days passed and all was going well. The visitor from this world and the resident from another world seemed to be getting along. That was until one Monday: the last of his commission. James was due to arrive on the Tuesday, so Haines drove himself to the establishment. That night he went to sleep as usual. Nothing seemed amiss; even his ghostly visitor was silent. In the early hours he awoke, feeling he was bouncing up and down in bed. He sat and turned the bedside light on. At that moment, the bed, with him in it, shot across the room a good three yards or more. Birch is happy to attest that Haines does not have a reputation for being lily-livered or faint-hearted. But now his courage left him and he spent the rest of the night in his car, waiting for security to open the establishment later in the morning.

When he made it inside, he was much surprised to see James, whom he had thought was travelling down that morning. In fact, James's duty had been changed and he'd arrived on the Sunday. Before Haines could speak, James got in first.

'Bloody hell. Good to see you, mate. Don't go to the cottage. Went to bed Sunday night and the bloody ghost tucked me in.'

Several hours later, after an exchange of stories and hypotheses, Haines, James and two burly soldiers went to the cottage. It took the strength of all four to move the bed back to its original position.

There is an interesting postscript to this story. A couple of years after James and Haines had been scared witless, a teenage lad who was visiting the UK required babysitting. He and his minders were lodged in the cottage. James was among the team. Towards the end of the week, the lad asked James who the old lady upstairs was. James, quick as you like, said, 'Oh, she's the cleaner.' That seemed to satisfy the young lad. James, of course, knew there was no woman in the building.

One day, Haines was on the phone to Birch when he caught sight of a ghost standing next to him. It promptly disappeared. Birch heard a shout of surprise over the phone. Haines is used to these apparitions, but this one caught him off guard. The two joked later that the ghost, when socialising with his friends later, chuckled and said, 'I gave Ainsey a fright. You should have seen him jump.'

On another occasion, Haines rang Birch and, while discussing the events of the day, saw the ghost of a female walking and bending in his garden. As Haines had not seen a ghost all day, he blamed Birch for creating this energetic situation. Birch chose to ignore the comment. 'Perhaps she was smelling the flowers,' was his somewhat flippant remark.

During a visit from Haines, Birch was talking to him in the back garden and enjoying a coffee. His back garden is Haines's smoking room. Haines was telling Birch about an incident the previous evening. He had been watching TV and he had felt his toes being tickled. There had been no obvious physical cause for this. Assuming that one of the local spirits was having some fun, Haines had told the joking spirit to stop. The phenomenon had not stopped. At the same time Haines had seen an array of golden lights moving around the room, a phenomenon not uncommon in the Haines household. While this story was being recounted, the two friends were joined by Haines's son, Harry.

Harry spoke of a much more unpleasant apparition that had appeared to him the previous night. Retiring to bed at the end of the day, Harry had suddenly felt extremely hot physically, as though he were burning up. This was despite the fact that this was a cold February night and the window in Harry's bedroom was open. As Harry had become aware of this odd situation, he had seen a figure of a man in his bedroom doorway. The apparition had not been of anyone he knew. He had stood and stared in

Harry's direction. As Harry had stared back, he had noticed that the man had a scarlet slash across his forehead extending from his right eye socket, the eyeball of which was missing. The figure had disappeared, but the unpleasantness of the vision had unnerved fifteen-year-old Harry, so much so that he had switched his TV on and remained awake in fear for some time before falling asleep. Haines said that Harry's face had been white with fear the next morning.

As Birch listened to the story, he had the feeling that this figure had been a shadow from the War of the Roses, the final battle of which had been fought in Tewkesbury: home town of the Haineses. Birch also said that the previous night had been a full moon and thus a period of high psychic energy. It may be, he added, that such manifestations are more common at such times.

Tewkesbury had suffered grievously during the floods of July 2007, which could also have upset the balance of psychic forces in the area. In addition, water is a very powerful transmitter of energy.

That same evening, Birch told the above story to the meditation group which meets at Hazel's house. There was a consensus that the Haines house could be cleared, but not by anyone in the group. This was backed up by advice given to Hazel from intuitive sources. Haines does not feel the necessity of clearing his house at the moment. He sees the ghosts as sometimes humorous and entertaining guests. This may change if son Harry is further frightened.

Before we leave Haines's back garden, there was another fascinating event that occurred just prior to Birch's trip to Carnac. Birch and Haines were sitting at the garden table, drinking coffee and chatting. Haines interrupted and pointed inside the sitting room. The windows were closed. Through the glass, he saw a figure of an elderly man. He wore a cream-coloured smock. Haines was much impressed by the kindly face, which was sun tanned and deeply lined. His eyes were striking in their compassion and wisdom. It was a lovely face. The figure looked in Birch's direction. From his right side, Haines heard the name 'Elwyn', a name he had never heard before; it made little sense to him, and none to Birch. But Haines was certain that this energy was attached to Birch, and not to him or his home.

Not long after, Birch made one of his regular visits to his dear friend Audrey, near London. Audrey asked him if he realised that he was being shadowed by a spirit energy. His name, Audrey said, was Elwyn. Audrey said she felt that Elwyn was there to accompany Birch on his visit to France, especially to Les Alignements de Carnac. Birch had not told Audrey of the experience in Haines's garden and Haines certainly hadn't told her. He'd never met or spoken to Audrey.

Birch has a sense that Haines has a role to play as a communication channel between these discarnate beings and people in this reality. This role will have to wait until he is able to release some of his business commitments.

Margaret, a friend of Birch's, had a friend, Molly, who passed away at the age of ninety-nine. Molly and her husband did great work unknown to most people around them. They would visit buildings, particularly old ones, to clear ghosts or earthbound spirits. They were particularly drawn to work in churches and cathedrals.

Molly said that many of these spirits were grouped around the flags of military regiments that often hang in religious buildings. From a mystic's point of view, this flag placement is rather bizarre given that these places are supposedly celebrating the Prince of Peace. Anyway, back to the ghosts. This grouping of the ghosts around military flags made sense to Molly. In times past during battles, the soldiers would be called to the colours at particularly difficult times of the conflict. Thus in death, or their dying agony, the spirit of the soldiers would naturally be drawn to the symbol of their loyalty. In addition, perhaps their last living moment would have been in the vicinity of the flag, maybe holding it or looking at it in their death agony.

So throughout the land of Britain, unknown to those not sensitive to these energies, discarnate spirits of soldiers would continue to be grouped around this last vestige of their contact in the material world. No doubt they would be looking down with interest on the congregations worshipping the Prince of Peace, and the marriages and funerals taking place below. Most incarnate people would be blissfully unaware of this interest above them. Molly was of the opinion that all such flags should be withdrawn from religious buildings in order to remove this particular infestation. Molly and her husband did this largely unsung work for sixty years.

Hazel, another friend of Birch's, was visiting a dying friend in the local hospice. As she sat and chatted, without warning, Hazel was taken into an enhanced form of consciousness. She saw the room she was in absolutely packed with discarnate entities. These beings wore clothes from all ages.

She was particularly struck with the roundhead soldiers. The hospice was in a very old building.

And now to the story of the paper clip ghost. Jaqueline Birch would gently joke with a work colleague who would stay late in the office that she should 'be careful of the ghost'. Perhaps sensitivity to the psychic atmosphere helped create this joke in her mind before experience of the phenomenon? This comment soon rebounded on Birch's wife a little later. One evening she found herself alone, working late. As she bent over her desk, a paper clip dropped out of thin air onto the desk. She looked up. There was no returning colleague playing a joke on her. The office was completely empty of incarnate beings, apart from her. There were no shelves nearby that could source such an event. Muttering under her breath, she bent her head and returned to her task. Immediately another paper clip dropped onto her desk close to her head. A discarnate entity was clearly having some fun at her expense. 'Oh, leave me alone,' she spoke in an exasperated fashion. This was precisely what happened and the dropped paper clips stopped dropping.

A little while later, the opposite happened to Jaqueline whilst she worked during the normal working day. She was performing a task which required opening a file of papers, removing the paper clip from the documents, performing an administrative task and then replacing the paper clip and closing the file. As she went through the routine, paper clips began to disappear from Jaqueline's desk. Four times in succession this happened. Becoming fed up with this game, Jaqueline went to a colleague's desk and retrieved a large box of clips, making sure that she kept an eye on them. The paper clip ghost stopped its activities at this point. The game was over.

There were times when Jaqueline was required to work late, on her own, in the office. Regularly she would feel cold draughts wafting around her when no doors were being opened and closed, and no windows were open. In addition, there would be unexplained noises similar to a crack, with no apparent physical cause.

Those readers who have read *So You Think We're Alone?* will remember the story of Oscar the cat. For those who haven't had the pleasure of reading this fine offering, here's a summary. Oscar lived in a care home. He was not a particularly friendly animal to the living, but he did have one particular talent. He knew when one of the residents of the care home was about to die, even when the well-trained staff had no idea that the death was about to happen. He would sit with the dying person until they had passed away; only with dying people would he make such a contact. Subsequent to publication of *So You Think We're Alone?*, Birch was told of a person who possessed an ability relating to dying people. This person worked in care homes and hospitals throughout her working life. She also possessed the ability to see ghosts. When a person was about to die, they would be joined by female apparitions dressed in black; usually there were a number at each death. Of course, this person was the only one who could see these ghosts. The assumption was that these spectres were there to help the dying person over into their next world.

Sophie tells this story from her homeland in Malaysia. Next door to her family home in a rural village is a mysterious space. Tradition has it that a house once stood there, occupied by a wealthy and influential family. The story continues that the head of the family instructed his son to kill a specially prepared goat. It was then to be spit-roasted as an important focus of a feast. The son ignored the wishes of his father and, instead of the goat, killed a dog which was prepared and cooked. Unfortunately for the son, his subterfuge was discovered when the partly cooked body began to bark. The father was mortified at the shame that this deceit had brought upon his family. So distressed was he that the father prayed for the family to disappear. The invisible realms acceded to this bizarre request. Family and house did, indeed, disappear, leaving an empty space next to Sophie's family's property. Perhaps this reminds us of the old saying, 'Be careful what you wish for. You just might get it.'

The final chapter of this tale occurred when Sophie was a young child. She remembers walking around the mysterious empty space with her grandmother, who would conduct a conversation with an invisible person in a low guttural tone, different from her normal voice. The impressionable child was told that one of the invisible men had formed an attraction to the grandmother and had retained that emotional connection for decades.

Sometimes it is necessary to do very little in order to change a negative situation. Back to the Haines household at the time when Harry was awakened to find a ghostly male figure with disfigured face standing in his doorway. Some days later, wife Jacqui awoke to find a heavy ghostly energy lying on top of her. That same night, soon after getting into bed, Haines felt as though ghostly spiders were climbing along his arm towards his face. This was very frightening for an arachnophobe, which Haines is.

Harry awoke in the morning to find his darts placed in the bedroom dartboard. This was very puzzling and frightening for a young teenager, as he was always careful to put his darts away in their box each night.

The next day, Haines rang Birch, recounting the tale. The latter immediately offered help. As Birch put the phone down he felt nervous about his precipitate offer. He rang a friend, Hazel, for support and input.

As Birch prepared for his own bed that night, he tuned into the Haines family house, asking the cosmic forces to fill the house with light, raise the vibrations, giving the family a restful night. The next day, Birch rang Haines to be told that there had been a quiet and restful night in the house. Soon after, Birch spoke to Hazel, who confirmed that she had tuned into her guidance and been told that there was nothing to be done by her or by Birch. Events in the Haines household bore that guidance out, for, from that time on, there was no further occurrence of unpleasant ghostly happenings in the Haines household. So was Birch's short visualisation sufficient to help the cosmic forces clear the above negativity, or is there some other explanation? Certainly Birch's normal reaction to such a request would be to go to the house, play his Tibetan bowl and perform reiki or other healing modalities. This time, of course, it was not required to do any of those.

In another story, a girl could not believe the reasons given for her mother's disappearance. Her father's claim concerning the mother's supposed running away with an Italian lover simply didn't ring true for the daughter. There was some intuitive impulse niggling away in her psyche that there was something really wrong with the story. The girl had heard her mum and dad arguing. The very next day, her mum had not been there. She did as much as she could to persuade adults to listen to her doubts. She confided in her class teacher, who took no action. This failure stimulated the girl to create the story that she was being bullied. She wanted to get the headmistress's attention. The headmistress informed social services. Later that month, the mother's body was discovered, hidden in the family home.

The girl's suspicions had been heightened after a dream in which she had opened a cupboard door and her mum's body had fallen out. The girl, gathering her courage, had entered the cupboard in waking life expecting to find her mother's body there. In fact, the body had been hidden in a casket in the garden. The father confessed to killing his wife and was arrested and charged. Was the daughter influenced by her mother from another realm? Did the girl, through her own intuition, sense that the crime had been committed? Is there some other explanation?

Birch was woken one night by a woman bending over him. He assumed that it was his wife, Jaqueline. Suddenly there was a movement from his left where Jaqueline slept. The woman bending over him disappeared. Jaqueline was choking from a condition where, from time to time, her breathing tube is blocked. On this occasion she did not need assistance other than reassurance from her husband. It seemed to Birch, when reviewing the event later, that the woman from the psychic world had been a Good Samaritan making sure that assistance was available in this potentially serious condition.

Bryan happened on this phenomenon whilst on a course during one of his regular trips to the US. He was resting in a bedroom when this very strange and fascinating event happened to him. Without warning, a strong, muscular arm moved across his chest. It was so real that he could see the veins on the arm. It certainly wasn't his arm. The arm wasn't attached to anything, though. Suddenly the powerful arm lifted him off the bed, two to three feet into the air. Let us be clear about this: Bryan had not been meditating or sleeping. He was in normal objective consciousness when this happened. After some seconds, maybe a minute, he was gently lowered back onto the bed and the arm disappeared. This was an entirely physical event, with Bryan in full knowledge of what was happening. Bryan pondered on the meaning of this throughout the rest of the day. He felt strongly that this arm had belonged to the Master Jesus. Beyond this he couldn't fathom the meaning.

Bryan shared this with a fellow course member. A little later, after Bryan had returned to his room, this fellow put his head around Bryan's door.

'I know what this means. You were taken down from the cross,' he said.

Ah, thought Bryan. *This is of profound significance. I have come to the end of a phase of suffering in this three-dimensional existence.*

This is not a ghost story per se, but it is a fascinating psychic event. It demonstrates the type of phenomenon that can be experienced by the practising mystic.

On the subject of being sensitive to ghosts, Birch believes that it is important to set aside any fear concerning the phenomenon. For those interested in developing such links, sensitivity and confidence, as well as belief, are paramount. Birch remembers a time when he was a young boy, trembling in bed in an old farmhouse while on holiday. He had just been told a ghost story. The farmer's wife had recounted a tale of an old man who would regularly walk around the farm for his daily constitutional. The day that his funeral had taken place in the church opposite the farm, the farmer's wife had heard the tap, tap, tap of his stick. She had turned to see the dead man's ghost walk through one wall of the farm kitchen and out through the opposite wall. He was taking his final walk before his body was interred in the ground.

So why aren't most people sensitive to this phenomenon? One answer is that our social conditioning denies the existence of ghosts, so we don't see what we don't believe. To explore this further, here are two stories from *The Gentle Art of Blessing* by Pierre Pradervand.

Harvard University conducted an experiment in which two groups of kittens were raised from birth to near maturity in two rooms. The walls of one room were painted in black and white vertical stripes. The other room was painted with horizontal stripes. When set free, the cats brought up in the room with horizontal stripes knocked into everything vertical: chairs, table legs, trees. They were incapable of discerning anything upright.

Humans are similar to the cats in this regard. We have been conditioned to filter all reality through our senses. In 1520, Ferdinand Magellan arrived at the Tierra del Fuego at the tip of South America. The ship's company was surprised that the Del Fuego Indians did not see the boat entering the bay. Nothing in the natives' experience had prepared them for the idea of vessels that were like huge floating houses. Canoes represented their seaborne reality. They were liberated from this blinkered view when taken onto the ships.

And now Birch and Haines found themselves in disagreement.

'No, Clive, I don't want to include my stories. This book is about you,' said Haines.

'I disagree. Yours will help to broaden the debate,' replied Birch, gently.

Haines gave in, so here are just two of his experiences. Let's hope Birch was right and they do broaden the debate.

Not so long ago, Haines and his business partner were overseas. With a couple of hours to spare between meetings, they visited the museum. They walked from gallery to gallery, enjoying every moment. As they wandered in their unstructured manner, they became separated. Totally unexpectedly, and without warning, Haines stopped. He felt an odd sensation, slight disorientation, slightly off-balance. Step one pace in any direction and the sensation disappeared. On stepping back to the spot, the sense returned. *Odd.* There was an overwhelming aroma of herbs.

Haines decided to experiment in a way he never had before. He called for his friend, who was not sensitive to spirits. Haines guided him to the spot of disorientation.

'I'm rocking. What's this all about?' said the partner.

'Not sure. Can you smell anything?'

The partner sniffed the air. His blank expression turned to mild excitement. 'Yeah, I can smell herbs.'

'Me, too.'

'What's going on?' The partner seemed excited.

Should I, or should I not? 'Well, mate, I think we're in the presence of a ghost.'

'No!' He was incredulous.

'Well, yes, uh… take a look over there.' Haines pointed to the corner of the gallery.

'Nope. Can't see a thing.'

Haines could see a woman very clearly defined. Although she appeared slightly transparent, he could see her features and clothing. Her hair, features and eyes were dark. Her dress was long, reaching to the floor of the gallery, and green. But, for Haines, what struck him most was her smile. She was looking straight at Haines and smiling warmly. He felt drawn to take a chance. He walked across the gallery and put his arms around the ghost's waist. This was a first. The ghost didn't seem to mind one little bit.

'Come over here,' said Haines. The partner didn't need to be asked a second time. 'Put your hand in there.' Haines nodded to a point inside the circle he'd made with his arms.

'Bugger me!' The partner was wide-eyed. 'It's freezing. I can see my breath.'

The ghost didn't seem to mind this intrusion. She continued to smile. Interestingly, and maybe even significantly, she didn't look at the partner throughout this event. She kept her eyes on Haines. Also strangely, even as they left the gallery, he could still see her standing in the same spot, still smiling. She seemed to be in no hurry to leave.

As they discussed the encounter over lunch, both men felt they had been fortunate enough to enjoy a very positive experience. Maybe the risk Haines had taken had been worth it?

The next story seemed insignificant to Haines at the time. Birch had a different view. Late on a summer's afternoon, Haines was walking around his garden enjoying the heat of the sun. He was thinking about his business; in fact, he was miles away. Haines was happy and relaxed; the last thing on his mind was a ghost.

In the garden there is a large terracotta Vietnamese pot-bellied pig. Those with a need for detail will want to know that it is called Ho Chi Minh. Ho sits a foot away from the conservatory wall. As Haines passed by, he caught a glimpse of a spectral hedgehog between the pig and wall. He did a classic double-take. Still he saw the hedgehog, but not clearly. The creature was transparent and white-grey in colour. Haines was just four or five feet away. Haines attached little significance to the experience until he told Birch.

Birch was fascinated. *But why?* Haines couldn't see any reason for this being anything out of the ordinary. What so interested Birch was that the ghost had been a wild animal rather than a domestic creature. It seems that this is significant to Birch. He had never heard reports of a ghost of a wild animal before.

One final comment on the subject of ghosts from an eminent academic. Archie Roy is Emeritus Professor of Astronomy and Honorary Senior Research Fellow in the Department of Physics and Astronomy at Glasgow University. On a British television programme, some years ago, he made an interesting observation. He suggested that, sooner or later, the scientific community would have to at least acknowledge the possibility that the mind can exist independently of the body.

This is from *The Coincidence File* by Ken Anderson.

> In *Coincidences, chance or fate?* I told strange tales of ghostly presences that appeared to bring comfort and hope to men whose lives were in peril. The first concerned three British officers trekking across Turkey after escaping from a prisoner-of-war camp in World War 1. All swore they were joined by a mysterious stranger whose very presence encouraged them to push on against the odds. In the second incident Antarctic explorer Sir Ernest Shackleton and two companions crossed South Georgia Island in a desperate attempt to find help for their marooned party. All felt they had been joined by a fourth person whose presence was reassuring.

Birch asked the question: could these figures have been projections of their own desires or were they genuinely joined by a discarnate being guiding and comforting them?

Paula's Adventure

Fascinating story from close to home

The town of Tewkesbury looks, from the outside, a pleasant but unremarkable English market town. However, it served as a backdrop to one of the most puzzling and challenging of Birch's experiences. The central figure in the story, Paula, is a busy mother of two. She has a healing practice in the town. She is also a woman of remarkable resource, as we shall see. Some years ago, the Inland Revenue (now HM Revenue & Customs) attempted to bully and threaten her over the payment of taxes that they demanded from her. She replied that she would take the might of the Inland Revenue to court over the dispute.

'No solicitor will take your case,' they jeered at her.

'I will represent myself,' she replied, undeterred.

After three years of dispute, Paula won her case against the tax authorities and was awarded £8,000. She calls herself stubborn and sees it as a somewhat negative trait. Birch has sought to reassure her. Without that quality, she would not have received justice from the over-mighty bureaucracy. So, this is the quality of the person at the heart of this story.

Paula works hard as a holistic therapist. Her speciality is healing people who have bad backs. She has a natural affinity to healing this element of the physical, and is well known in the town for her skills.

The series of events began to unfold on a bank holiday Monday. Paula had a full day of clients. There was nothing unusual in that, except close to the end of the day she felt exceptionally tired, had a headache and felt 'off-balance'. She put it down to work pressure.

On Tuesday, when she got out of bed, she felt as though she had been run over by a bus. She struggled through the day. During the course of the evening, a friend said to her, 'You don't look good.'

Paula replied, 'No, I don't feel right.'

Given the character she is, Paula brushed it off and returned to the treatment room to finish her shift. When it came to complete her last massage of the evening, she could hardly lift her head and hands. Somehow, through sheer determination, she finished the task.

Upon rising on Wednesday morning, Paula stumbled out of bed in a foul mood and burst into tears: most un-Paula-like. *I don't want to help people any more. I am 'up to here' with it all.* Paula describes the feeling as being very intense. That day, when she was giving a healing to the friend mentioned above, the friend suddenly said, 'Paula, your face changed as though you were another person.' The friend, who was herself a healer, offered to send Paula some distance healing when she reached home. Paula readily agreed. She was heartily fed up of feeling so poorly, although she doubted whether any good would arise from this distance healing.

By this time, Paula was beginning to feel that there was some energy, a strong force, within her being. But she had no idea what it was. Later that same day, Paula received a text from the friend claiming that there were two energies attached to Paula's being and that Paula's energies were much reduced in strength. Paula, at this point, couldn't relax. She describes the feeling as akin to 'a cat on a hot tin roof'.

The friend rang Paula again the next day, telling her that she had sensed a negative thought form which had been removed and a stronger negative entity that was more difficult to clear. This entity had mocked the friend by telling her consciousness, *You aren't strong enough.* Amazingly, Paula had received the same mocking message in her consciousness. Later that day, the friend claimed to have removed this entity. However, on the next morning when Paula woke, she had what appeared to be two sucker marks on her neck.

After the claim that the entity had been cleared, Paula turned to domestic matters. She switched on the vacuum cleaner, which refused to start, as did the microwave. The latter blew when not in use. Paula's dad, an electrician, claimed that there must have been a power surge.

Paula went to visit a good friend, let's call her Friend 2, in a nearby town. Without knowing why, Paula spoke to her more roughly and nastily than she had done in the past. This behaviour was totally baffling to Paula. After picking up Friend 2 in her car, Paula practically threw her out on the flimsiest of excuses.

'Oh my God, Paula, what is wrong with you?' wailed Friend 2.

On the way home, the car broke down. She got out and spoke to it. *Please get me home.* With that, the car promptly started. Later, Paula took the car to a garage, which could find nothing wrong. Paula felt that whatever was happening to her was increasing her energy at this stage. She rationalised the electrical breakdowns by saying to herself, *accidents do happen.*

The next Friday arrived and Paula was in the shower. She was jolted by an almighty bang. Rushing from the shower, she could find nothing amiss in her domestic surroundings. Later, her father arrived to work in the house.

'Paula, you had better come here,' Father shouted to her from the treatment room.

When she entered, her jaw dropped with amazement. The room had been trashed. Certificates in their frames had been thrown on the floor and smashed. Her reiki certificate, particularly prized, was ripped beyond repair and the frame broken. She was upset by this particular destruction as she had put much effort into gaining this certificate. Glass was strewn across the floor. A glass bowl was snapped in two. There was no other person in the house.

Paula recounted this violent, indeed frightening, occurrence to a friend, who advised Paula to protect herself. Paula looked up the subject of possession on the Internet and downloaded a prayer of protection which she immediately began to use. She could identify with many symptoms of possession that were mentioned on the Internet. This included blockages on one side of the body including nose, ears and eyes as well as pain in the shoulder. She played Tibetan bowl music on a CD to lighten the atmosphere. She didn't feel threatened in any way and got on with clearing up the room.

Paula, being the character she is, challenged the entity to do its worst. 'Come on, bring it on,' she shouted. There was no response.

The situation quietened down for a couple of days, although she still felt out of sorts and angry. The next day arrived and Paula went to a prearranged healing session. During the session, the healer said that Paula's energy levels were low, but didn't mention that he sensed any negative energy.

'I pick up that your strength is phenomenal,' the healer said. 'It takes a lot to stop you.'

The healer began the session and asked Paula what she sensed, what she felt and which colour was prominent in her consciousness.

'Black,' she replied.

The healer continued with the session. As he did so, Paula felt the dark energy becoming more prominent. She couldn't see it, but she felt it. She became aware that the dark energy wished to communicate with the healer. Through Paula's mouth came the deep tones of a masculine voice.

'Do you know who I am?' It seemed to be mocking the healer. 'You are not strong enough to get rid of me.'

Paula then spoke to the dark energy. 'If you have something to say then say it yourself.' Paula refused to be a messenger for this darkness. She sensed that if she had acquiesced, then it would have an even stronger hold on her. She could feel its energy in her voice and throat, but she didn't know why this was so.

Paula looked at the healer, who was by this time as white as a sheet. The frightened healer asked Paula to help. 'The two of us are strong enough,' he said.

The healer attempted to send the unwelcome energy to the light. The entity laughed. Paula realised it wasn't going to go. The healer called on Archangel Michael and his sword. The healer said that he would trap the entity in a box, after which he would pierce the box with Michael's spiritual sword to destroy the unwelcome one. Both humans, by this time, were mightily shaken. Paula told the healer that the energy wanted to speak to the healer in its own language. The healer replied that, on a scale of one to ten, the power of the entity was eight. Both recognised that it was extremely unpleasant. The healer then asked Paula to hold a book, which she did without flinching. The healer looked relieved. The book was the Holy Bible.

But how did all this come to Birch's attention? Jacqui, Haines's wife, had a pre-booked reiki session with Paula. It was then that Paula confided in Jacqui. That evening, Jacqui told Haines, who didn't like the sound of the story one little bit. Haines had never met Paula but sent her a text anyway. He asked if he might be able to help. Paula replied to the text. As Haines was reading the reply, he heard a voice.

'It's me. Tell her it's me.'

'Who are you?' he asked, slightly taken aback.

'Sarah. Tell her it's Sarah.'

Haines was confused. *What to do?* He resorted to his mobile phone and sent Paula another text. *Does the name Sarah mean anything to you?*

In a very short time, the mobile rang. It was Paula.

'How did you know that?' she asked.

'Know what?'

'Sarah. How did you know about Sarah?'

'Well, actually I don't know anything about Sarah.'

'I've been writing the name Sarah on my pad all day. Doodling, really. For some reason I've been trying to write the name without the pen leaving the paper.'

Haines explained the reason for his question.

'But I don't know any Sarah,' said Paula.

Wow. Haines had been outside during this exchange. He now saw a young woman leaning against the heavy wooden garden table. She was in her early twenties, contemporarily dressed, jeans, shoulder-length hair, around five foot four and attractive, pretty. By and large there was little to indicate that Sarah wasn't really there at all. The only visible clue was that Haines could see right through her. She raised her right hand and pointed to the east.

'Paula, do you live between the town centre and the motorway junction?' asked Haines.

'Yes. Why?'

He explained what he was seeing. It seemed possible that the spectre was pointing towards Paula's house. The vision said nothing. Haines assumed that this was Sarah and she had contacted Haines so he could tell Paula. Birch agreed with this interpretation.

From that day to this, Haines has had no further contact with Sarah.

A couple of days later, Haines, Jacqui and their son, Harry, arrived at Paula's house with Birch. Jacqui was there for a healing, the others to sense the energy. Birch had had the intuition that he should take his Tibetan bowl.

All five stood in the healing room as Paula briefly outlined the story. Haines and Harry, both sensitive beings, felt very uncomfortable in the room, but nothing more. Haines was certain he could not sense a ghost. But all was not well. Both Haines and Harry began to feel nauseous, then very sick indeed. Harry went white.

Birch listened to Paula's story, first-hand and in full. Eventually, Birch picked up the Tibetan bowl and began to play it. As the sounds died away, Paula said that she felt better, as did Haines. Harry still sensed negative energies in the room, and he looked distinctly unwell.

Before they left, Paula was able to add a postscript to the Sarah story. She explained what had happened the previous evening. She had met her friend, Lesley, to share a glass of wine and a natter. During the evening,

Lesley had interrupted the flow of their conversation. It seems the interruption went like this:

'Paula! Your face is changing shape. You're different. What's happening? You aren't Paula, you're Sarah.'

It would be easy to say that Lesley had reacted to hearing about the Sarah event. However, Paula had kept it to herself, not mentioning it to Lesley, or anyone else for that matter.

Birch arranged to return the next week and work in Paula's house. This he did, working in the treatment room, the sitting room and Paula's bedroom. She felt better immediately afterwards, but nausea returned on the following two days. During Birch's work on the second occasion, another electrical problem presented itself. The electric kettle refused to work. Other electrical appliances were also dead. None of the switches in the fuse box had been tripped. Paula manually tripped a switch off and then back on. All the electrical appliances resumed normal working, except for the kettle. On a later occasion, Paula said that as she entered the treatment room, it was as though she were being physically choked.

This is from *No More Secrets, No More Lies* by Patricia Cori:

> Imagine, too, that if another soul essence decides it wishes to journey through the cosmos by 'attachment' to you – then you can become a host for a soul-merging with another human being, extraterrestrial, or entity travelling upon the ethers.

Greatly puzzled by the apparent failure of different healers, including himself, to eradicate this mystery energy, Birch went into meditation in order to seek further help from his guidance. What he was told was so different from the assumptions previously made that he sought advice from another experienced mystic. Birch had worked with him previously and had great confidence in him. Without having had anything given away to him, this mystic confirmed the guidance that Birch had received. For the moment, Birch decided to keep his counsel until after his next healing session with Paula. This was scheduled for the following Wednesday.

At their next session together, Paula started by telling Birch about her contacts with two psychics. The conversation began with Paula saying to Birch, 'At least you are sane.'

Birch replied, 'Thank you. Many people say I am crazy.'

Paula recounted her odd adventures with the two psychics. The first one had been in a classroom environment with a man who claimed to be a crystal healer.

'I can clear millions of souls of their traumas on this planet and others,' the healer proclaimed in the session.

Oh, yeah? said Paula to herself.

The extravagant claims continued after the session. Interestingly, Paula noticed that this man did not look her in the eye. He would make eye contact with others in the group, but not Paula. Now, we are starting to become aware that Paula is coming into her power, but it appeared that the ego of the man could not deal with this energetically powerful lady. She also noted that the man's leg started to tremble in her presence.

Subsequent to this session, the crystal healer telephoned Paula, making extravagant claims concerning her energy levels. He also claimed to have cleared eighteen entities from her being. By this time, Paula was aware that this man was not necessarily the healer he claimed to be, and realised that the biggest thing about him was his ego.

'I have attached a healing photon' (whatever that is) 'to your solar plexus,' he said.

'If you conduct any healing you should ask the intended recipient's permission,' Paula countered. It was time for Paula to distance herself from the alleged healer's advice.

On a whim, Paula picked up the Yellow Pages telephone directory, found a tarot card reader's telephone number and called for an appointment. When Paula arrived at the tarot reader's house, she was a little alarmed that the session was to be held in his garage. She was also faintly uncomfortable in the man's presence.

'OK,' he said, 'I will give you a reiki healing, but first of all you must take off all your clothes.'

Paula, being the sensible person she is, refused and started to look round for an escape route. He then tried to hypnotise her, saying, 'Look into my eyes.' The freaky thing that Paula saw as she stared at the man was the appearance of his face as it changed into something different and more sinister, as though he were being taken over or changing into another being.

Paula successfully made her escape. A friend later told Paula of other woman who had been to sessions with this man and had been persuaded to take their clothes off. Paula went to the police to make a complaint. The conversation in the police station went something like this.

'I wish to make a complaint against a man.'

'Did he touch you?' asked the policeman.

'No,' replied Paula.

'Did he prevent you from leaving?'

'No.'

'Did he lock the door when you were inside his house?'

'No.'

'Then there is nothing that we can do.'

The policeman didn't even make a note.

'So,' said Paula to Birch. 'Those were my two experiences. As I said earlier, I am pleased to see a sane person.'

After she had recounted this, Birch asked Paula to sit while he told her of his guidance concerning the psychic attack on her person.

'Have you heard of an entity called the shadow?' he began.

'Not at all,' was the reply.

Birch continued. 'Everyone on the planet has one. It is the sum total of all the elements of character that we don't like about ourselves. The shadow grows from our self-denial, from bewilderment, from past shames and perceived weaknesses. It becomes an entity within its own right, buried within us and unexplored. At some point all those on a spiritual development path will encounter their shadow. The shadow must be dealt with through love rather than fear.'

Paula listened intently. 'That would explain why the entity knew what I was thinking as soon as the thought popped into my head.'

'You can work with integrating your shadow into your normal consciousness, or go to counselling. Emotional therapy worked for me.' Birch concluded by explaining an experience he had had with his own shadow and how he had worked at dealing with it. 'If you need any more help, call me.'

The last part of the session consisted of Birch playing his Tibetan bowl in Paula's healing room and then giving Paula reiki healing. One remarkable event during the healing occurred when the double doors at the end of the healing room burst open with no human intervention. Paula's jaw dropped open. Birch gave himself a wry smile and remembered a similar event that had occurred as he had ridden his bicycle. The story of that event is told in *So You Think We're Alone?*

Birch left Paula's house, perhaps for the last time, bearing a present of a beautiful crystal pyramid.

Birch assumed wrongly that he had finished with working with Paula. He pushed the work that he had done with her to the back of his mind and got on with other projects. One day he received a call from Haines. The conversation went something like this.

'Have you seen the *Echo*?' asked Haines, referring to the local newspaper.

'No.'

Haines emailed a copy of the front page of the previous day's *Echo* to Birch. Its jaw-dropping headline featured a spat that Paula was having with a local vicar. The latter had arranged for a beauty session to be conducted in the local church hall. The session was open to those who wished to experience a number of techniques. Various beauty therapists had been invited. The invitation was not open to all, however. Paula had offered to give reiki healing as part of this healing day. The offer had been rejected by the vicar on the grounds that he did not know where the energies with which Paula was working had come from. Not much investigation there, then. Paula was incensed that she had been excluded on zero evidence. It seemed that the priest was frightened of even making the most preliminary study of Paula's skills. The result of this rejection found its way into the aforesaid *Echo*, which responded with a blazing front page headline. **Local Therapist Accused of Witchcraft,** it trumpeted.

There the whole thing came to a halt. Paula had the opportunity of continuing the campaign with an interview on regional TV. She declined the offer. The story, however, energised Birch to give a critique of the religion which so rejected Paula's skills. Here it is.

Haines says that there is much that is good about the Christian Church. Birch knows that he is correct. There are some things that Birch feels need to be said by an outsider who has an alternative perspective of spirituality. The sect of the Christian Church that found itself at odds with Paula has a number of challenges that contributed to the confrontation, Birch believes.

A number of the issues have historical roots. When the Eastern Roman Emperor Constantine embraced Christianity, it was for political rather than spiritual reasons. This was in order to develop and retain unity within the empire. From a mystical point of view, intention is a vital component of any work, whether mundane or spiritual. The mundane original purpose of politics would create an energy that would be embedded in the newly adopted religion. This is a subtle point.

The New Testament of the Holy Bible was created from religious tracts of the time. Some were included. Others that did not fit the then-current political paradigm were excluded. Still others were mistranslated as the various books were translated over the centuries, from ancient Greek to Latin to English. The depth of the spiritual insights and understanding was not the most important reason for inclusion.

The original intention of this religion would follow it throughout the two millennia of its existence to date. Throughout history, the Christian religion has immersed itself in the political life of the day. It is almost as though it cannot help itself. The hierarchy of the faith, it seems to Birch, is pulled into working with political life as a fatal attraction. Birch uses the term 'fatal attraction' because he sees it almost as a knee-jerk reaction from the original intention and it detracts from the spirituality of this faith. Many people are aware of the abuses of the Inquisition. This blood-soaked Inquisition is still in existence today and thus still carries the energy of its abusive past, polluting the whole of the religion. It is significant that the present and previous popes have apologised for abuses of the past. Are they aware that the faith is still carrying the dark energies of its history? We may never know. There is much more that could be said here, but let us leave it there in order to explore other issues.

The above paragraph refers to elements of this faith before the emergence of the Anglican sect. This branch of Christianity developed and emerged as a result of the activities of King Henry VIII in England. Again it was a response to a political situation, this one arising from Henry's quarrel with the Catholic Church based in Rome. Henry was adept at marrying and divorcing at regular intervals, a tendency that the Catholicism of the sixteenth century baulked at. So Henry devised his own offshoot of Christianity in order to create a religion that would justify his mundane actions. Ironically, although some claim Henry became a Protestant on his death-bed, he advocated Catholic ceremony and doctrine throughout his life. Royal backing of the English Reformation was left to his heirs. The Anglican sect was also a partial product of the Reformation, during which a number of Protestant sects in Europe broke away from Catholicism. So politics continued to greatly influence the formation of this religion.

We will now move forward to the First World War. Up until this point, the Anglican sect was the predominant religious movement of Great Britain. At the end of that conflict, ordinary people were searching for answers and reasons for the most appalling slaughter conducted on an industrial scale. The Church manifestly failed to provide a lead or supply comfort to those who were crying out for answers to the enormous pain. That failure began the Church's slow decline in membership and the deterioration of its authority. It is now facing extinction. This extinction will be as a result of its inadequacy, of the unbalanced energetic roots of its formation and of its failure to redress its energetic imbalances. This is an energetic and mystical perspective.

In recent times, the Anglican faith has been called 'the middle class at prayer'. Sadly, this church allowed itself to become embedded in the class structure, much to its detriment morally and for spiritual energy consequences. Birch's grandfather, Charlie Ruck, suffered grievously in the 1930s from the impact of unemployment. He was a fine man. He would have described himself as a member of the working class. Charlie was totally turned away from religion when the then Bishop of Gloucester uttered insensitive comments concerning the working class. These statements included the point that the unemployed should be confined to the workhouse, a demeaning and much hated place of incarceration.

So where are we today with this debate? By its own admission this church is in crisis. Church attendances are falling (what mere attendance has got to do with genuine spiritual work, however, escapes Birch). The church has lost most of its moral authority. It has attempted to turn its back on its theological confusions. Very few people listen with attention to its pronouncements. Archbishop Desmond Tutu, one of the heroes of the fight against apartheid, a senior and respected member of this church (Anglican Church of South Africa) has said, 'The church is obsessed with sex.' By that he means there appears to be a never-ending internal debate agonising over the moral probity or otherwise of homosexuality, whether practising homosexuals should be allowed to be members or priests, and whether women should be allowed to be bishops. This internal navel-gazing is conducted against a backdrop of spiritual hunger and searching among the population at large, social disharmony and rapid change. Madness, madness!

So what is the perspective for the future of the Church? At a mundane level, the Church demonstrates the signs of one that is past its sell-by-date. It doesn't appear, from an outsider's perspective, to possess a clear message that has relevance to the people in this society. It demonstrates little leadership. Its hierarchy is at odds with itself. It is unable to distance itself from a material establishment. All in all, it is a physical disaster. So why does it continue to survive? From Birch's view, the genuine and deep spiritual perspectives of thousands of adherents keep it grounded in a genuine and pure reality. This is the true essence of this faith as Birch sees it. The rest of it is bunkum, grounded in a dogma and theology that makes no sense to ordinary people and has zero spiritual value to them.

Two quotations which may be used to further the arguments of the church follow.

> Love never fails, but whether there are prophecies they will fail. Whether there are speaking in tongues they shall cease. Whether there is knowledge it shall vanish away.
>
> Corinthians 1:13

> Many will say to me in these days lord, lord, have we not prophesied in thy name and in thy name cast out devils and in thy name done many wonderful works and then I will profess unto them, I knew you, you that work iniquity.
>
> Matthew 7:22-23

Birch's friend Doug, a Biblical and ancient Greek scholar, comments on mistranslation from the early versions of the Bible. This is from the ancient Greek version of Matthew verses 16-18: *You are Peter. On this rock I will build my congregation.* This early work does not say *I will build my church*, as appears in the King James Version of the Bible. Nowhere in early works does Jesus instruct that churches should be built, or priests and hierarchies created. This is clearly a subsequent development created in the consciousness of men.

The priest excluded Paula from his church on the grounds of her being a 'witch' without exploring her healing skill and personal spiritual value. He is required to carry all the above perspectives, whether he is consciously or unconsciously aware of them. Perhaps, in that case, his attitude and approach are not surprising.

Of course, Christianity is not the only religion that immures itself in past warped perspectives. Birch watched a TV programme which demonstrated the sad plight of a baby, born in India, with two faces. The family of the child struggled desperately to cope with the traumatic existence of this little soul. Sadly, the child succumbed and died after a few weeks. The local Hindu priest refused to officiate at the funeral because the family of the dead child were of a low caste. What a way of adding insult to injury. Eventually, a priest from an adjacent community was persuaded to officiate.

Everyone is doing their best, whether they be priest, guru, pope or mystic. After we have had our say, it is important to have compassion for others and ourselves.

Let's finish Birch's part of this debate with three quotes. The first is from *Anna, Grandmother of Jesus* by Claire Heartsong.

> Organised religion furnishes only one context through which eternal truths can be expressed. It resembles crutches: often necessary, but temporary at best. At the present stage of human history and collective level of consciousness certain forms of organised religion are certainly useful and necessary. The great religions of the world have furnished societies with an ethical dimension indispensable to human progress. But who, if he or she has the choice, would not prefer to walk without crutches, or to spring from the diving board and swim? This is the reason that for many great spiritual teachings of humanity, truth resides first and foremost in demonstration. In the truth lives a state of consciousness and not in dogmas, rituals, or sacred books.

The next two are from *The Disappearance of the Universe* by Gary R Renard.

> Jesus was repeatedly accused of blasphemy. It's even in the Bible. I guarantee you that if he were here he'd be accused of exactly the same thing today – and by Christians. Don't expect us to shy away from heresy or blasphemy any more than he would – we don't have any problem rattling people's cages. We have no investment in what you think about us. We are free to be teachers and not politicians. We don't have to suck up to you so you can feel all warm and fuzzy about us instead of learning something. Your approval of what we say is not required. We have no need to be popular. We have no stake in manipulating the level of form so we can make a tale told by an idiot appear to be going our way.

> For god to create the imperfect must either mean that he was imperfect or that he deliberately made those who were so they could screw up, be punished by him, and suffer here on psycho planet.

Runes and Mantras, Words of Power

Protection and more from the spoken word

Birch clutched the steering wheel and blinked in an effort to stay awake. The drone of the engine seemed to be mocking his battle with sleepiness. He breathed deeply and made noises in his throat to try to keep himself alert. It was 3.30 am and he was driving along a virtually empty motorway. He even wished for a few oncoming headlights, which would have been a welcome stimulation of his senses.

As a gesture of friendship, he had offered to drive two friends to Gatwick Airport (re-christened Airwick Gatport by some wags, until the constant repetition of the joke had become boring, as repetitions do). It had been later when second thoughts had entered his mind. The passengers were to catch the very early morning flight.

Ah, it's time to change motorways, he realised with a start, jolting him out of his near-reverie.

He accessed the slip road which climbed upward and circled to the right in a tight curve. Suddenly he was confronted by an enormous truck on his left, labouring up the tight curve. With a supreme effort, he concentrated on the task in hand, to keep himself, the car and the sleeping friends in the back of the car in one piece. As he negotiated the tight bend, into his mind flashed a word that was strangely familiar, yet had no meaning in the English language. He successfully negotiated imminent danger, eventually arriving at Gatwick. All the while the word flashed across his consciousness.

Birch dropped his sleepy friends off at the airport and returned home. On his return, he called a friend: an expert in the use of runes, an ancient symbolic practice. Birch sensed that this friend had spoken of this rune some time before, perhaps years before.

The conversation went something like this.

'Hello, mate,' said Birch. 'This word came into my consciousness while I was driving early on today. I think that it is a rune. If so, could you tell me what it means?' Birch then told his rune friend the word.

'That word is the most powerful rune of protection there is. How did you know when and where to use it?' his friend replied.

'I didn't,' said Birch. 'It presented itself to me. I didn't call on it.'

After Birch put the phone down, he thought hard about the lesson to be learned from this experience. It came to him that, after this powerful experience, it was time to work with this rune, to use its energy when appropriate and in a positive way. This could be another tool in his mystical toolbox.

And so it proved. This particular rune, used as a mantra and in another way, became one of the powerful and useful elements of Birch's healing and psychic protection work. One of his experiences of using the power of sound through this mantra occurred when he visited an elderly lady of similar mystical beliefs to himself. She was living in sheltered accommodation. She recounted that she was being troubled by someone entering her flat when she was not there and stealing her books. She suspected someone who had access to her apartment and was theoretically honest to all in the outside world. Nothing could be proved.

Birch had worked with a rune on a number of previous occasions as a protective instrument, drawing its shape in the air and chanting its name. He did this for the elderly lady around her flat, building the vibration of protection. She later reported to Birch that the thefts, and probably the unwelcome entry to her flat, had ceased immediately.

From the *Futhark* by Edred Thorsson:

> According to most scholars, the runes were ancient symbols used in writing, mainly on stone and metal. These symbols bore religious or magical significance for the people who inscribed them.
>
> Each rune has a threefold nature, which is also the threefold essence of the secret slumbering within it. The points are:
>
> Form (ideograph and phonetic value)
>
> Idea (symbolic content)
>
> Number (its dynamic nature)
>
> They describe energy flows and states as related to the self, to the planet, and ultimately to the multiverse.
>
> The runic system may well have been fully developed by as early as 200 BCE.

Everything in the universe has its own vibration. These vibrations can be influenced by powerful magical words or mantras. Mantras, quite often syllables from the classical Indian language Sanskrit, are thought forms representing divinities of cosmic powers which exert their influence through sound vibration.

Scholars tell us that mantras originated in the Vedic religion of India. They later became an essential part of the Hindu tradition, also considerably used in Buddhism, Sikhism and Jainism. Mantras are commonly used in various spiritual movements today. They are intended to deflect the mind from illusion and material inclination and are usually externalised by chanting. Birch is of the view that the use of sound and mantra far precede the religions above. Humanity has been using all types of magical processes for as long as its awareness has been tuned to manipulating the environment.

The New Testament Gospel According to St John starts, 'In the beginning was the Word, and the Word was with God, and the Word *was* God.' (Birch's italics.) If the mantra is coupled with intention, then the vibration of the sounds contains that intent: that thought form, which has an influence on the result. The sound is the carrier and the intent is embedded in the sound. Mantra is a truly magical process that can work wonders.

Jacques Rangasamy confirmed an insight Faye had into the power of the mantra ROM. Faye had a dream in which she was looking across a ravaged landscape at an approaching horde of enemies. She was constantly keeping them at bay by repeating ROM. In contrast, Audrey received the strongest vibratory response by intoning the word SOL. She realised that this mantra was the old word for the sun and that, in our consciousness, this consists of entwined suns: as always the duality of creation to complete the whole. Audrey also found great power when intoning SOL whilst at the same time concentrating on the bone marrow.

Audrey reminds us of the link with myth, which teaches us esoteric truths in a way that is acceptable to our objective consciousness. She talks of the myth of Orpheus, the legendary Greek master of music, poetry and art, who was beheaded. His head floated down the river, eventually arriving at the island of Lesbos. As the head floated, it sang, and all that heard the song were enthralled and reached attunement with the gods. Audrey also works with the words THEO and ADONI, which mean 'lord'. In a book by Eduard Sure, the mantra TAO was quoted as the first sound uttered by evolving mankind. It was a prayer, to the higher faculties and dimensions, in gratitude and unity.

Margaret White tells a story of the power of mantra. She was leaving a spiritually based weekend course to drive home. The weather was appalling, wet and windy. The motorway was unpleasant, full of spray with reduced visibility. As she drove, her eye caught sight of a car apparently stranded on the side of the road. For some unknown reason, she slowed her car as she approached. To her great surprise, she recognised one of her fellow course attendees standing next to the car. She pulled over and stopped.

The fellow ran over and gratefully jumped into the passenger seat of Margaret's car, on her invitation. He was soaked through. He was profuse in his thanks. 'My car has broken down. The idea came into my mind to chant the word of power we both know, and then you turn up.' Margaret was able to drive the fellow home, with both being tickled pink by the unusual communication.

Mysterious Facts and Fictions

Unexplained and strange energies

Tracy sat bolt upright in bed. It took seconds for her to unscramble her thoughts and organise her mind. Out of a deep sleep, she had been suddenly brought back to everyday consciousness. What was going on? Wayne, her partner, continued to sleep soundly, snoring gently next to her. As she became aware of herself and her surroundings she realised that she was feeling distinctly uncomfortable. Her skin and the air around her felt cool but her body was aflame with heat. It was as though her whole body were being microwaved. This was the only way that she could describe the sensation. She sensed that all the liquids in her body were being dried out. This drying out and physical discomfort were caused by a source that she couldn't identify. She felt that all her cells were vibrating, but in disharmony with each other. Her body was in destructive mode. Sleep was elusive and when it came it was fitful. Once wakefulness was achieved at the end of a troubled night, it was a fight to regain full consciousness. The final unpleasant experience was related to her mind, which felt as though there were a disassociation between it and the remainder of her being. 'Spaced out' would be a simple way of describing it. It was as though she were floating above the bed.

Across the city in the heart of England, hundreds if not thousands of people were experiencing the same phenomenon. Night after night the same thing occurred and re-occurred. There would be a break of some days, and then the same middle-of-the-night discomfort would return. Inhabitants of a nearby town started to experience the same. What was the source of this mystery internal heat? No one could explain. To this day, the unpleasant, apparently unhealthy and slightly frightening phenomenon continues.

There were only two outside circumstances that seemed to link with the strange heating. It seemed that certain cosmic cycles linked to the switching on of the heat. These cycles included the new moon, full moon and quarter days (equinoxes and solstices). For some unexplained reason, the cycles of the moon and the sun ran concurrently with the start and finish of the strange discomfort. But there seemed to be other occasions when people were subjected to these phenomena: when important and significant political events occurred and announcements were made by the government. What was the cause and why did these anomalous phenomena happen at all? Because of their strange, inexplicable and widespread occurrence, many people started to question the events, and some made the connection to the outside circumstances. The mystery remains unsolved.

Overnight and without warning, large poles appeared. Atop each was a bulbous protuberance. The metal structures were forty to fifty feet high and were not conventional light or camera poles. They appeared to be some sort of transmitting or receiving aerial of a type that is uncommon. Their true purpose is unknown. Each pole was accompanied by two large metal cupboards, one on each side. A resident of the town asked the chief constable what they were. The chief constable said he didn't know. Another resident sought enlightenment from the town's Member of Parliament. He didn't know, either. So if these supposedly well-informed public figures had no idea what they were or who put them there, who did know? They were not amateur structures. This mystery is also waiting to be solved.

One 5th November, Bonfire Night, the crashes and bangs of fireworks, the happy cries of children around bonfires, the sizzling of meats on barbecues proceeded as they do every year on this day. The only difference on this occasion was that a sinister event was about to unfold. Suddenly, in the same town, a riot erupted. Many youths started to rampage, throwing fireworks. Innocent people going about their business were abused by the out-of-control youths. The situation became so serious that the police closed off both ends of the road where the riot was taking place. It became necessary to send in many police officers to re-establish control. Never before had there been such an apparently co-ordinated riot. The story became stranger and stranger. It became clear that the riot had occurred in a road where one of the mystery poles was situated. Was there a connection between the strange pole and the riot? Was there a more simple explanation for the riot? Perhaps local people connected with the frightening event can throw more light on the story.

Our story now moves to the troubled land of Iraq. Demonstrators were approached by a US army tank. This tank, however, was different from those that one sees regularly on television. This was no M1A2 Abrams or Challenger 2. The top part of the vehicle had no turret or gun. What it did have was a strange, shield-shaped structure. As the vehicle rumbled towards the crowd, the demonstrators stopped in their tracks. This halting was not due to the approaching threat alone. They were experiencing strange, unfamiliar sensations. They realised that their bodies were heating up uncomfortably. This heating was not felt from outside, but it was as though it were being generated from inside the body. The crowd broke and fled. Where have we heard of this phenomenon before?

Are all these events connected? Is there a single cause?

This is a good place to include some other issues which interest Birch.

INVISIBILITY

Birch's experience of invisibility occurred some years ago. With a friend, he was practising an exercise to achieve this state. First he took a seat, while the friend watched him from a distance. The friend was able to see the pillows on the sofa behind Birch. Next it was Birch's turn to view. He went into the required concentrative meditation and the friend started to fade from view as he sat in the chair that Birch had recently vacated. Birch became so excited by what was happening that he shouted out. The shout immediately brought him back into normal awareness and the friend returned to his normal rotund bulk. Physically, this process bends light rays around a physical object such that the object becomes invisible when the enhanced meditative state has been achieved.

CYCLOPES

Years ago, Birch read a fascinating story concerning an ancient Cyclopean race which, allegedly, inhabited this planet hundreds of thousands of years ago. Their purpose for being was to develop a form of consciousness so that their whole race could be raised up to a higher dimension, above this material third dimension. This process was associated with the letter L. Using this process the race would go through a change, from this reality into the one that they wished to enter. Thus they would move from one energy vibrational level to another.

According to www.tpub.com, 'The phase of a wave is a specific point or benchmark along the wave. A phase shift is an observable repositioning of this benchmark between successive transmissions.' Further help is found at www.mind.net, which gives a moveable pictorial demonstration of how phase shift works in a wave pattern.

They were successful, according to the writer, and disappeared en masse from the Earth to their new destination. It has been said that their immense underground cities are still silently waiting to be discovered. From this story we have inherited the myth of the Cyclopes: the one-eyed monsters which, in reality, were advanced beings. Birch believes that individuals can attune to the consciousness of the Cyclopean race through racial memory and through the akashic record.

Audrey believes that the word 'Cyclops' refers to their spiritually opened third eye. There seems to be a persistent folk memory of a race of giants inhabiting this earth. Audrey believes that the L is another form of 'EL', another name for God. She also found that intoning the mantra 'EL' gave it great power.

Birch tuned in to the Cyclopes and perceived one of these beings looking back, through time and space, to the Earth. His third eye was very bright and focussed. Birch received the message that these beings lived underground in order to avoid harmful solar radiations that played upon the earth. Birch was also told that there were comparatively few of the Cyclopean race in relation to humanity's current population. Therefore it was easier for them to work co-operatively on this great adventure. In addition, they were of greater mental, psychic and spiritual development than most of current humanity.

Birch wonders if living a subterranean existence helped them live long lives.

There is a book by Sure which says that the original mankind was almost transparent and had an eye in the middle of the brow which allowed awareness of higher and lower vibrations. Whether the story is true or not, we may never know, but it can be used as an aspirational model for the future. This story can be looked upon as a metaphor for the aspiring mystic, for our struggles for self-realisation, for service to higher spheres, other people and the planet.

Drunvalo Melchizedek in *The Ancient Secret of the Flower of Life* vol. 1 says…

> The Neters (Gods) are concentrated on the time when we go through a certain stage of resurrection, which is a rapid biological change into a different life form. They're holding an image of that transition as they're walking along the line, then suddenly the line comes to an end and there's

a 90 degree shift [L shape] upward, and they're walking perpendicular to their first direction.

This 90 degrees is a very important part of this work. The 90 degree turn is crucial to understanding how to make resurrection or ascension real. The dimensional levels are separated by 90 degrees; musical notes are separated by 90 degrees – 90 degrees keeps coming up over and over again. In fact, in order for us to enter into the fourth dimension (or any dimension, for that matter), we must make a 90-degree turn.

HIGHER-CONSCIOUSNESS

The higher-consciousness realm is the abode of vast psychological forces. When in this realm we are not consciously aware of our beings, for we are absorbed on a much larger scale. We have direct access to these vast forces and are not forced to see through a dark glass. Therefore, in this mode of consciousness, it is much easier to manipulate the physical environment and to do it from a set of higher laws with direct access to strong forces.

A friend told Birch of a cosmic consciousness experience where she saw her existing material existence as a tiny part of her total reality. Although she had relationships in this existence, they made up a very small part of the totality of her being in the cosmic consciousness state.

Miguel Ruiz says that, in his view, mankind will need the whole of the Aquarian age to raise its consciousness.

Birch's intuition said to him, *You will live for ever.* This took him aback, so much so that he felt the need to check that it wasn't his ego fooling him. It wasn't. Some days later the corollary of that insight came into consciousness. It said, *Who mentioned living in a body for ever? You, and every other person, lives in consciousness for ever. When you lay aside this body there is no change in consciousness. The body is not the primary consciousness. The spiritual element, the soul, the higher-self, God, whatever you want to call it, is the consciousness for which there is no end.*

According to Ross Heaven in *The Spiritual Practices of the Ninja*, Masaaki Hatsumi, the thirty-fourth Ninja Grand Master, wrote:

> In every encounter or experience, there is the potential for gaining our enlightenment, the possibility of finding that one missing piece of the puzzle that brings about illumination. It is our own mind that determines the experience.

THE CURRENT RELIGION

During one of his daily walks, Birch pondered on the question: what is the foremost religion in this country today? As quick as a flash his intuition said 'football'. (Soccer for our US friends.)

For the most part, the head of religions is God. The heads of football clubs, in the English Premiership at least, are the saviours. These are the elite band divorced from contact with the flock of ordinary believers, the fans.

The Premiership clubs used to be headed by boards of directors, but these are increasingly being replaced by the saviours. The saviours fly in and rescue football clubs from anonymity, financial meltdown and, worst of all, relegation to the lower leagues. These saviours are mostly from other realms, chiefly Russia and the USA. These saviours are the generators of emotional energy in this football religion. They are the popes and archbishops who function through lower order intermediaries. The managers and coaches of the various teams are the bishop and canon surrogates. This is the pecking order.

We now come to the players who are idolised by the faithful fans, the priests and gurus of this worldwide religion. As in any religion, at the bottom is the faithful flock. These are the fans, powerless, except for shouting in their religious excitement at the ceremonies and taking part in singing the anthems or cursing members of competing sects, otherwise known as other teams.

The football match is the ritual played out endlessly in the same way, week after week, month after month, year after year, even century after century. Everyone is committed to the cause: the haves, those in the power positions mentioned above; the have nots, relatively powerless fans. The latter are given to reliving the glory of their religious experience and passion, laid out for them by the haves. The haves clear up by taking the money from the have nots. This sounds cynical, maybe, but this view might just ring a bell.

The structure of the football religion is laid out and maintained by the founding fathers, the sport's governing bodies. The proselytising texts and bearers of the good news are the newspapers, particularly the red tops, constantly trumpeting the joys and sorrows and reinforcing the importance and continuity of the true faith. Through emotional involvement and the excitement of their team, individuals satisfy that big emotional need unaddressed for modern humanity by the major religions. This idea probably works for other sports and activities on twenty-first-century planet Earth.

MOVING HOUSE

A friend emailed Birch one day, puzzled and concerned that a proposed house move was apparently being blocked at every opportunity, despite the need of the friend's family to move to a new location. The friend was a deeply spiritual person and had exhausted every meditation and visualisation technique in order to facilitate the move.

Birch replied that he would help by performing his own meditation to try to locate the blockage. He did as promised, entered a meditation and was immediately presented with a vision of a very old deep sink for holding water. The sink was almost full of water being held there by a plug. Without thinking further, Birch reached in psychically and pulled out the plug. The water poured out. A little while later, the purchase was completed without further hitch. Whether his meditation helped or not, Birch will never know.

Jacques Rangasamy, the man at the centre of the Temple Study Group, says that those people who are of a mystical and spiritual persuasion create a temple in their home without realising it. They do this with their thoughts, meditations and vibrations from their beings. So it may be necessary to deconstruct this temple by ceremony and reconstruct it in the new home. All our thoughts and actions create a very powerful environment around us, whether we are aware of it or not, or whether we are spiritual in our thoughts or not.

This may be part of the reason for our feelings of comfort or discomfort when we enter a room or house for the first time. Birch felt very comfortable when he first entered the flat in which he currently lives. The previous occupant had been a musician and a teacher: a very pleasant person. His vibrations could be felt in every room.

For their part, Haines and his wife had to invent a coping strategy at their home in Tewkesbury. At one time they entertained regularly, with guests joining them for dinner. (They have desisted in this recently, since the floods of 20th July 2007 destroyed the ground floor of their home. The house doesn't feel the same any more.) However, after eating, the diners would retire to the sitting room for coffee and talk. Here was the problem. The Haineses found it very difficult to get rid of their guests. Some would actually say they didn't want to leave, they were so comfortable. There was a sense of peace, tranquillity and comfort, even a feeling of safety in that room. There were a few occasions when Haines actually had to ask guests to leave, since it was long past their bedtime.

Haines also agrees with Birch's sense of rightness in a home. He recalls the occasion when he and Jacqui were house hunting in the south of France. Local estate agents had been given a tight brief of their needs. Yet the very first house to which they were sent was totally off brief. It could not have been more off brief in any respect. The moment they entered the 800-year-old house (the brief stipulated a new property), they knew it was right for them. In the shortest possible time within the French buying/selling system, they had bought it.

Some months later, Haines asked the estate agent why she had ignored the brief and sent them to that particular house. It should be said that, prior to Mr and Mrs Haines arriving to view the house, the agent had never met them. They had just spoken on the phone and communicated via emails.

The agent smiled coyly in a very un-French manner. 'I am not sure. It just seemed right for you. It was an instinct thing, I think.'

An unconvincing reason, but true nonetheless. She was right. The family loves their French home. It feels right to them and everyone who visits it. (Oh, and, by the way, Haines has spotted three ghosts there. A medium friend recognised the same three plus two more. Harry refuses to go to the house because one of the female ghosts upstairs gives him a hard time when he's in bed. Harry sees her watching him from behind the floor-to-ceiling curtains. And she can be very noisy on occasions.)

EFFICIENCY AND HAPPINESS

In a dream, it came to Birch's awareness to explore the contrast between efficiency and happiness. In the business environment, processes and procedures become more and more scientifically based, which creates more things and services for less work, in theory. A side-effect of efficiency is the reliance on cold, dry formulae over the flexibility and intelligence of people. The more scientific that business processes become, the more divorced these processes are from humanity and its wants and needs.

This has created much stress and alienation among the workforce. So called burnout becomes an issue when individuals are so drained of mental and physical energy that they cannot function effectively, if at all, in their employment role any more. Birch suffered from this in his business life. His immune system became so compromised that he suffered the onset of a viral condition that took months to clear.

He was recently reminded of the work-stress issue and of a parallel experience of Nelson Mandela. He had been incarcerated for twenty-five years by the South African authorities of the time. The thing that amazed Birch when he saw Mandela leave prison was that he looked fresh and healthy. OK, Mandela hadn't been in a normal prison, but his life had been severely restricted for that time. When asked why he looked so well after this experience, Mandela said that the secret for him was to do some mental, physical and spiritual work every day. Thus he exercised balance in his daily life within the limits of imprisonment.

This is the crucial element that is missing in the hectic business life and indeed normal daily living: the notion of balance in all levels of our being. Returning to Birch, he was fortunate enough to be able to distance himself from his stressful business life, and was able to work in a more constructive and energising way. For many, working life is a chore, something to be coped with, something to be completed and then held at a distance, something to be placed out of one's mind wherever and whenever possible. This is the legacy of scientifically-based work systems.

Whilst briefly working for a public service, Birch came across a number of people who hated their job but were sticking it out until they were entitled to their pensions. This was usually years into the future. This is madness. What a waste of time and morale. No one can deny the advantages that many scientific advances have given mankind: DNA processes in forensics and the wonder of the computer, to name but two. The picture is not all doom and gloom. However, a balanced approach is needed when dealing with technology and working life.

Fortunate is she or he who has work which they enjoy, of which they are proud and which produces results that are further motivating. A major reason why Birch is so content with his spiritual path is that it has led him away from drudgery, misery and those things that no longer serve him, including dead-end workplace situations. Instead, his new direction has presented him with opportunities for employment, personal development and social activity.

'WE WEREN'T EXPECTING YOU'

It is important that we learn to laugh at ourselves. This spiritual work can become most serious. There is nothing wrong with that, but it does need to be balanced with humour. A friend on a similar path to Birch told him this story recently.

During floods, a man of deep spiritual interest was trapped on the roof of his house. A party waded through the rising water to rescue him. As the rescuers approached, the man standing on his roof waved them away, saying, 'I don't need your help. My spiritual guide will rescue me.'

The waters continued to rise, so a boat was sent to rescue the man. As the potential rescue approached it was dismissed with the shout, 'I don't need you to rescue me. My guide will provide the necessary help.'

As a last desperate measure, with the waters lapping the top of the house, a helicopter was sent. It too was sent away.

The inevitable happened, and the man drowned. When he ascended to the spirit world, he met his guide, who said, 'You shouldn't be here; I don't understand it. I sent a rescue party, a boat and then a helicopter.'

And so to China…

China

Peeping through the curtains into China

One day, at the annual Hawkwood Retreat for the Temple Study Group, Birch entered the dining room for a well-earned (according to him) and delicious lunch. As he entered, one of his fellow Temple Study Group members, John, called him over.

'I've been reading some of Edgar Cayce's work,' said John. 'He says that China will be the new home of the Christianity of Man. What do you think?'

Birch said that he would meditate on the matter and contact John at a later date. This he did, having returned home a couple of days later. This was the information that he received from his guidance.

As far as Edgar Cayce and other seers are concerned, they view trends and events that don't necessarily pan out in the manner described.

As for China, there is an enormous amount of spiritual hunger among the people. Since the communist revolution, the government has done all it can to suppress religious and spiritual thought in order to control the masses. One can draw an analogy between the slave culture that the Chinese people are enduring and the slavery that the Jews were subjected to by the Roman authorities at the time of Christ. In three-dimensional reality, every thought and action is the signal for the equal and opposite reaction to occur. Therefore suppressed spirituality causes it to rise even stronger because such spirituality is an implicit part of the human condition.

Underground Christianity is already on the rise in China. This is due in part to the suppression and partly to China's industrialisation. This unconsciously sucks in the energy and thought patterns that the West absorbed in its 2,000 years since the life of Christ. This is as inevitable as night following day. The power of the underground movement is such that the Chinese authorities will find great difficulty in suppressing it. It is like the hydra: cut one head off and another one rises elsewhere.

The authorities are already secretly concerned about this movement.

Many people will be surprised by the power of it as it breaks to the surface. The source of the power is the spiritual will of the people.

Consider the defeat of the US by the peasants of Vietnam, and the defeat of the fearsome Red Army by a few thousand ragged tribespeople in Afghanistan. The source of the victories was the spiritual will harnessed by the peasant peoples. How the situation will develop in the future, only the angels know. As the Chinese curse says, 'May you live in interesting times.'

Birch informed John of his insights, which harmonised with the latter's perspective.

One of the sensitive issues about which the Chinese authorities are aware has historical roots. Incompetent responses to natural disasters make the government nervous. Recent heavy blizzards at Chinese New Year 2007, when 100 million people were on the move, were mishandled by those in charge. People froze at railway stations with no food or toilet facilities. The Chinese know very well that this has happened on at least two occasions before, causing government collapse in the eighteenth and nineteenth centuries. One advantage for this enormous country is that they have a great sense of history, for 'those that ignore history are doomed to repeat it' is a much-used but apt quote. The response to the recent earthquake has been entirely more energetic and focussed.

We have spoken concerning the importance of history in Chinese present-day society, so what are the historical links shorn from the Western ex-imperialist rhetoric? The following is taken from historian Professor Jonathan Spence's Reith Lecture, broadcast on BBC Radio 4.

Western contacts were made with China by the English government-sponsored trading ships of the East India Company sailing from India. The first contacts were violent, particularly on the part of English sailors who were not given the trading links they were looking for. There was violence and admiration at the same time. The population of China at this time in the eighteenth century was 170–180 million, much smaller than it is today. Language was seen by the Chinese at this time as a protection, so foreigners were forbidden to learn it. The incoming Westerners were also forbidden from moving inland or from entering the cities. In order to create trading links a form of pidgin English was developed. This patois consisted of Portuguese, Indian and English words, supplemented by Chinese grammatical forms. In this way traders could communicate. This was a fascinating linguistic structure.

The English tried to reason people out of their culture in China. (There is no way that this could ever have been successful. More recently the US tried to reason Iraq and Afghanistan into their version of democracy after first invading. The resulting carnage indicates the lack of success of that approach.) After 1805, religion began to spread. Protestantism was in the vanguard, followed by Catholicism. The Bible was translated into Chinese.

Initially there was a failure of balance of trade. The Chinese did not want the goods the Westerners had on offer in exchange for silks and spices. The Western-initiated Opium Wars were to pressurise China, who saw their forces defeated. The Nanking Treaty of 1842, bitterly unfair from the Chinese perspective, was imposed. Even today this period is taught in Chinese educational establishments as the beginning of modern China. One wonders if this is one reason for the suspicion of foreigners that bedevils Chinese thought even today. One modern Western diplomat said that negotiating with the Chinese is like bargaining with a tiger over the price of its skin.

The Chinese began their own migration into southeast Asia, then to the Caribbean and Latin America. From 1850, migration continued to California, to Washington, into the deep- south of the US and to Liverpool. Chinese nationals came to the UK, brought by the Blue Star shipping line, as sailors and engineers. By 1880 or 90 English was forcibly taught in China at the behest of English military power. Confucian thought was translated into English, and English texts translated into Chinese. Racial slurs and discrimination in Japan, the US and the UK caused China to boycott goods of countries that treated them badly.

The last Chinese dynasty fell in 1911, leaving a weak Chinese Republic. Chinese cleaned up the battlefield in World War I, running prisoner-of-war camps. British power never recovered after the collapse of UK forces in Singapore. After WWII, large numbers of Chinese were repatriated back to China from the UK without legal redress. 'History is given to those that are visible' is an apt quote for that abuse. There were a large number of Chinese casualties on both sides in the US Civil War. The causes for Chinese suspicion of the Western countries and their motives are thus manifold.

Dr Joseph Needham (1900–1995), an eccentric scientist and academic, fellow of Caius College, Cambridge, changed perspectives of Chinese civilisation. Before Needham, Western countries perceived China as in the periphery of civilisation. Needham opened Western eyes to the sophistication of Chinese civilisation and the length of time for which it had functioned. Its achievements included the invention and use of gunpowder, mechanical printing and the magnetic compass. Needham based himself in Chungking, now a city of 38 million people. Needham is the best-known Englishman in China.

The upsurge of Christianity in China has generated millions of adherents to the Roman Catholic sect of Christianity. The Chinese government is not only attempting to control this, but is extremely wary of the Vatican with its political power base and influence, as well as its proselytising fervour. The traditional philosophy in China is, and long has been, Confucianism. It is a system that has survived countless attacks, not least the cultural revolution of the 1970s, and is being recycled by the Chinese government, according to Professor Spence. Confucianism is particularly Chinese. One of its tenets is an awareness of the dangers of speaking out, which would rest comfortably with an autocratic, repressive regime.

Perhaps it would be useful to reproduce these extracts from Wikipedia giving some background to Confucius and Confucianism.

> Confucianism is an ancient Chinese ethical and philosophical system originally developed from the teachings of the early Chinese philosopher Confucius. It focuses on human morality and good deeds. Confucianism is a complex system of moral, social, political, philosophical … thought that has had tremendous influence on the culture and history of East Asia. Confucian doctrine remained a mainstream Chinese orthodoxy for two millennia until the 20th century … when it was attacked by radical Chinese thinkers as a vanguard of a pre-modern system and an obstacle to China's modernisation, eventually culminating in its repression during the Cultural Revolution. Since the end of the Cultural Revolution, Confucianism has been revived in mainland China … As with many other prominent figures such as Jesus, Socrates, and Buddha, Confucius did not leave any writings to put forward his ideas. Instead, only texts with recollections by his disciples and their students are available.
>
> Generally speaking, Confucianism is not considered a religion by Chinese or other East Asian people. Part of this attitude may be explained by the stigma placed on many 'religions' as being superstitious, illogical, or unable to deal with modernity. Many Buddhists state that Buddhism is not a religion, but a philosophy, and this is partially a reaction to negative popular views of religion. Similarly, Confucians maintain that Confucianism is not a religion, but rather a moral code or philosophic

> world view. Many 'religions' practiced in East Asia such as Buddhism and Taoism can be considered as 'not religions.' There is a much more blurred line between religion and philosophy in non-Western thought. Most of the Western distinction is in fact a relatively recent phenomenon resulting from the Enlightenment period unique to Western Europe. Therefore, it could be said that while Confucianism is not a religion by Western standards (even according to Asian adherents) it is a religion in the East Asian sense of the word.

The above explanation is useful in order to understand the background to the amazingly deep culture of China. The Confucian view of the importance of roles and ritual is most interesting and apposite for Western societies in this present era. Problems with young people in our society are, at least partly, due to failure to enthuse many of them with effective roles and positive ritual behaviour, in Birch's view. Young people are presented with antagonistic role opportunities through sport and aggressive entertainment. It is no wonder that many of the younger generation feel lost and disconnected from society. So many young people would perceive themselves as losers in the game of life.

The point made in the Wikipedia paragraph concerning the lack of written material left by Confucius and other spiritual leaders is an interesting one. Written texts underwrite the status quo in religions. They are a way of keeping adherents in line, as well as promulgating the faith. The verbal tradition used by Confucius, Jesus and others is much less prescriptive, allowing the listener to form their own opinion, to integrate that which is being proposed through speech into their psyche. This approach is liberating to the listener.

In a guided meditation concerning China at an Imaghi meditation group meeting, Birch received a vision. He saw that the dragon energy (a particular energy associated with China) had been unleashed to such an extent that it was thrashing around, out of control. The Chinese government, despite appearances, was not in control of the situation. The uncontrolled industrialisation in the country was a major cause of this.

Birch was also told that the successful hosting of the Olympic Games was a double-edged sword. Thousands of people with different mental constructs to the Chinese thought processes would be entering the country. This invasion of foreigners was a potential Trojan horse. These foreigners would have thoughts contextually alien to the controlled mass consciousness in this ancient country. This would leave its mark. Thoughts are things. Until then, the Chinese government had been successful in keeping out unacceptable influences through harsh punishments and a rigid educational regime.

The torch procession of the Olympic flame paraded through the streets of foreign cities was another process, invoking further strength to the powerful dragon energy. The fiery torch flanked by macho Chinese security guards was feeding this increasingly aggressive energy and was itself another form of dragon consciousness. The Chinese authorities, imbued with their repressive materialistic thoughts, didn't have a clue what they had unleashed. The yang macho dragon forces needed to be balanced with a loving calm aspect if they were to return to a harmonious condition. Would political change be generated in China as a result of the games, as occurred in South Korea after the 1988 games? The population of South Korea had thereafter been much more willing to criticise the government. A Chinese acupuncturist living in the UK told Birch that the Chinese people do not support the government, and that human rights suppression plus improvement of the economy are ways the regime attempts to retain power. The Olympic Games were an apparent external success. Where the games were to be held, repressive measures were used to clear the area of people. They were expelled from their homes and businesses to live in near concentration camp conditions, because they dressed and lived poorly and would thus have been a poor advertisement to the foreigners. This is not the action of a compassionate society.

Birch believes that it is useful to balance the negative, apparently unchanging perspective of the Chinese government. It is a fact that the number of death sentences have halved from around 8,000 annually since legal reforms were introduced in 2007. In the past, many death sentences have been carried out for non-violent offences such as fraud. Prisoners were shot in the back of the head, allegedly. Waiting behind the scenes were medical teams who would remove the organs of the dead for transplant to those needing them.

The whole intriguing phenomenon of transplanting organs from one person to another has surfaced in the West as well as China. There is now considerable evidence that patients who have been recipients of another person's organs sometimes take on aspects of the personality of the donor. Vegetarians become meat eaters. Passive people have suddenly become much more assertive. There have been a number of cases reported in the

British press. In these cases, there is the issue of trauma transferred, from a person violently killed or who has died after a long and painful illness, to the transplant recipient. A report surfaced in the US press emanating from Hilton Head, South Carolina. A man received a heart transplant, successfully living and later marrying the donor's widow. Amazingly, he died the same way that the donor did: from a self-inflicted gunshot wound. In a report in the *Nexus* magazine, a 37-year-old woman received a kidney from a deceased 59-year-old man. The woman claimed that she had suffered a personality change, becoming, unnaturally for her, short-tempered. Her literary tastes changed from light, low-brow novels to heavy Russian authors. It was claimed in the article that academics in the United States had named the condition 'cellular memory phenomenon' in order to explain the personality changes. The only case recognised by the scientific community, it was alleged, was that of a fifteen-year-old Australian girl whose blood type changed following a liver transplant.

For Birch, this issue demonstrates the holistic nature of the human. He believes that all of our physical, psychological and emotional natures are stored in each cell of our body. We are thus holographic in nature. The issue of blood transfusion is a little different. Such cells only live for a few days in the body. Therefore, any transferred characteristics will quickly disappear.

Perhaps we have strayed some way from the China debate. Nevertheless, it is important to consider the holistic nature of humanity.

Given Birch's assumption that the Earth is a living being, one wonders what the repercussions of underground nuclear tests are. Both the US and China have involved themselves with this obscene practice in recent times. The living Earth, or any living being, would respond to such an assault. China recently suffered a terrible earthquake, and the US has had catastrophic flooding on and near its Caribbean coastline. Is there a retributive element to these disasters? Perhaps we will never know. Sadly it is the ordinary citizen who suffers, whatever the cause of the issues.

OK, let us return to the China debate. Birch believes that there is another aspect of the Tibet issue. The Chinese political leadership believes that Tibet is part of its country. There is much criticism in the West of the invasion and occupation of this ancient mountain country; rightly so. There is the pervasive and mistaken perception that pre-invasion Tibet was a haven of harmony and spiritual succour, ruled over by a beneficent religious regime. The truth was the absolute reverse. A small caucus of elite families and religious leaders ruled, with a cruel rod of iron, over a populace of serfs and slaves. The majority of the population was uneducated and uncared for by the rulers. Most were condemned to lifelong servitude and abuse. In some respects, conditions for the poor improved under the Chinese. Education and health care, as well as freedom from slavery, were introduced. The Chinese, however, were unable to separate themselves from cruel and inhumane punishments for those who didn't fit with their rule. Their suppression of the Buddhist religion is another cause of great resentment. The Tibetan culture, inextricably linked to their religion, is thus suppressed to the point of destruction. The Dalai Lama, chief Tibetan religious leader in exile, has expressed interest in Western ideas of democracy and social systems. Thus things may change if the Chinese leave.

So what is the point of this diversion into Chinese and Tibetan history? A meditation group with which Birch is familiar is working on a weekly basis in order to make the Chinese system of governance and administration unworkable in Tibet. The upshot of government failure would be withdrawal from the mountain country. This type of focussed visualisation has worked at least once in another case. Birch continues to watch this with great interest.

It seems to Birch that China, as a nation, is going through the birth pangs of a change in consciousness, as many nations are. These pains are manifested, in one way, through the natural and human disasters that beset this country. They include the Sichuan earthquake on 12th May 2008 killing tens of thousands, many of them children. There were thirty-nine dancers killed in a more recent night club fire, the health of 50,000 children was affected by contaminated milk, and there were the deaths of Chinese cockle pickers and students in the UK. Social pressures are manifesting between the rural poor and big business. Poor farmers say they are having their land stolen by building speculators and corrupt local politicians. This phenomenon is not restricted to China. The same is allegedly happening in India.

Politics and the Mystic

Return to living in this world

The death of democracy is not likely to be a death by ambush. It will be a slow extinction from apathy, indifference and undernourishment.

Robert M. Hutchins

George Orwell said that some ideas are so stupid that only intellectuals can believe in them. Communism was one example and liberal imperialism is another.

Richard Koch and Chris Smith

Birch's visit to Brittany inspired this chapter. This inspiration came from guidance rather than his objective mind. As he sat down he didn't have a clue what should be written. Trusting in his guidance, he heard the whisperings arise in his mind which started the process. Other inspirations arose from his knowledge and experience. The following is the result.

Society, including politics, could be argued to be a compromise at the lowest common denominator. This is based on explicit and implicit agreements worked out over long periods of time. Society is structured so that most people can get by just enough to keep everything moving. Within that, there are obviously attempts to make society more co-operative and creative. The mystic is working from an internal code that may or may not be harmonious with societal structures. Thus, working in society is sometimes convenient for the mystic, sometimes not.

The trick for the mystic is to work inside the structure, but also work from one's personal highest perspectives. First of all it is important that we get out and vote. For a mystic a vote is a form of energy, an input to the total energy of votes cast, an input to the aspirations of the voting public. Each vote is saying, *In you I place my trust for the next few years to care for the interest of this country and its citizens.* Politicians, no less than anyone else in the public eye, thrive on the energy directed towards them from the public. It is part of the food and drink of the persona. Have you ever come across a shrinking violet politician? It is difficult to find one. Whether the politicians use the energy to boost their egos or not, they will be aware of the energy flow. It is a euphoric high, similar to the adrenaline rush experienced by an athlete or that experienced by someone who has successfully overcome a danger.

The energy and the power of the role of a politician is heady stuff indeed. No wonder that they have to be dragged, kicking and screaming, from their privileged position at times. Witness recent prime ministers. This is another reason to get out and vote. It is one of the few means, as limited as it may be, that the individual possesses for controlling the power position of politicians. Many people feel that a vote is wasted, that it won't make a difference. They feel that the corruption, double standards, lying and alienation from the nation's wants and needs cannot be reversed. This is an attitude to be challenged at every opportunity.

It is on these issues that Birch and Haines have more than the odd discussion. Birch believes that societies and nations, perhaps none more so than England, can adapt and heal themselves. Haines, an optimist by nature, has lost his optimism in these times. He believes Blair, Brown and their governments have done irreparable, irreversible damage to English society, its structure and cohesiveness. History shows how good England is at absorbing and integrating newcomers. By and large, it has done this by itself without the need for heavy-handed legislation, political correctness and the subjugation of the needs and identities of the existing peoples and their communities. What Haines now sees is ghettoisation and government-sponsored division; white and black, Christian and Muslim.

Maybe Haines's fears have been justified. Just one week before this chapter was penned, the results of a survey were published. One in five English people now wish to live elsewhere. Haines places the destruction of English society firmly at the feet of New Labour and its dogma. Yet we, the electorate, have allowed the government to commit this social vandalism.

This is the era of the instant fix, the sound-bite, the wearing of make-up by politicians for the camera: spin and PR done to death. The following is from *The Disappearance of the Universe* by Gary R Renard.

> ... but you do realise that Lincoln could not be elected today? He didn't have a good speaking voice and he actually took the time to think about the answer to a question. If you did that in a debate today, you'd be called stupid. Imagine having a thoughtful answer instead of a clever, pre-written sound byte.
>
> It's all style and speed, and what does that do for people except tune them more and more into the madness?

And this is from Jacques Rangasamy:

> Very young infants and parrots learn rude words more easily than they do sensible words. This is because profanities are usually uttered with passion, with the energy of feelings and they register more readily on the receptive consciousness of young infants and that of parrots. The tone of voice often contradicts the content of some politicians' speeches, which makes it wise, if one is at all inclined, to listen for any resonating sincerity in their words with one's eyes closed.

Nothing could be dearer to the wishes of those that would rule us for their personal or group interest than the electorate switching off, giving their power away. There is a cynical statement that Birch has heard which says, 'Don't vote, it only encourages them' (meaning politicians). This is the politics of despair. Burke wisely told us, 'It is necessary only for the good man to do nothing for evil to triumph.' Birch heartily agrees with this.

Birch's grandfather was an ordinary working man who, in the 1920s and 1930s, fought peacefully for the rights of what was then called the working class. This was a success. As a result of the pressure exerted by millions of working-class people, coupled with external events such as the two World Wars, the ordinary person advanced in freedom, education and material wellbeing. This forced the elites of the time to retreat somewhat. It seems almost archaic and anachronistic to write of the working class, a term that legitimised the status of millions of people in the UK between the 1920s and the mid 1980s. It seems to be a term that is no longer relevant in a society that is affluent, increasingly multi-cultural and much more concerned with world issues. The working class idea was corrupted in the end, Birch feels, by greed and narrow-mindedness of the representatives of the class as they gained political and industrial power.

The reality of multi-culturism was brought home to Birch recently. He was giving a chi gong class in a city close to his home when he realised that here was a man from a Western background teaching a Chinese health system to Hindus and a Sikh.

Now ordinary people need as much as ever to express themselves politically. Besides voting, actions such as writing to one's political representative, attending political events such as marches and becoming knowledgeable about political processes at home and abroad are favoured by Birch. He thus involves himself with the political process. There are other positive moves that one could make, not the least of which is standing in an election if one feels strongly enough and has the courage. It is vitally important that politicians be made aware of feelings about important events on the part of ordinary people in the country.

So could the control tendencies and fears of those that would rule us today have echoes of the working-class entertainment in Victorian times? Prior to the 1860s, the music hall, the entertainment of the lower and working classes, was a participative arrangement. There was much rowdiness and communication between the entertainer on stage and the audience. The performers entered from the auditorium, assisting the participative system. This boisterous pattern was controlled by a loud-voiced master of ceremonies who would sit on the stage behind an official-looking table and wield a gavel to impose discipline and order on the proceedings.

This participative movement was a threat to the establishment. The music hall was now a place for the 'great unwashed' to demonstrate their empowerment. This could not be allowed to continue. Changes were imposed on theatres, using the threat of hall owners losing their licence. If you have a 3,000-seat hall of entertainment, you will need to fill it to avoid bankruptcy. A much more anodyne process was imposed where the master of ceremonies was removed and the various acts were introduced by a numbering system at the side of the stage. This was where the phrase 'your number is up' originated. Performers now entered from the side of the stage. Birch became aware of the psychological separation impact of this in one of his chi gong classes. Due to the large number of students in one class, he retreated to the raised stage at one end of the hall in order to perform his instruction. Instantly he sensed the separation between him and his group of students. The music hall customer now became a passive observer. The ruling classes could relax in the knowledge that this potential force disrupting their management of society was now neutralised. This was very much akin to that passivity-inducement modern control mechanism: the television. As Lao Tse said, 'The people are difficult to govern; they are too clever.' Everything changes but nothing changes unless good men do something.

Andrew Marr, the political commentator, called Arthur Scargill, the ex-miners' leader, a 'deluded insurrectionist'. Birch likes the word 'insurrectionist' because this is what we should all be, according to him. The process of insurrection is striving for a better system and should be part of a mystic's raison d'etre.

In order to balance the negative image of Arthur Scargill, here is a positive story. Birch's friend Faye worked for the diplomatic service for many years. At one time she had responsibility for organising social events in the British High Commission in Delhi, India. She thus had access to those with the highest political status. A highly placed trade union official was in the High Commission with a delegation of other trades unionists. There was a relaxed meeting in the High Commission bar. The high official was introduced to many people. At the end of the meeting, this official went round to every person saying how much he had enjoyed meeting them. He addressed each by name despite having met many people and only been introduced once. This is a different slant to the hard-line trade unionist portrayed in media presentations. Faye was impressed with this side of the man. Faye is not a person easily impressed.

Appearances can be so deceiving. Winston Churchill called Mahatma Gandhi a *half-naked fakir.* This was an insult which rebounded on the great man, as Gandhi was at the centre of the British Empire falling apart in India. This *half-naked fakir* was a man of great intelligence as well as personal courage and spiritual insight. By Gandhi's successful mobilisation of the Indian nation over the iniquitous salt tax, the death knell of the greatest political system of the time was sounded. How did Gandhi do this? His now famous walk to the sea, which he started with a few followers but which was joined by many thousands, created an energetic resonance that a powerful empire could not resist. No one was killed on the march. There was no violence, simply the building of a coherent will and energy. This scrawny little septuagenarian took salt from the sea and ate it, thus breaking the law of the time. Such powerful symbolic acts worked through at the level of the mass consciousness, causing revolutionary change. Mystics can create their own changes with an insurrectionist attitude.

This is all very fine and dandy, Birchy, you may say, *but what has this got to do with the spiritual life?* It has this to do with it. The more intensely that we work on spiritual matters, the greater is the tendency to become driven inwards to our inner-self. This is almost inevitable. In order to return to balance as a human being, it is important that we function and operate in the mundane world. We have a part to play. The age of the anchorite in his cave and the monk secluded in the monastery is not the way forward for the aspiring mystic.

First of all we do this by merely being. By the very nature of what we are, we influence those around us. Every human being resonates to a certain vibration. All the years, lifetimes that we, as mystically inclined persons, have struggled to refine our vibration, leave their mark and influence on the world and people. Birch believes that this influence is beneficial.

Sometimes we do not have to do anything; simply being in our normal consciousness is enough. Birch's friend, a powerful healer, was asked to perform absent healing by a person suffering. A little time later, the sufferer thanked Birch's friend for the healing that he had done. In fact the friend had done nothing. He had forgotten. It could be argued that the healing was spontaneous, or as a result of the placebo effect.

Wikipedia says that:

> Placebo effect is the term applied by medical science to the therapeutic and healing effects of inert medicines and/or faith healing manipulations. When referring to medicines, placebo is a preparation which is pharmacologically inert but which may have a therapeutic effect based solely on the power of suggestion.

Sceptic.com says 'placebos may be sugar pills or starch pills. Even "fake" surgery and "fake" psychotherapy are considered placebos'.

It could be, however, that the friend's vibrations were enough once the request for healing had taken place. The request may have attuned the person in need of help to the natural healing vibration emanating from the friend.

Secondly, our inner work will give us insights and a clarity that will be of benefit to society, the environment and local and national politics. Mystics are no more important than any other person; however, they are engaged on a unique path that can be a source of benefit.

Thirdly, as with those of other persuasions, mystics can speak their truth, write to politicians on matters of importance and become active in peaceful ways. Several years ago, Jaqueline and Birch went on a peace march protesting against the upcoming Iraq war. Up to 2 million people protested against the impending insanity. It made no difference to the attack. However, Birch believes that public opinion was affected by the march. It was not simply the march that created the change, but the energy created by it: synergistic energy on a grand scale.

Let's return to the 'it is necessary only for the good man to do nothing for evil to triumph' idea. We refer to the Adam Curtis TV programme *The Trap: What Happened to Our Dream of Freedom?* In this programme it was stated that current politicians saw their job as delivering simplistic, selfish needs, which has led us, is leading us, into a political world without meaning. As aspiring mystics we have meaning in our lives. This is an important point. In individual and group work, mystics are the antithesis of this *world without meaning*. They are the opposition. So let's be active.

It isn't necessary for the opponents of bad politicians to be other politicians. Birch remembers that during the 1980s the major opposition to the political policies of Margaret Thatcher seemed to be the stand-up comic Ben Elton. A man of great wit and personality was almost single-handedly standing up to what Birch and Elton considered abusive policies. Opposition politicians at the time were limp and impotent. Haines, a great supporter of Thatcher, unsurprisingly takes quite a different view; *cometh the hour, cometh the man*, or, in this case, the woman.

Oppositions create the energy for change. Light and dark, positive and negative, yin and yang: out of the stress of opposites, ideas, options and solutions can arise. Isaiah Berlin, who grew up in the British establishment, was a political philosopher of the 1950s. He spoke of individual freedoms and how to protect them. He said:

> Political systems should be created to restrain politicians who would lead us to tyranny ... We must never come to believe that our current political system is the final solution. This is the antithesis of the current political myth that what we call democracy and currently experience is the final solution. It should be viewed as the beginning and not the end.

Two thousand years ago, Lao Tse said, as previously quoted, 'The people are difficult to govern; they are too clever.' This is no less true today than it was in ancient China. We should certainly be difficult to manage. It is a vital element in the battle for making politicians aware that they are servants of the people rather than the masters.

This offering is from Jacques Rangasamy, relating to the current politics being in the pocket of mega-money:

> Other columnists analysing the current economic crisis in America attribute the cause not only to unfortunate economic mismanagement or to 'natural misbehaviour of market forces'. They blame mainly the carefully crafted fiscal policies that powerful governments and international corporations have introduced, and their deliberate styles in the exercise of power and privileges. Some columnists argue that the same governments and international corporations devised or approved over two decades ago fiscal policies that they knew carried the risk of destabilising the financial market and causing the current debacle of many pension schemes and the turmoil in the housing market. But they chose to prioritise the creation of wealth for the few above the welfare and economic security of many, and rationalised their decisions by asserting that the new wealth would trickle down the socio-economic pyramid and benefit in the long run the wider population dwelling at the bottom. Such, however, is not the experience of the dispossessed and chronically destitute.

If the above is true, so much for the welfare of the majority being the major concern of Western democratic governments.

A recent Radio 4 programme spoke on the subject of hypocrisy in political life. It claimed that it was not as reprehensible as some claim, especially those in public life. The programme's commentator said that, due to public pressure in democratic and Western democracies for politicians to exhibit higher moral standards than the ordinary citizen, they, the politicians, retreat into hypocrisy. In truth, they are no more or no less moral than the norm. Hypocrisy, it was argued, gives them space to function. We are all hypocrites to some degree, therefore this human trait is an element of our reality rather than entirely negative. The parallel was drawn between hypocrisy in democracies and the behaviour in tyrannies where thought and action was so constrained that not even hypocrisy could function.

This argument is another one to legitimise the status quo, it seems to Birch. For the mystic, this cannot be acceptable. In our beings we are constantly striving to eradicate our negative traits. Once society accepts that the present imperfect behaviour pattern is acceptable, then the path of devolution, rather than evolution, is entered. The whole energy pattern in this reality is working against that. We are on an evolutionary path. Individuals, groups and organisations that hang onto the old ways are doomed to disintegrate. This is typified by the crises that are being experienced by political, financial and religious organisations.

One saving grace is the public concern over the quality of politicians in this country. Higher standards of behaviour and attitude are expected. The previous ten years have seen an unprecedented blitz of public relations from politician to public. Birch's view is that voters have seen through much of this particular hype. The previous prime minister of the UK, Brown, Birch believes, expected things to go on as they had done in the last ten years. During his period of office this was not the case. Similar to the leadership of Gorbachev in Russia, leadership slipped away from Gordon Brown's control. (That was so until the 2008 financial crisis. As in many other crises, the known is viewed as the preferred option, hence Mr Brown's then-rise in the popularity polls.) The British people expect more than they were given in the past. This is a positive move in the mass consciousness. An apt quote here might be 'you can read the face of the heavens but you cannot read the signs of the times'.

Birch saw the film *V for Vendetta* on DVD when he was in America in 2008. One character in the film says, 'People should not be afraid of their governments. Governments should be afraid of their people.' Birch didn't agree with the idea of advocating fear in the relationship between government and people. However, he found the sentences powerful in the context of the film and they caused him to think further on the relationship between the two. The character was speaking of the balance of power between the two. The idea that the balance of power should be with the people was an attractive one to Birch. Even with democratic governments this has not always been the case. When elected politicians start with the best intentions, the heady aphrodisiac of power can take them away from a balanced relationship with the citizenry. Ideally the trend of our democratic law making and systems should be in the direction of transferring power back to the people. In the UK the trend has been the other way. It has been the trend of the electorate in this country to put powerful leaders in place. As they have become more confident in their leadership role there has been an insidious haemorrhage of power to the central government. This has taken decades to happen.

The story in *V for Vendetta* concerns an anti-hero who aims to blow up the British Houses of Parliament, and other buildings, dressed as Guy

Fawkes. For those outside the UK, this man was a historical figure who did indeed try to blow up the Houses of Parliament in the seventeenth century. He failed. The object of doing this in the film was to shake the British people out of political stupor into which they had sunk. It was set in the near future when Britain had become a fascist state. The film had an interesting impact in the US, which surprised Birch given its very English style and presentation. As a protest against the current political leadership, hundreds of people dressed as Guy Fawkes, a decidedly English anti-hero, gathered at the White House. This was clearly a political protest. It seems that the most unlikely communication patterns can have a profound influence on the mass consciousness.

Sometimes things and people are not as they first seem. Birch's friend Mary tells of an intuitive guidance which was written up on the Internet. This guidance claimed that Hugo Chavez, president of the Republic of Venezuela, and Vladimir Putin, then Russia's prime minister, were both working in a way that was unknown in the West. Neither of the two had good reputations in the West, with some justification. However, the guidance said that they were difficult people in order to enable themselves to free their countries from the grip of alleged illuminati. The latter are those that would rule us, it is claimed in some quarters.

The Disappearance of the Universe tells us:

> ... people who waste their lives fighting the battle of 'good versus evil', when what they're really seeing out there in the world is merely symbolic of the conflict between right-mindedness or good, and wrong-mindedness or evil, that is occurring within their own split minds. Save your airfare and forgive. You'll get to heaven a thousand times faster in the process ... Now you must learn that only infinite patience produces immediate effects.

Blood, Bones and Plasticity

Have they completely taken leave of their senses, or...

The information, insights and inspirations in this chapter are the joint work of Audrey and Birch. Along with Haines, they thought long and hard about including this material. It consists of deep spiritual and subtle elements that need considerable meditation and reflection. On balance it was decided that it should go in.

The authors would also like to thank Faye plus Ian, Louise and Shaun for their contribution.

This is from *Don't Underestimate the Power of Your Blood* by Karen S Clickner, from theherbaladvisor.com:

> There is great power in your blood, and the strongest tides on the planet may actually be within your own body. Many times we underestimate the essential quality of our blood and our circulation, a vital mistake when evaluating any body condition.
>
> Without the body's blood supply, your cells would not have food, oxygen, water or waste-removal. Your hormones would never reach their target tissues and power your physiology. Your food would never leave the intestinal tract. Your nerves would never tell you everything about the world around you. Your brain would cease to function ...
>
> This system [circulation] also shares fluid with the lymphatic system in the form of plasma enabling immune cells to be transported ...
>
> Whole blood is made up of two portions, blood plasma and blood cells. Plasma is a watery connective tissue, which carries the blood cells. It is about 91% water and 9% dissolved substances such as plasma proteins, electrolytes, enzymes, nutrients, hormones, gases and waste products.
>
> Blood cells make up the rest of the blood. These cells can be complete cells or they can be cell fragments, which will then be recycled to make new cells. 99% of these cells are erythrocytes or red blood cells ... they contain the oxygen-carrying protein haemoglobin, which gives blood its red pigment and brings redness to the skin ... Erythrocytes also have a strong

> immune capability because of the specialised proteins that are found on their surface.
>
> Leukocytes or white blood cells can generally live for several months or years, but many live only a few days or hours, especially during an infection. This is because our leukocytes are concerned primarily with mediating our body immunity and protection ... Once they leave the blood and diffuse into interstitial fluid, they do not return to the blood, but instead are picked up by the immune system.
>
> The third type of blood cell is a platelet, also known as a thrombocyte. These cells help stop blood loss from damaged blood vessels by forming a sticky plug while at the same time releasing chemicals that promote blood clotting. They have a very short lifespan, usually about 5–9 days. Blood loss must be quickly controlled, localised and stopped, in order to prevent our bleeding to death.

It is interesting to speculate on the divine right of kings, well entrenched in human consciousness even to this day. We know that the hype has always given power to those who claim to be royal, but it must have been more than that originally. The members of such families, and many others, have worked with the idea of bloodlines either consciously or unconsciously. Some claim that magicians in the distant past worked to create exceptional properties in blood. From this arises the concept of blue blood. It may be that royal families believe that they perpetuate themselves from the holy family. By that we mean the family of Jesus Christ. Such a system has been able to satisfy, in the past, the emotional needs of the people. Cromwell couldn't capture the hearts of the English people and was succeeded by another monarch.

An astrologer recently told Birch that the British royal family seem to co-ordinate some of their major events with solar eclipses. Prince Charles announced his divorce from first wife, Diana, through a parliamentary announcement, and was married to his second wife around a solar eclipse.

Another story concerns the effect of a solar eclipse on animals. Birch's lawyer neighbour Demelza tells the story of a visit that she made to a wildlife park during a solar eclipse. As the eclipse reached its high point, an eerie silence pervaded the entire park. All the animals went completely silent. The staff and public in the park were amazed. This silence was unknown during daylight hours. As the eclipse passed, all the members of the cat family set up the most fantastic crying and yowling. Leopard, panther, lion cubs, all created an incredible wall of sound. The other animals continued in silence until much later before normal chatter and noises resumed. What was there about the solar eclipse that caused the animals to behave so out of character? Were they aware of the cosmic event happening above their heads? What influence was it having on them?

Unfortunately, this wildlife park is now closed as further planning permission was refused. Local people claimed that wildlife should be in the wild. This is fine in theory. However, all the animals in this park were those that had been passed on by zoos and other wildlife establishments which could not accommodate additional newborn animals.

Kingship/queenship and its relation to blue blood may have something to do with higher initiation. Anyone speaking of blue blood usually feels that they have something of which to be proud. This notion of initiation is one of anointment by a priest, the representative of God, similar to crowning with cosmic fire. Jacques Rangasamy speaks of the Master Jesus at Chartres as being crowned with solar glory.

The following are quotes from www.plim.org:

> Some believe that accumulated tribal knowledge and wisdom of all previous generations is carried through the blood.
>
> Magic plays an important part in mankind's worship of various deities and the spirit. Since blood represents life, it was believed that by offering up blood or using blood in some rituals it has the power of passing on this principle of life, giving power to protect, heal and create. For example, many gentiles would drink blood of sacrifices believing they could obtain some type of spiritual attributes from the substance. Killing an innocent baby and drinking the blood was thought [of] as a way to obtain the principle of innocence.
>
> ... Even at the time of the Messiah, Pilate mixed human blood with the blood of animal sacrifice (Luke 13:1). Again, it was thought that human blood increased the efficiency of their rituals to their pagan gods.
>
> Under the law of Moses, Yahweh allowed for one instance of justifiable murder. A victim's family could take vengeance on the perpetrator who killed their relative. In fact, many gentile nations and tribes believed in this means of carrying out justice from the inception of man. According to the *Dictionary of the Bible* by James Hastings: 'The practice of blood-revenge is one of the most widely spread customs of human society, and is by no means confined to the Semitic races, although it is still found in full vigour among the Arabs. By the Bedouin of Sinaitic peninsula, for instance, the vendetta is kept up to the fifth generation.'

How did the blood become such an important mystical matter? We know about its physical manifestation, but there is something else behind all this. Does the importance of the blood originate in the creation of living matter?

There is a cosmic law: *as above, so below*. This law operates in humanity when we attempt to develop ourselves and to consider the questions of life and death and our reasons for incarnating. This is akin to shining a bright light, which is a masculine energy, into our deepest subconscious. The feminine responds by helping us to find answers as we move on our path towards wholeness. So the masculine and feminine interact within our beings, creating the dynamic creative tension. This law operates on physical and spiritual levels.

On a long-haul flight some time ago, Birch watched a film about the legend of Nosferatu: a tale about the stealing of human blood in order to maintain the life of a monster. Birch wondered at the time whether this was a mythical interpretation of the practices of certain lower-energy individuals of the past and present. He now also wonders if the defencelessness of the victims in the film indicated the relative power position of certain blood initiates compared to the powerlessness of the mass of humanity who are not privy to the secrets of the blood. Birch believes this is the perception of the past and is being changed by the combined work of mystics and those of good will. Perhaps the function of the Nosferatu myth is to serve as a warning to humanity? In a subtle way, might it penetrate the unconscious and help to protect against future abuses?

Also in the film, there is the issue of the vampires moving from place to place on the Earth, from lairs which have been contaminated by them. It could certainly be a metaphor for the corruption of the Earth wrought by humanity as a result of its industrial processes and negative thought forms. This raises an interesting point concerning the positive Earth power locations such as Teotihuacán, Palenque and Chichen Itza, all in Mexico, and others. The story makes the point that certain places on the Earth are corrupted and centres of dark, negative forces. Birch maintains that the places mentioned are centres of the light. Perhaps from the perception of both sides, the dark and the light, these places are centres for the fight against each other. From this tension and friction between the two grows the opportunity for development and change in the consciousness of humanity.

As Birch travelled in Central America, visiting pyramid cities and places of the ancient spirituality, he was struck first by their very high vibrations. However, he was also aware of the low energies of the feeder towns close or next to them. Teotihuacán has the megatropolis of Mexico City one hour's drive away. Birch reckons that Mexico City is not completely negative, but it does have problems. Tulum and Palenque are both ancient places of power with low-vibration towns next to them.

Interesting also is the sacrifice of the heroine figure in order to draw out the vampire into the light and thus destroy him. Perhaps here is a pointer to the power of the female energy and its potential to combat dark forces which are aggressively masculine in nature. In many myths, Nosferatu, Dracula or Frankenstein for instance, the evil entity is masculine. These dark forces have power and dominion over the male elements but can be defeated by the female.

In the saga, the monster rips out the heart of the heroine on her wedding night, thus, on this occasion, conquering the powerful female energy through the destruction of one of her most powerful symbols.

Audrey believes that the feminine aspect acts as a facilitator in bringing about desired evolutionary effects, after first having nurtured them. This is one of the messages in the Cinderella fairy story. The heroine overcomes resentment and envy (of the ugly sisters) which results in her fairy godmother (the divine feminine) appearing and granting her wish to go to the ball. There, her dreams come true. She meets her prince, takes the male into herself so that the female and male become balanced, and is happy ever after. That is, she becomes an integrated being.

In the Sleeping Beauty fairy story, the wicked fairy (the destructive Kali feminine energy) attempts to deny Sleeping Beauty her life. The good fairy (the divine feminine) cancels the spell. Sleeping Beauty then sleeps until the prince, battling against the odds, seeks her out and awakens her. In the Greek myth about the Minotaur, Ariadne advises Theseus to use a ball of twine to find his way out of the maze after slaying the Minotaur. Thus she facilitates his mastery over the negative forces.

It would be interesting, in these allegedly enlightened times, to develop a mystical myth demonstrating the power of the feminine and its challenge to the lower, dark forces today. It could be that there are such myths in the Superman, Spiderman, Batman and other superhero characters. Of course these are all aspects of the masculine. Wonder Woman is one of the few female characters in this genre. There is also the myth of

Jack and the Beanstalk: 'Fee, fi, fo, fum, I smell the blood of an Englishman.' So what is special about the blood of an Englishman?

> Bone marrow is the soft tissue found in the hollow interior of bones. In adults, marrow in large bones produces new blood cells.
>
> There are two types of bone marrow, red marrow and yellow marrow. Red blood cells, platelets and most white blood cells arise in red marrow; some white blood cells develop in yellow marrow. The colour of yellow marrow is due to the much higher number of fat cells. Both types of bone marrow contain numerous blood vessels and capillaries.
>
> At birth all bone marrow is red. With age more and more of it is converted to the yellow type. Adults have, on average, about 2.6Kg (5.7lb) of bone marrow, with about half of it being red. Red marrow is found mainly in the flat bones such as hip bone, breast bone, skull, ribs, vertebrae and shoulder blades and in the 'spongy' material at the proximal end of the long bones femur and humerus. Yellow marrow is found in the hollow interior of the middle portion of long bones.
>
> In cases of severe blood loss, the body can convert yellow marrow back to red marrow in order to increase blood cell production … Many of the symptoms of radiation sickness are due to damage to the bone marrow cells.
>
> Bone marrow is a source of protein and high in monounsaturated fat. These fats are known to decrease cholesterol levels resulting in a reduced risk of cardiovascular disease, prompting some to make bone marrow a dietary staple.
>
> http://en.wikipedia.org/wiki/Bone_marrow

Birch details two exercises for energising the bone marrow in Appendix Two.

This is from Wikipedia:

> Bones are rigid organs that form part of the endoskeleton of vertebrates. They function to move, support and protect the various organs of the body, produce red and white blood cells and store minerals.
>
> Because bones come in a variety of shapes and have a complex internal and external structure, they are lightweight yet strong and hard in addition to fulfilling their many other functions. One of the types of tissues that make up bone is the mineralised osseous tissue, also called bone tissue, that gives it rigidity and a honeycomb-like three-dimensional internal structure. Other types of tissue found in bones include marrow, nerves, blood vessels and cartilage. There are 206 bones in the adult body.

> Bones can serve to protect internal organs, such as the skull protecting the brain or the ribs protecting the heart and lungs. Bones can act as reserves of minerals important for the body, most noticeably calcium and phosphorus. Bones are important in the mechanical aspect of hearing. All bones consist of living cells embedded in the mineralised organic matrix that makes up the osseous tissue. Bone is not a uniformly solid material but rather has some spaces between its hard elements.
>
> The hard outer layer of bone is composed of compact bone tissue, so called due to its minimal gaps and spaces. This tissue gives bones their smooth, white and solid appearance, and accounts for 80% of the total bone mass of an adult skeleton. Compact bone may also be referred to as dense bone or cortical bone.
>
> Filling the interior of this organ is the trabecular bone tissue (an open cell porous network also called cancellous or spongy bone) which is composed of a network of rod- and plate-like elements that make the overall organ lighter and allow room for blood vessels and marrow. Trabecular bone accounts for the remaining 20% of total bone mass but has nearly ten times the surface area of compact bone.

The Placebo Response by Howard Broady says that 'Live bone is one of the most dynamic tissues in the body'.

In Tibetan monasteries, and in St Katherine's Monastery, the bones of deceased monks and sages have been preserved for centuries. It is believed that the accumulated wisdom of these holy people is stored in their bones and can be accessed by the sufficiently attuned living.

This is from the Lonely Planet's Egypt Travel Guide:

> Tucked into a barren valley at the foot of Mt Sinai, the ancient St Katherine's Monastery has been a place of pilgrimage since the 4th century. It traces its founding to about 330AD, when the Roman empress Helena had a small chapel and a fortified refuge for local hermits built beside what was believed to be the burning bush from which God spoke to Moses. In the 6th century Emperor Justinian ordered a fortress to be constructed around the original chapel, together with a basilica and a monastery.

From ancient times this monastery, and the work done inside its walls, have obviously been considered important.

This is from *Tan Tien Chi Kung* by Mantak Chia:

> In many indigenous cultures, bones are considered especially sacred and are, even long after a person has died, preserved with great care, as they are believed to contain the spirit of the person as well as the spirit of his or her

ancestors. It would seem as if the people intuitively knew that the bones are the generators of the substance of life and need therefore a special attitude of reverence.

One day, there was an interesting insight during a dark skeleton meditation. It came to Birch that it was possible to change the skeleton to a plastic state, and then change the molecular structure to such an extent that one could move through solid objects, such as walls, or become invisible. This is a different route to the invisibility exercise outlined in *So You Think We're Alone?* Children will be born, probably already have been born, with this alignment and will not need to work in this way in order to achieve success. If enough individuals create this new vibrational blood and bone frequency, it will have a profound effect on the mass consciousness. 144,000 is an appropriate number, in Birch's view. This is the one hundred monkey effect.

These ideas could be used by those of the dark persuasion to instil fear, but it is an entirely natural phenomenon. Once the plastic state has been achieved through the dark skeleton meditation exercise then, by visualising the shape, being or object that one desires to move into, one makes the conditions for the change available. One would also need to be in an altered state of consciousness, albeit self-controlled, to facilitate the change. To return to one's original state, one would visualise it. Audrey believes that, although the form changes, it retains the original consciousness that set it in motion.

The shamans of Africa use bones for divination. Lion shamans use the bones of special lions to see happenings and to enter a state of psychic coalition with the consciousness of the great beast. Through this, the ancestral king lion is able to communicate with lions living in the present. Also it is written that a lion shaman claimed that gold should not be extracted from rivers because the Earth needs this precious metal for its life. Perhaps this is akin to our need for the beautiful sunlight? Birch wonders if this Earth need includes gold dug from it.

Further to the development of our bones in this work, Dr Gabriel Cousens has compiled many studies pertaining to the crystalline properties of the human bone structure. In his book, *Spiritual Nutrition and the Rainbow Diet*, he reports that bones can receive and emanate electromagnetic fields in the same manner as other crystalline structures. These fields can affect cell nutrition, cell function, enzyme activity, energy transfer and other internal activities. For the Taoists, the bones are a secret key to stabilising the life of the spirit within the human body. Before this can be achieved, the bones need to be cleansed and their vibratory rate raised to a more refined level.

Birch feels that the processes of plasticity of the body have been used by master beings to create a body without going through the issue of pre-birth, birth and maturation. It is said that the master Babaji (Indian holy teacher) spun a new body when one was needed for him to work on the Earth. Birch wonders if this process could also be used to prolong physical existence indefinitely, for centuries in some cases. The reason would not be just to prolong existence, but to complete the work of the spirit. It is claimed that the Count of St Germain lived for centuries, never appearing to grow old. It could be that, if what is said about him is true, he utilised the same principles.

There is the cliché, 'I can feel it in my bones.' Without work on the bone marrow and the blood cells it produces, the vibratory rate of the whole body cannot be raised or be able to function with the higher frequencies.

Audrey works with the mantra ORTHO, which is the prefix from orthopaedics, the branch of surgery concerned with the spine and joints. In the Greek language this word means 'straight'. She also works with the mantra IONA, which has strength and creates a spiritual and peaceful, but charged, feeling. The mantra LUNA invokes the feminine goddess principle. Audrey believes that ORTHO and SOL are the two main mantras for stimulating energy in the bones. SOL brings to mind Sol Invictus, the winter solstice celebration in ancient Rome.

Birch has worked with a meditation adding the mantra ORTHO, silently repeated. He found it to be a vibration from humanity's distant past. So ancient was it, Birch saw his skull and in particular the top part of his skull elongating and moving forward in relationship to his torso. Although he couldn't see the outer form, he had the sense of being in a dinosaur or very intelligent insect body. Immediately afterwards, he received a vision of a praying mantis-like insect. This creature was very large; much larger than a human.

The energies created in the skeleton meditation, detailed in Appendix Two, can be used in conjunction with the energy of the Earth. The forces of gravity and magnetism can be used as part of the transmutation. If one uses the Earth as an ally rather than a cruelly treated servant, the highest transmutation can be achieved. This transmutation can be achieved by slipping sideways into a form which is invisible. This is not the same as the Spencer Lewis process of bending light rays around the physical body, as outlined in *So You Think We're Alone?*, but is instead a matter of minimising form in 3D reality so that light rays move past an ultra flat array of molecules. The vibrations can thus be speeded up so that they move into a higher energetic state and are thereby invisible. This image reminded Birch of video footage and photographs of beings and objects that are not visible to the naked eye.

There is a profound cosmic law called the Law of Assumption which allows those proficient in such techniques to assume a physical state or to appear in a location other than the one they are currently physically in. This law can be used in conjunction with the plasticity state to create an enhanced condition over and above those mentioned above. Could the rash of sightings of wild carnivorous animals, puma-like, in a number of geographical areas, be of shape shifters satisfying their blood lust in an acceptable way as far as society is concerned? Or is there some other explanation? There are so many reports that, as always with oft-repeated news, the public curiosity wanes through boredom.

Audrey believes that some shamans have this shape shifting ability and knowledge. She had an intuitive flash in which she saw an animal shape superimposed on the pillar in the underpass where Princess Diana was killed. The driver, speeding away from the paparazzi, lost control as he saw this frightening image. She surmises that, perhaps, someone with access to these skills wanted her out of the way and used this magic. This would have been in addition to physical methods that were used to achieve such an end. Audrey once had the experience of seeing herself as a sailing ship. She felt the wind in her sails, the water under her keel, and laughed with joy to be a conscious boat.

There is an interesting aspect of the blood of Christ entering the Earth. By this shedding of sacred blood, transmutation of humanity could take place. However, it was necessary for this transmutation to remain hidden until conditions were ready for changes of energy patterns on Earth and in humanity. The shedding of the blood created an unbreakable link between the Christ consciousness and the nascent possibilities for human consciousness. Previously, Birch feels, the Christ consciousness was only available to avatars (spiritually wise men). After the shedding, this consciousness became available to all. The consciousness has its part to play in aiding the forces of light in the battle with those that would oppose the light. The forces of light were defeated at the time of Atlantis, hence the mess around us now. The forces of light can now prevail.

While working on this section, Birch looked in the mirror and saw his image as part human and part lion. He felt that this being was overshadowing him in order to inspire him in some way; not the only time that he has been overshadowed in this way. He also feels that this being is one of his future selves. See *So You Think We're Alone?* for further reading on the way reincarnation works for Birch.

Some time ago, Birch was reading a letter from his great friend and fellow worker Audrey. He read that, one day, Birch might write a book. A book that had been next to him, but not close, moved and fell off the seat on which he sat. No one else was around. *So someone out there thinks that it is a good idea. Fine.*

Many years ago, Birch received a vision of a lion lounging in a very relaxed way on a grassy bank. 'You will write a book,' said the feline. Nothing could have been further from Birch's thoughts at that moment. He was more interested in leaving for the pub for a couple of beers.

'What would I write about?' asked Birch.

'Write about your experiences,' replied said lion person.

Birch forgot all about it as he plunged back into the maelstrom of life. *Well, here you are, Birchy, assisted by the lion person* (who is perhaps a future Birch self?), *writing about the psychic nature of blood and other matters.*

There seem to be a number of communication levels when dealing with discarnate entities. We could call level one the situation where we become aware of such entities but do not have communication beyond sensing their presence, visually or otherwise. This has been Haines's experience with contact with many of the ghosts that his awareness has presented to him so far. The second level is one where a one-way communication is opened, as well as a visual contact made. Birch's contact with Paramahansa Yogananda as described in *So You Think We're Alone?* would be on this level.

A third level is where a two-way communication occurs as outlined above in the lion person experience. The final and arguably the highest level is where an overshadowing takes place on a permanent basis. The alleged overshadowing of Jesus by the Christ consciousness is an example of this enhanced, high-level communication. Birch talks here of the positive contact wherein the discarnate being is assisting the incarnate in completing her or his objectives, both spiritual and mundane.

Birch admits to having some doubts concerning publicising these matters in this chapter for a number of reasons. Firstly, there is the issue of the power of these energies that can destabilise the unprepared and the unwary. Secondly, there is the issue of the consequent danger of misuse. Thirdly, there is the issue of linking the raising of these energies on a mass level in such a way that they link to the changes in consciousness of humanity and the Earth. This third point is positive.

In the public realm, no longer will it be possible to keep secret the powers of the blood. Birch tells of those who seek to keep this knowledge secret. As the energies around us increase exponentially, no longer will it be appropriate to keep anything hidden. In fact, it will become impossible to do so.

Audrey had an insight which told her that crystals have a part to play in this work. We turn now to *The Crystal Bible* by Judy Hall.

> They have been used as for ornamentation and as a symbol of power for thousands of years. But such crystals were valued for more than their beauty – they each had a sacred meaning. In ancient cultures their healing properties were as important as their ability to adorn. Crystals still have the same properties today.

Subsequent to Audrey's vision, Birch had an insight of his own. As he mused over the idea, the single word 'citrine' welled up from within his consciousness. This is what *The Crystal Bible* has to say about citrine:

> Citrine is a powerful healer and regenerator. Carrying the power of the sun, this is an exceedingly beneficial stone. It is warming, energising, and highly creative. This is one of the crystals that never needs cleansing. It absorbs, transmutes, dissipates, and grounds negative energy and is therefore extremely protective for the environment. Citrine energises every level of life. As an aura protector, it acts as an early warning system so that action can be taken to protect oneself. It has the ability to cleanse the chakras, especially the solar plexus and navel chakras. It activates the crown chakra and opens the intuition. Citrine cleanses and balances the subtle bodies, aligning them with the physical. Citrine is one of the stones of abundance. This dynamic stone teaches how to manifest and attracts wealth and prosperity, success and all good things …
>
> Psychologically, citrine raises self-esteem and self-confidence, and removes destructive tendencies. It enhances individuality, improves motivation, activates creativity, and encourages self-expression. It makes you

> less sensitive, especially to criticism, and encourages acting on constructive criticism …
>
> Mentally citrine enhances concentration and revitalises the mind. It is excellent for overcoming depression, fears and phobias. Citrine promotes inner calm so that wisdom can emerge …
>
> Emotionally citrine promotes joy in life. It releases negative traits, fears and feelings at the deepest levels …
>
> Physically citrine imparts energy and invigoration …
>
> Citrine is an excellent stone for energising and recharging. It is highly beneficial … and reverses degenerative disease. Citrine stimulates digestion, the spleen, and the pancreas. It negates infections in the kidney and bladder, helps eye problems, increases blood circulation, detoxifies the blood, activates the thymus and balances the thyroid.

For those who wish to study crystals in some depth, Birch heartily recommends this book.

With reference to the potential healing qualities of citrine, Jacques Rangasamy says that the grief of the mother is stored in the spleen and the anger of the father is held in the liver.

So citrine, the yellow stone, is associated with the solar plexus. There is a connection and correspondence here for meditation: citrine, solar plexus, sun, yellow bone marrow. Now, making an intuitive leap, could there be a connection with the moon energy? Could this connection be an orange crystal, navel, moon, red bone marrow?

It was suggested to Birch that he meditate on citrine in the Earth as this would be much more powerful than working with single stones above ground. Ian, yet another friend, received an insight that citrine forms the skeleton of Gaia, the Earth mother, holding her highest vibrational energy. Birch wonders if citrine could be connected to the Earth's bone marrow. The marrow of humans is sometimes yellow, as is the colour of citrine.

In a later vision, Birch saw Earth energies coursing around the citrine skeleton in the same way as they do in the human body. This process is detailed in the bone marrow meditations described in Appendix Two.

This book is not about providing answers. It does pose questions for the individual to use on her or his path, should they so wish.

The reign of Akhenaton, the Egyptian pharaoh, was deemed a failure by many. His spiritual mission was to bring the concept of the one god into human awareness. Within a short time he was overthrown by those of the dark persuasion. Was this a victory for dark forces? Absolutely not. Although an apparent failure in the third dimension, Akhenaton bought the awareness codes of light into the akashic record for humanity to access later. He was truly a preparatory light for the Master Jesus, that great being whose ministry has been subverted by those of little understanding.

> Ye hypocrites, ye can discern the face of the sky and of the earth; but how is it that ye do not discern this time?
>
> Luke 12:56

Back to Akhenaton's purpose and its relevance to this book. There are a number of issues for which Birch does not attempt to provide answers. For one thing, he doesn't possess the answers, and for another, we all have our different answers to issues that we face. They are all equally valid. This includes elements in this chapter and the one entitled 'The Feel-Good Factor – A Different View'.

OK, this finishes quite a heavy chapter. Nevertheless the times are right for this material to be externalised. This is Birch's intuition.

Earth Work

Working with our inner earth friends

When Birch returned from his latest trip, his friend Mary thought it a good time for the team of three to pick up a new project. In a meditation with Mary and Joan, Birch was inspired to work with Earth-associated energies and beings. Mary initiated this after listening to Birch reading an astrological piece on trends for the future.

During the meditation, a being came to Mary. It appeared as a venerable old man, Father Earth. Another male being also made his presence known. This one was a father elemental, king of the fairies, a composite king of all the elements. Birch empathised with these visions as he had his own insights: to work more with the masculine after a number of years developing his feminine being.

Joan's vision was that trees possess much healing, with the roots going deep into the Earth for healing purposes. She became more aware of the eucalyptus in her own garden and its part in this healing. The three were told, from meditative sources, that animals received healing from trees through the roots. Joan saw pockets of non-human beings living deep in the earth. They were urging Joan to centre healing through them. These beings are working in their own way but would benefit from co-operative ventures with sensitive humans. Later, Birch was given the communication that the beings would feed energies back, through the three, to humanity on the surface. The purpose of this particular process was to make humanity more sensitive to Earth and her beings.

During the same meditation, Birch saw the trio working in a cave with a crystal at its heart. There was water in the cave that had never seen the light of day. Energy was pulsing in circular waves outward from the trio and the cave, working its way through the Earth in the same way that a stone thrown into a pond causes ripples to spread outward in perfect circles. When Birch asked his inner-self where this energy was coming from, he was told that it emanated from the galactic centre.

In a subsequent meditation, the trio was told by cosmic inspiration to walk psychically in tunnels and caves in order to ground the energy with intention. This is such an important part of manifesting this power in the third dimension. In these subterranean places, ancient energies are stored to be stimulated in the present. Mary was told to work from her cave containing the crystal.

Dragon energy is the old pulsating energy of the Earth. People walked in more enlightened times following the dragon lines. In meditation, the trio was inspired to send the energy and information gleaned from the tunnels and caves down the dragon lines on the surface. Birch, without being aware of the subject for the meditation, turned up wearing a shirt with a dragon on the front. (Haines really needs to speak to Birch about his dress sense.) Subsequently, Joan saw the energy being absorbed by the trees from the dragon lines, transported up to the branches and leaves. Then the energy was taken by the birds to be disseminated in a wider context in nature.

Until recently, two white stags lived in rural parts of Britain. These animals are said to be endowed with great spiritual power. One of these animals lived in the Forest of Dean. Both animals were known to local people who kept quiet to protect them. Unfortunately, they were not successful. Both animals were brutally slaughtered. The killing in the Forest of Dean was made to look like an accident, although it was apparent to those who discovered the body that this was not the case. Both stags had their heads cut off, presumably to be used as trophies. The body of one was hung from a tree.

Mary completed a meditation in which she saw the stags alive and well in another dimension. An ancient king was blessing them with a sword. First he held the point of the sword up, and then down. The animals spoke to Mary, saying that they were perfectly fine in their new abode, although they would have preferred to continue living in the third dimension. The good news was that they were now working, in their present dimension, with healing the land. It has been reported that a white fawn has been born in the USA in order to replace the slaughtered stags. This animal has been taken to a refuge for its protection. Recent reports say that two white stags have been spotted in the UK, one in Scotland and the other in Suffolk.

In another meditation, Birch was given an image of the yin and yang symbol. A diagram of this symbol appears in *So You Think We're Alone?*

The difference in Birch's vision was that the dark element was a beautiful golden colour instead of the usual black. The white of the normal figure had been replaced by a luminescent ivory. The whole figure shone with a brilliance that indicated it was a projection from the cosmic realms.

The object of the meditation was to take the symbol around the Earth in visualisation. However, the image took on a life of its own beyond Birch's objective control. Birch watched the visualisation unfold itself. The luminescent yin yang symbol was absorbed into the Earth. The Earth and symbol were the same size, as Birch observed them as though from space. Eventually all that was left was a re-energised Earth. The planet had received a gift from cosmic sources.

As the three, Mary, Joan and Birch, developed the Earth work meditations and visualisations, they started to work as a seamless whole in conjunction with the Theos animal energy work and the healing meditations for people (Theos is discussed in detail in *So You Think We're Alone?*). This seamless combined energy was utilised by Mary on a trip to the sacred stones at Avebury. Mary went deep into a visualisation at this place as her companions roamed the site. At the end of it, she was approached by a wide-eyed young man sporting multi-coloured hair.

'That was amazing,' he said.

Mary did not have the opportunity to quiz the young man concerning his enthusiastic comment, as her friends had returned. They were not quite on the same spiritual wavelength as she was, and they were obviously keen to leave the site quickly. Mary quickly told the young man to tune in to the stones. As she left, she saw the young man lost in meditation inside the circle. He had got the message.

It is believed by some that Anna, grandmother of Jesus, lived for six hundred years. For much of her life she inhabited an underground city under the pyramids. So it is alleged in *Anna , Grandmother of Jesus* by Claire Heartsong. One reason given for her great longevity was her living inside the Earth, plus the regular performance of powerful meditations. This city is, allegedly, huge in size, stretching from the pyramids to the port of Alexandria.

The following is also from the above book and concerns a story of one of Jesus' initiations in Avalon, Britain.

> At this ancient well, my sixteen year old grandson [Jesus] met with his uncle Joseph, who was clothed in the white robes of a Druid high priest. He led the nephew through a labyrinth devoid of light, except that born of the

> sun within the soul. In a chamber of great crystals both massive and tall, the young initiate was left alone to meditate beside a small inner lake which reflected his every thought and feeling. Into the cold water he plunged, diving deep into the abyss, until a faint light began to shine in the distance.
>
> No longer breathing as does a human, Yeshua surrendered into the remembrance of his soul having taken the form of a dolphin. Upward through a narrow passage he swam, until his body broke through the dark water. Emerging from the deep, shivering with cold, he found himself in a cavern, sealed from the world above. Over the doorway, written in the ancient language that his uncle taught him, were the words of Thoth-Hermes, 'As above, so below'. Seeing a beckoning light beyond, my grandson crossed over the towering door's threshold. Great beings, over seven foot tall in stature, arose from great stone benches to greet him.
>
> ... Then, one of the beings took him by the hand. This one was ancient, several thousand of earth years old. Yet his translucent face shone with a sparkle of wit and sublime wisdom. Torak announced that he was one of the high priests who had survived the sinking of Atlantis ...

The above passage is significant for it details the fact that living inside the Earth creates a potential for enormous spiritual development. It is not a prison environment for those of great spiritual awareness. Upon reading this, Birch was reminded of the Cyclopean beings. There was also the significance of underground water that had never seen the light of day, which had played its part in a Birch, Mary and Joan meditation.

One day, the three were discussing the puzzling great reduction in the bee population on the Earth. Joan subsequently meditated on this problem, for a problem it surely is. Pollination of plants is dependent on this undervalued part of the animal kingdom. The message that Joan received was that the bees had departed to another realm of existence because they could no longer withstand the continued pollution of the Earth.

'How will humanity survive without such pollination of plants?' asked Joan.

'Different ways will be provided,' she was told.

A psychic channel, Matthew, who sends messages from another realm, said that the plant devas would take over this task in the short term.

Mary, Joan and Birch attended a meditation group called Imaghi, supervised by Paul Hover. The group was asked to work in order to protect the Earth physically. As the group moved into the meditative state,

Birch contacted a spiritual being connected to the White Brotherhood (a group of spiritual enlightened beings), as he had been asked to do.

The group was asked to create a fountain of light energy from their centre, which was to cascade around the Earth. As Birch visualised this, his awareness was immediately taken out of the room and he found himself viewing the Earth from space. The Earth was, by this time, surrounded by the protective energy, golden in colour. Birch likens it to the image of an apple, with the source of the golden energy up-welling and cascading from a core that penetrated the centre of the Earth. Paul later linked this image to one of Birch's previous visions of a crystal at the centre of the Earth, co-ordinating energetic activity on and above the surface. As Birch continued to observe psychically, he saw the golden protection creating a protective blanket, much like an atmosphere. His intuition told him that the protection was required to counteract rays and particles that were being, or about to be, thrown off by the sun. The sun was undergoing its own initiation in these enhanced times and, although consciously aware that it could cause damage to the Earth by this activity, was unable to negate all the potentially harmful effects. The golden energetic protection settled until it stabilised to a constant and balanced blanket.

At the same group meeting, the members were asked to psychically attune to some work that was allegedly being done by scientists who were secretly attempting to access energy of the Earth. The reason for this scientific work was an attempt to bridge the looming energy gap that was, and is, becoming a major challenge for humanity. Birch meditated on this issue with the other members. His guidance told him that a being was projecting energy through him that would clarify what was happening in the scientific community and would assist in creating more positive outcomes from this work. He was told that this energy projection would assist those scientists who were working to harness this energy from an altruistic perspective for the benefit of humanity. Secondly, those energies thus far generated from this scientific work that were harmful to the Earth would be balanced. Thirdly, those scientists that possessed the propensity to use the knowledge for power and ego reasons would be blocked from doing so and would be directed into failing theories. Fourthly, the resonance of the Earth would be rebalanced. The impact of this work was to create a resonance in the Earth similar to a bell, which would be the Earth's normal state. If the resonance of the Earth were not rebalanced, this would create a potentially disastrous situation.

Scientists are not aware of the full ramifications of the work in which they are involved. Paul had previously been informed that the energy created by the scientists had mutated into a dangerous form when it had penetrated underground spaces, tunnels and caverns. Birch was also told that the potential risks of this work for the Earth were so serious that higher powers would intervene if necessary. It was important that the ameliorating energies be projected through humanity, such as members of the group and others, in order to balance the karmic debt. If the higher forces were forced to act without human support, this would have potentially serious karmic results for humankind.

Birch was further informed that this energy had been previously misused in this universe, resulting in the blowing up of a planet called Marduk. The residue of this explosion is still evident in the universe. The higher forces would not allow this to happen to the Earth. Lessons had been learned on higher planes.

Mary Earle, a member of the group, was concerned about a visit she was due to make to London the next day, and the necessity of her travelling on the Underground. As Mary expressed her concerns, Birch immediately had the insight that her travels on the Underground were important for this work. Her very presence would ameliorate the impact of these powerful vibrations. Further, if she tuned in to them, she would assist the process of disposing of them completely. In fact, although Mary had not realised it up to this point, one of the reasons for her being there was to perform precisely this function. Birch also intuitively sensed that the energies generated were in a pulsed form and, once in open space, the pulses would break up, creating a disharmonious, dissonant condition.

Immediately before the meeting, Birch's friend Mary saw the most amazing sunset. She felt that it was otherworldly and preparation for the meeting.

Friend Sylvester and others were dancing paneurhythmy, a Bulgarian spiritual circle dance system, in Ashridge Forest. As they danced, Sylvester received the intuitive message that a being in the Earth was absorbing the energy that was being generated by the humans involved in the dance. So dance is one way of generating energy and healing for the Earth. This has been well known to so-called backward societies for thousands of years.

In a healing meditation for the Earth, Mary was approached by a being, half gnome-like and half crow-like in appearance. It told Mary that its job was to break down the leaf mould and rotting vegetation in order to create new soil. It asked for assistance as it, and fellow beings, were profoundly affected by pollution. The being requested that Birch perform the Chinese medicine wheel ceremony in the wood. This ceremony invokes the five elements of the Chinese system. These elements, energetic signatures more precisely, are earth, water, wood, metal and fire. The three friends were happy to agree to perform this ceremony, for, as Birch often says when thanked for his spiritual activities, *it is what I do.*

So You Think We're Alone? The Legacy

Following up and strengthening

Since the book *So You Think We're Alone?* was published in January 2007, a number of people have told Birch that they were enthused by one or a number of the subjects contained therein. Most felt drawn to one of the psychic or spiritual elements. There was one who found a different inspiration.

Jaqueline worked with a colleague who dominated her husband. She ruled the roost in terms of lifestyle, holiday and all aspects of their relationship decisions. He was squashed and had been so for years. Jaqueline loaned her colleague a copy of the book, which the colleague ignored. But it was picked up by the husband. It was as though a light were switched on in his head when he read the stories of travel contained in the book. Within weeks he had decided to visit Thailand, alone, where a friend lived with his Thai girlfriend. The wife tried all the old pressure and blackmail tricks in order for the old order to be re-established. None of it worked. He went. Jaqueline blamed Birch for the husband's foreign adventure in what many people say is a moral den of iniquity. Birch blames the cosmic forces for inspiring him to write in the first place. Do you remember the old military adage 'never volunteer'? Well, in this case, Birch does not intend to take responsibility for another's actions. Perhaps the experience would be beneficial for both people in their future life. Birch certainly hopes so.

It later transpired that the couple had decided to separate and divorce. They are now in their fifties and had been together since the age of fourteen. Who outside the relationship is to say that this decision is right or wrong?

When *So You Think We're Alone?* was published and a modicum of marketing had been completed, Birch assumed, wrongly as it turned out, that he was finished with it and the energy of its messages. At the end of

November 2007, he developed a very painful condition in his right leg. It became extremely stiff and was impossible to ignore. Various healing modalities were tried and all failed to complete a cure, although the condition and pain were relieved to some extent. Massage, chiropractic, conventional medicine, all were visited with limited healing results. At the end of January, three months after the onset of the condition, it still bedevilled him.

On a visit to Audrey, she of the akashic record contact abilities, Birch asked his friend to explore the condition from a psychic point of view. Audrey immediately came up with a link to the life Birch had at the time of the American Civil War. In this conflict he had fought in the Confederate Army having been born and brought up in the state of Georgia. With her psychic sight, Audrey saw Birch and a friend lying on the edge of a copse of trees, just before cessation of hostilities. They were relatively relaxed, expecting a quick return to their homes and their loved ones. Most of the opposing armies had disbanded. Sadly and tragically, they were to be part of one near-final drama of the conflict. Unknown to them, a bitter and hard-hearted member of the Union Army, a sharpshooter, had spotted them. This man, dark of intent, had murder in mind. *I will kill two more of the bastards*, he whispered to himself, *before it becomes illegal.*

He took aim and shot dead Birch's friend and companion. Birch, oblivious to the danger around him, tried to attend to his doomed friend. The Union sharpshooter circled around the pair and shot Birch in the leg. Before he could kill Birch, he was called away by a comrade. So in a physical sense Birch survived, 'lingered' would be a better word, to continue that particular incarnation. He staggered back to his home town with the aid of a stick supporting the damaged leg.

So Birch had his answer. From that moment, he knew that visiting Georgia, and the sites that were significant, would somehow expurgate the pain and suffering from his DNA. The karma would be repaid, and Birch would move further towards wholeness. Birch believes that the energies now entering this third dimension are increasing at a great rate. This energy enhancement is bringing old wounds to the surface for many of us to deal with. It may be relevant that as soon as Birch had decided to visit Georgia, the site of his past and present pain, he discovered an exercise that helped the leg condition and it started to heal. Or perhaps the two are not connected at all.

Bryan told Birch that he knew of a life of his as a slave owner or dealer in historic times. One day he awoke to find the image of his slave owner/dealer self lying next to him in bed. This earlier part of him, Bryan, was very dark skinned with thick curly hair. However, the eyes were as they are now, in Bryan's current life. It certainly brings a whole new meaning to 'be careful who you get into bed with'.

It will be apparent that Birch and many people around the world are believers in reincarnation. This is a humorous story that amused Birch. An old friend's husband passed away. After her sad loss she was befriended by a male mystic. Eventually the male mystic made a pass at Birch's friend but was rebuffed. The fellow made a final plaintive plea. He asked Birch's friend to marry him in a future incarnation. This proposal takes the concept of delayed gratification to a whole new level.

There is another twist in the reincarnation debate. In 2008 Birch became a grandfather for the first time. When the baby, Bella, was approximately ten weeks old Birch sensed that his deceased mother was attempting to contact him from the realm in which she now resides. At that time Birch was unable to make contact or extract any sense of the attempted communication. Birch spoke with friend Faye for guidance. Faye's intuition informed her that the attempted communication was connected to Bella. Later that same day, the thought suddenly hit Birch that Bella was to be the reincarnation of his mother. At such a young age the soul would not have fully surrounded the young baby's body. Whether this is true or not may become more evident over time. It is interesting to speculate on the mother becoming the granddaughter. Later, friends Mary and Joan felt that Birch's mother would not reincarnate into the body of Bella but would act as an out-of-body advisor. They called it overshadowing. The reason they gave was the timing of the mother's attempted communication with Birch, which had been after Bella's birth. They felt that the attempted communication would have been before the birth if the intention had been to enter Bella's body as the resident soul.

For those who have read the previous book, you will recall the chapter on the rise of animal consciousness through the mechanism of the Theos wave. In that chapter were quoted numerous examples of the change in animal behaviour observed as a result of their changed consciousness. Here is an example of animal sensitivity to earth energies. It is a reported fact that in times past in Muslim countries, the builders of sacred structures would observe where animals would gather together and construct in that place. They believed that the animals could sense the most harmonious vibrations.

Seismologists claim that it is nearly impossible to predict the timing and place of an earthquake. Yet three weeks before the 2008 Chinese quake, the water level in a pond 350 miles from the quake's epicentre dropped dramatically. Three days before the horrendous event, thousands of toads appeared on the streets of Mianzhu city. This is a city where 2,000 people died in the disaster. Hours before the quake, zoo animals in Wuhan began to behave strangely. And then there's the story of the wildlife park during the eclipse.

In a meditation, Joan received the information that the vast majority of the bee population was leaving the planet for good. The illness afflicting the species throughout the world would destroy the population and it would not recover. Mary later confirmed this information from a book that she had read which gave in-depth information. It was said that bees had originated in the Pleiades and incarnated on Earth in order to experience the linking of spiritual and physical existence. During Atlantean times the bees had been respected by the human population who had only taken a proportion of their honey, allowing the bees to retain that which they needed for harmonious existence. The book said that the bees were now leaving the planet because, at the level of their mass consciousness, they were sick at the abuse of being used as a human resource as part of an industrial process. They were now returning to their source.

Mary, Joan and Birch's meditations have indicated that the Theos wave of energy is working in three ways. First, it works to develop and raise animal consciousness. Second, there is a healing modality which assists physically, mentally or emotionally sick animals to heal. Third, its protective mode gives animals a buffer if they are threatened with abuse by other animals or humans or if they are under threat of extinction as a species.

The following is an example of animal consciousness that is of a high level. Birch is not claiming that Theos energy is solely responsible for this particular remarkable behaviour.

> A German shepherd dog has saved his owner's life by dialling the emergency services. Buddy had been taught to press a pre-programmed button in case of trouble and duly hit it after owner Joe Stanlaker suffered a seizure. The operator heard whimpering and barking, traced the call and sent paramedics to the house in Scottsdale, Arizona.
>
> http://lifestyle.aol.co.uk/2008/09/18/buddy-the-phone-dog-saves-his-owner/

Audrey saw a snippet on TV news concerning a dog that could sense its owner's imminent grand mal epileptic attack forty minutes before the onset. The owner, who had been able to check it out, said that the timing was to the minute. Conventional science is at a loss to explain the phenomenon. Audrey is of the view that the dog reads the owner's aura, which is radiating and warning of the condition long before the physical attack.

The dog's owner went on to say that the epilepsy had been the ruination of her life before the dog had become part of her life. Previously she had decided not to have children. The woman's confidence grew with the support of her canine warning system. She subsequently gave birth to and successfully raised several children. The animal would lick and gently bite the hand of its owner as a warning of an impending attack. The psychic dog also had another talent. With its mouth it would fill and empty the washing machine in the owner's house. It is interesting to know that dogs are now used to support the deaf and wheelchair-bound as well as the blind in the UK.

When Audrey lived in Africa a friend told her of the intelligence displayed by a Siamese cat. The son of the house was woken up one night by the cat biting his toe. The son got out of bed to discover an intruder in the house. Thus a cat can be a valued guard dog.

Audrey tells of her youth when she grew up on a farm. A member of the family had a young baby who would be put in the garden to enjoy the fresh air. The garden was next to the field where the bull was kept. One day the baby's mother went out into the garden to check on the baby. She shrieked with fear and amazement at the scene that confronted her. There before her was the bull, which had broken through the fence and was gently licking the baby's face.

This next story is from an unattributable source. Steve Ford searched frantically for his beloved dog Jo Jo, a Labrador retriever, after being told he had been hit by a car outside his home. Unable to find him, he called the Audubon Animal Hospital to tell them that Jo Jo had been injured and that he would be bringing him in, if he could find him. But Jo Jo had already admitted himself. Following the accident Jo Jo had apparently run about a mile from Ford's home to the animal hospital. He suffered bruises but no broken bones. Jo Jo stays at the Audubon when his family is away.

The following quote is from *The Elephant's Secret Sense: The Hidden Lives of the Wild Herds of Africa* by Caitlin O'Connell:

> Elephants are the only other species other than humans and Neanderthals known to have a ritual around death. They show a keen interest in the bones of their own kind (even unrelated elephants that have died long ago). They are often seen gently investigating the bones with their trunks and feet, remaining very quiet. They also bury their dead. Elephants that are completely unrelated to the deceased will still visit their graves. When an elephant is hurt, other elephants (also even if they are unrelated) will aid them.

An issue of the *Pleiadian Times* bases the following story on *Elephant Destiny: Biography of an Endangered Species in Africa* by Martin Meredith:

> [He tells of] an occurrence about a typical elephant death ritual that was witnessed by a South African biologist who had studied elephants for over eight years. The entire family of a dead matriarch, including her young calf, were all gently touching her body with their trunks and tried to lift her. The elephant herd were all rumbling loudly. The calf was observed to be weeping, and made sounds that sounded like a scream, but then the entire herd fell incredibly silent. They began to throw leaves and dirt over the body, and broke off tree branches to cover her. They spent the next two days quietly standing over her body. They sometimes had to leave to get water or food, but they would always return. Occurrences of elephants behaving like this are common throughout Africa. On many occasions they have buried dead humans or aided them when they were hurt.
>
> George Adamson recalls when he shot a bull elephant from a herd that kept breaking into the government gardens of northern Kenya. George gave the elephant's meat to local Turkana tribesmen, and then dragged the rest of the carcass half a mile away. That night, the other elephants found the body and took the shoulder blade and leg bone and returned the bones to the exact spot the elephant was killed. A large variety of animals display what appears to be 'sorrow' through body language, posture, and actions although seeing elephants standing over a body, burying them, refusing to leave, and their trunks being observed hanging limp certainly seems evidence that perhaps much deeper and complex emotions are involved.

Birch has persuaded Haines to recount the strange story of Haines's connection to a very special blackbird. This story came to light after the two friends had talked of the ghostly hedgehog in a chapter above.

'What's that got to do with ghosts?' said Haines, perplexed.

'Maybe nothing, but while we're on the subject of wild creatures, this story broadens the scope of discussion. In any case, it's fascinating, interesting and touching,' Birch countered.

Put like that, how could Haines refuse? One Saturday, he was working in his garage. At the far end of the garage is a large window. A blackbird flew through the open door at an alarming rate. Seeing the light through the clean window, the bird flew into it. In panic, the bird kept flying into the glass, flapping its wings and colliding time after time. It was a pitiful sight. With great care, Haines eventually managed to catch the bird, being careful not to damage the wings. He carried it into his back garden and opened his hands, expecting the bird to fly off. It didn't. Instead it just sat there, looking straight ahead. There it sat for several minutes. Haines assumed it was traumatised, stunned and scared witless. He was relieved when the bird eventually flew off. But this was not the end of the story.

Immediately, blackbirds started nesting in his garden. That, in itself, probably meant nothing. But much more surprising was the behaviour of the birds. Every year since, blackbirds have approached Haines, provided he is alone. The male seems to bring his young to introduce to Haines. They show no fear, coming within just three feet of him. If he approaches them, they stand their ground, never hopping or flying away. Again, Birch finds this significant. Haines just sees it as odd, but secretly he rather enjoys it.

Up until recently, the blackbirds have been Haines's ever-present companions in his garden. Sadly, things have changed. The tree in which the birds nested, year after year, has gone. It was killed in the floods of July 2007 and had to be cut down.

But Haines leaves it to others to place significance upon this strange story. For him, he merely accepts it as a fact and is content with that.

As the Theos meditation and visualisation work has progressed over the last three years, one of the remarkable developments has been the involvement of other beings. Into Joan, Mary and Birch's consciousness, various beings representing different animal groups have presented themselves. Their role has been to be part of the group consciousness channelling the energy from cosmic realms. They then assist in the transmutation of that energy in a circle with the three humans. The final part is the transmission of the energy to the group of animals that each being represents. The three humans have decided that now is a good time to name them. This is in order for others who read this book to have the benefit of working psychically with these beings for the benefit of the animal kingdom if they wish. An additional benefit could be raising the awareness of those humans that have a responsible role with the animal kingdom.

The event that persuaded the trio to name their co-workers occurred during a meditation. The three were working with the Theos energy when Birch was approached by the Minotaur and encouraged to focus energy through his being in order to alleviate the suffering of bulls abused during bullfighting shows. We won't honour this disgusting slaughter by giving it the name of a sport. Birch recently read that European Community funds were being diverted to support this madness. What is our society up to? Has it no shame? The bulls have no chance. They are weakened before they go into the ring and then weakened further with lances into their lungs before the brave(?) matador appears. So this is a list of entities that Mary, Joan and Birch have been privileged to work with:

- A being that looks very much like Yoda from the *Star Wars* trilogy. This being has responsibility for those animals with sensitive hearing, for example horses, elephants, buffalo.
- A positive snake-like reptilian being.
- A being that appears to be a cross between a hawk and an owl, with responsibility for the bird kingdom. These animals spread the energy around the planet.
- A feline being similar to a lion. This being has links to Sekhmet, the Egyptian aspect of the creator /destroyer energy.
- A butterfly of light. Responsible for insects including bees.
- A calm pale being which has responsibility for rodents. Mary and Birch think that the actor Bill Nighy looks like this being. No insult, Mr Nighy, honest.
- A beaver that represents the beavers and duck-billed platypus. When this being presented itself to Birch it informed him that the two types of animals were related, at least energetically.
- Brigid, known as a saint by the Christians. She represents domestic animals including pigs and donkeys.
- A primate being. He appears warm and rounded with a face that is a cross between an old African and a gorilla form.
- A deep sea creature with a frog-like face.
- An amphibian which is also a frog-like being.
- A selkie representing seals and their connection with humans; also representing other sea mammals.
- The ancient salmon of wisdom representing particularly freshwater fish.

- A stag with golden antlers.
- An Ent-like being (see *Lord of the Rings*) which is a cross between animal and tree.
- The phoenix representing the link between air and fire elements.
- The Capricorn goat representing the link between the earth and water elements.
- Pegasus, the winged horse, representing the link between earth and air.
- The Minotaur possessing the best of both humans and bulls.
- The green man, symbol of natural fertility
- The unicorn overseer of spiritual development throughout the animal kingdom.
- A wolf pack together with a Native American spokesman. This pack runs with the energy, spreading it as do the birds.
- Ghobe, leader of beings working within the earth.
- Pan, the spirit responsible for nature in all its forms.

The following two spaces in the group, suggested by the beaver during meditation, have been made available for appropriate beings to join when they feel ready.

- A being representative of those animals that have lived on the Earth in the past. In a meditation following the beaver's suggestion, Birch saw this being as a dinosaur with wings. The outline of the being was picked out in light. At the same meditation, this being told Birch that he could represent future beings as well but would not do so.
- A being representative of animals that are future inhabitants of the Earth, or those that are already here and of which we humans are not yet aware. In the next meditation this channel was occupied by pure light. Perhaps a high being was using this channel to be part of this group.

It has been suggested by a number of sources that all beings that have ever existed on this planet, present or past, are connected to a band of energy around the planet. This energy band is a requirement for any species to exist here.

While Mary was on holiday in Pembrokeshire and paddling in the cool Welsh sea, she saw a seal that was intently watching her from the safety of fifty yards of sea away. Its head was bobbing up and down as it floated in its natural environment. Mary held eye contact with the animal for some time before the seal's head disappeared under the surface. On the last day of the holiday, Mary and boyfriend Mike went to the sea in anticipation of seeing a flippered friend. There was none. Before returning home disappointed, Mary, almost on a whim, called out to the selkie mentioned above. Immediately a seal appeared to them. This completed the holiday for the couple and they could return home contented.

Wikipedia has this to say about the selkie:

> Selkies are able to transform to human form by shedding their seal skins and can revert to seal form by putting their selkie skin back on. Stories concerning selkies are generally romantic tragedies. Sometimes the human will not know that their lover is a selkie, and wakes to find them gone. Other times the human will hide the selkie's skin, thus preventing them from returning to seal form. A selkie can only make contact with one particular human for a short amount of time before they must return to the sea. They are not able to make contact with that human again for seven years, unless the human is to steal their selkie's skin and hide it or burn it.

The format of our meditations (that is for Mary, Joan and Birch) varies depending on the insights, inspirations and guidance that are received once we enter the meditative state. We are never sure how the detail will work itself out. We have an overview and the rest fits into place without our conscious intervention. One time, when the group began to meditate on the Theos energy, Birch called it in and was asked to structure the meditation in the following manner. First it was suggested that the responsible beings mentioned above be called in to circle with the humans. Then the humans were asked each to select one animal that was symbolic of the consciousness developmental aspect of the Theos and place it in the centre of the circle. After a period of meditation the three were asked to place another animal each in the circle, this time one that would benefit from the healing aspect of the Theos wave. Later, the trio was asked to place three animals that would benefit from the protective element of the Theos in the circle. After the meditation, the three exchanged the names of the animals that they had placed in the circle for development, healing and protection.

For development, Birch chose the unicorn, which, during the meditation, changed into a horse. This surprised Birch because the unicorn is an advanced being and part of the outer circle of responsible beings mentioned above. He was informed by guidance that the horse would develop into the advanced being of the unicorn. Mary chose the white stag for this category, representative of animals that run and have cloven hooves. Joan also received the image of the unicorn, which was superseded by a cow. For the second category, that of healing, Birch chose a poor, sick-looking cat. Birch may have been partly influenced by Opal, Joan's cat, who regularly joins the little group for the meditation. Mary perceived a hare in this category: an animal significant to those with paws. Joan selected an elephant at this point. For the third section, that of protection, Birch chose a donkey, Mary a crane for migrating birds, and Joan chose a polar bear, significant to a group that is threatened by global warming. The three cannot say if they chose the animals or if the animals were chosen for them by other sources. It may be that the choice was made for a need that the humans were not aware of. It didn't matter who made the selection. What was important was that the meditation was done.

On the subject of Opal the cat, her behaviour is very interesting. Rarely is she in the room when the three gather for the meditation. As soon as the meditation is due to start she imperiously wanders in, jumps up to sit next to Mary, bows her head and joins in the proceedings. At the end of the meditation she jumps down and wanders into the kitchen to eat some food waiting for her; a job well done in the cat world.

The physical abilities of many animals are phenomenal in many cases, far outstripping humans. Here are two examples.

In 2007, a female bar-tailed godwit made the longest non-stop bird migration ever recorded. It managed the 7,145-mile trip from Alaska to New Zealand in nine days, without a single break for food or water. By the end of the trip, the brilliant bird had lost more than half of its body weight, and had survived by sleeping on the wing, shutting off half of its brain at a time while keeping the other half wide awake. All in all, the journey was the equivalent of a human running non-stop at 43.5 miles per hour for more than a week.

In 2005, a great white shark called Nicole (named after Australian actress Nicole Kidman) made a nine-month, 12,400-mile circuit between Africa and Australia. Nicole swam further than any other known shark, and the return leg of the journey set a second record: the fastest return migration of any known marine animal. Of course, humans also swim between distant foreign lands, but the nineteen nautical miles that separate England and France aren't quite in the same league.

Finally, just so humans don't become too immured in their superiority blanket, this is from the Reuters website:

> Australia's kangaroos are genetically similar to humans and may have first evolved in China, Australian researchers said Tuesday.
>
> Scientists said they had for the first time mapped the genetic code of the Australian marsupials and found much of it was similar to the genome for humans, the government-backed Centre of Excellence for Kangaroo Genomics said.
>
> 'There are a few differences, we have a few more of this, a few less of that, but they are the same genes and a lot of them are in the same order,' centre Director Jenny Graves told reporters in Melbourne.
>
> 'We thought they'd be completely scrambled, but they're not. There is great chunks of the human genome which is sitting right there in the kangaroo genome,' Graves said, according to AAP.
>
> Humans and kangaroos last shared an ancestor at least 150 million years ago, the researchers found, while mice and humans diverged from one another only 70 million years ago.
>
> Kangaroos first evolved in China, but migrated across the Americas to Australia and Antarctica, they said.
>
> 'Kangaroos are hugely informative about what we were like 150 million years ago,' Graves said.
>
> http://uk.reuters.com/article/2008/11/18/us-australia-kangaroos-idUKTRE4AH1P020081118

The chapter on reincarnation highlighted a number of Birch's lives sensed by Audrey. The following is a life of Birch's neighbour, Demelza. One friend was so taken by the story that he said it could be the basis of a novel. The story is told by Audrey to Demelza.

> In this life you lived in Spain or Portugal in a grape-growing area. You were the daughter of the owner of a vineyard situated inland, but not far from the sea. It was a hilly area with white-washed houses with red roofs. The religion was Catholicism in a timeless peaceful area. You were the only child of disappointed parents that really wanted a son to leave the business to. You had a good brain. Your father was controlling about who you married because the property passed to you. He kept a close eye on suitors. You were an independent girl who received a traditional education from nuns. You fell in love with a young priest. This was 'a passport to nowhere' in the culture in which you lived. There was a mutual attraction and you had a fling with the

priest. There was a child as a result of this union, which was a terrible disgrace. The priest was defrocked and banished. Your father went ballistic.

Your father forced you to marry the son of another vineyard owner. You had no choice. The affair was hushed up, the marriage rushed and your new husband pretended that the child was his. You went to live on your husband's estate. Life went on. Your husband died when your son was in his twenties. You and your son became heir to the combined vineyards. You were wrapped up in your son who, unfortunately for the family, was not interested in the vineyard business. He went to the big city to study architecture, leaving with the belief that the man you married was his father. You became a businesswoman and ran both estates by the time you were middle aged. You were very strong minded.

Your son was drawn to do charitable work in the city. He was not short of money. He made friends with others with whom he was studying. One of his new friends was a man studying medicine. They visited patients together. By an incredible stroke of luck, the pair visited your son's blood father who was dying. The son initially didn't know the relationship but the ex-priest did recognise him. The priest wrote a letter to you. Life had brought the three of you together again. The priest and your son had long philosophic discussions together. You visited the ex-priest and your son. When your son was told the truth he was shattered. You stayed with the love of your life until he died. There could be a connection between one of the men in that life and one in this.

The son couldn't bring himself to return to take over the vineyard and he married someone in the city. When you passed away, the land was sold. You knew this was coming and were very upset. You began to lose your grip on the workforce as you became old and frail. You felt the son had not given you the support that you needed. Politics in your country were changing. You were sad at the end.

Birch later visited a friend, Julia, after she had purchased *So You Think We're Alone?* She recounted some psychic experiences that occurred after she started to read the book. Three pages in, and a voice from within her spoke. *You are not making the most of yourself. Have faith in your abilities. There is much work for you to do.* Julia had been a healer, but had let this work drift away in recent years. Julia's intellectual mind recognised the value of this insightful information. This was a path which she had been avoiding in recent times. As she recounted the story to Birch, she felt energised by the impetus that the message had given to her life. She said she would start her healing practice again.

As Julia read the book further, she happened to glance out of the window. As she did so, across the blue expanse of the sky floated a cloud in the shape of a dolphin. It finally disappeared behind the spire of the abbey to the right of her window. On another occasion, another dolphin cloud presented itself. This time the mammal was going straight up out of a sea of cloud. So was Julia being inspired by the book? Was the experience of the book creating an altered state of consciousness in her being? Was she fooling herself? Is there another explanation?

Paul Hover said that he was puzzled about one aspect of the book. 'There was one chapter of the book that was missing,' he told Birch. 'In an early chapter you talk about meeting Jaqueline and then, much later, you are married. Where is the bit in the middle?'

Birch's response was that the book is a story, not necessarily following linear time. The people who appear in it are subservient to the demands of the unfolding events. The book is not a diary or a biography. The same is true of this sequel.

Paul laughingly responded by reminding Birch of a story told by Brenda concerning one of her books on channelled Pleiadian information. Becoming frustrated by the confused order in which the information was channelled to her, she was told by her Pleiadian sources to throw all the written material up in the air and let it land, apparently even further mixed up. When she examined the mixed-up material, it was in an order that was totally appropriate for the book. Brenda tells this story partly to demonstrate the humour that the Pleiadian beings employ.

Exit

Clive Birch signs off

As a computer programmer in the 1970s, Birch wrote his programs in modular fashion as was the practice at the time. Memory in computers was scarcer in those far-off days. He finished his programs with a module called EXIT. It made it easier for the logic to be performed and easier for those who came after him to make changes. So it seemed appropriate to him to finish this particular program with an exit.

OK, end of story. Birch hopes that you enjoyed it and found food for thought. As outlined in the opening remarks, the cosmic contract to complete three books is now complete.

As Birch reached the final chapter in his writing the first draft, he thought, *There is something missing here, concerning the heart of the book.* He was concerned enough to pass this message on to what he describes as head office. This is his description of those spiritual beings that advise and stimulate him in his writings. That evening he received a reply.

'Don't worry yourself, Birchy. The text is fine. This is not a "me, me, me" book. It is a book concerned with wider issues. The things that need to be in it are in it. You are finished with it. Pass it on to Pete so that he can work his magic with it.'

We all have our ways of seeking empowerment. The issues herein are Birch's way. More importantly, other people will find their own powerful means. Gandhi found his by peaceful, passive resistance that was so powerful it assisted in bringing the end to the most powerful empire the world has ever seen. The most disempowered people, when backed against a wall, will find a way.

Birch is reminded of a story by Mark Thomas. It concerned a demonstration against an arms trade fair being held in Australia. Demonstrators built a very large male member out of papier-mâché and mounted it on a flatbed truck. Secretly, they built a battering ram inside. At an appropriate moment, the papier-mâché object was directed at the doors of the arms fair and broke in. The previously hidden demonstrators poured out, causing mayhem among the arms dealers. The image of the abuse of the abusers, the arms traders, was poignant as well as humorous. This certainly was not passive resistance, but it made a powerful point. Birch is not normally a fan of sexual innuendo, but the scenario enacted was so meaningful.

This is Clive saying a big thank you to Pete. No one reading this, or our previous books, will be aware of the full range of talents of the man who put these offerings together. A world-class backgammon player, *Daily Telegraph* crossword expert, biker, adventurer, aerobatics ace, scratch golfer is Pete. All these talents have been laid aside to assemble my sometimes obtuse ramblings into coherent, interesting word pictures that have made it into print. Thus Pete's excellent writing skills have been the backbone of this and our previous offerings.

(A note from Haines, here, Clive. Scratch golfer? Hardly. I once went round a championship course in scratch. No one was more surprised than me. That was the day I hung up my clubs for ever. Thing was, on that fateful day I was playing my then chairman. That was a bit insensitive of me.)

Birch finishes with a few apposite quotations.

> Those who tread the path of love may suffer when their loved ones are taken from them. Those who tread the path of power may suffer when their power is opposed. But those who tread the path of wisdom find peace, for wisdom cannot be taken away. When wisdom is so powerful that it sinks into the subconscious mind and wells up again into the conscious, then it gives immunity from sorrow; for its light has banished darkness from every layer of consciousness.
>
> *The Initiate in the Dark Cycle,* by His Pupil.

> The idea that life was put together by a random shuffling of constituent molecules can be shown as ridiculous and improbable as the proposition that a tornado blowing through a junk yard might assemble a Boeing 747 from the material therein.
>
> Sir Fred Hoyle, 1915–2001, director of the Institute of Astronomy at Cambridge

> Learn the rules so you know how to break them properly
> Remember that not getting what you want is sometimes a wonderful stroke of luck

Open arms to change but don't let go of your values
Remember that silence is sometimes the best answer.

Dalai Lama

All that must be recognised, however, is that birth was not the beginning, and death is not the end.

The Disappearance of the Universe, Gary R Renard

WE WISH YOU EVERY BLESSING

Appendix One

The Cathar Prophecy of 1244 AD

The last of the Cathars was burnt by the Inquisition of the Roman Catholic Church at Montsegur, Languedoc, France in 1244, but they left the prophecy that the Church of Love would be proclaimed by 1986.

It has no fabric, only understanding.

It has no membership save those who know that they belong.

It has no rivals because it is non-competitive.

It has no ambition, it only seeks to serve.

It knows no boundaries for nationalisms are unloving.

It is not of itself because it seeks to enrich all groups and religions.

It acknowledges all great Teachers of all ages who have shown the truth of Love.

Those who participate, practise the Truth of Love in all their beings.

There is no walk of life or nationality that is a barrier. Those who are, know.

It seeks not to teach but to be and, by being, enrich.

It recognises that the way we are may be the way of those around us, because we are the way.

It recognises the whole planet as a Being of which we are a part.

It recognises that the time has come for the supreme transmutation, the ultimate alchemical test of conscious change of the Ego into a voluntary return to the whole.

It does not proclaim itself with a loud voice, but in the subtle realms of loving.

It salutes all those in the past, who have blazed the path but have paid the price.

It admits no hierarchy nor structure, for no one is greater than another.

Its members shall know each other by their deeds and being and by their eyes and no other outward sign save the fraternal embrace.

Each one will dedicate their life to the silent loving of their neighbour and environment and the planet, while carrying out their task, however exalted or humble.

It recognises the supremacy of the great idea which may only be accomplished if the human race practices the supremacy of Love.

It has no reward to offer, either here or in the hereafter, save that of the ineffable joy of being and loving.

Each shall seek to advance the cause of understanding, doing good by stealth and teaching only by example.

They shall heal their neighbour, their community, and our Planet.

They shall know no fear and feel no shame and their witness shall prevail over all odds.

It has no secret, no Arcanum, no initiation, save that of true understanding of the power of Love and that, if we want it to be so, the world will change, but only if we change ourselves first.

ALL THOSE WHO BELONG, BELONG;
THEY BELONG TO THE CHURCH OF LOVE.

Appendix Two

Bone marrow meditation

This is a bone marrow meditation that Birch has performed with great personal benefit.

He first drew energy in through the toes and fingers, then spiralled the energy around the bones, drawing it in and visualising the bones as the colour black for absorption purposes. He then worked with changing the colour of the bones to translucent purple with the marrow visible through the purple. Next he visualised the marrow but within the shape of the skeleton. Birch saw the marrow as bright red. As he chanted the mantra SOL internally he found the powerful energy focussing. Lastly, Birch visualised his aura as bright pink, which helped the love vibration to flow much more easily.

Consider the reason that people wear black clothes. Could it be that, consciously or unconsciously, they are absorbing energy from the environment and people around them?

Birch has used this second meditation many times in his chi gong teaching practice. This is called bone marrow cleansing. It strengthens the immune system, increases strength and density of the bones, stores chi and stimulates the transmission of chi through the skin and various acupuncture points.

There are four basic movements:

1. The meditating Buddha.
2. The cosmic being.
3. Wash marrow with one hand.
4. Wash marrow with two hands.

Stand with feet shoulder width apart or a little less, feet pointing straight and forward, knees and elbows relaxed, shoulders down and tailbone tucked in. The head should be upright (not leaning left, right, forward or back) and relaxed. Breathe through the nose with relaxed chest. Empty your mind of extraneous thoughts.

Visualise that you are standing on the core of the Earth. You and the Earth are one.

1. The meditating Buddha. Place both hands in front of the lower abdomen with fingertips touching. (You should be looking down at an arrow-head shape.) Hold the position for a few seconds, then slowly bring the palms of the hands together in prayer position in front of your heart.

With your eyes closed, visualise yourself in a large empty sphere. You are alone; it is peaceful, serene, tranquil; you are happy. You are the Buddha. Relax. Thoughts will come. Acknowledge them, let them go and return to your focus. Do this for at least half a minute. Lower your hands, very slowly, to your sides. Relax.

2. The cosmic being. Raise your arms to shoulder height, palms facing out, fingers pointing skyward. Stay relaxed. Your feet are still on the core of the Earth and your head is in the universe. Visualise that you are pressing against the edges of the universe. All your pores are open. Fresh healthy chi is blowing through them. Relax and breathe. Your hands are pushing without effort, left and right into eternity. Relax in this stance for up to one minute. Slowly lower your hands to your sides.

3. Wash marrow with one hand. Place the back of the left hand, fingers pointing down, on ming men (gate of life) about halfway up the lower back. Hold the right hand, palm down, over bei wei (hundred meeting points) immediately above the crown of the head. Lower the right hand slowly down the front of the body. Visualise the chi washing the bone marrow of each part of the skeleton as the right hand passes. It may help to name the part being washed in your mind as the hand passes. Finish with visualising the chi passing through the feet into Mother Earth. Change the hands over and repeat on the other side.

4. Wash marrow with two hands. Hold the hands, palms facing up, fingers almost touching, in front of the lower abdomen. Raise both hands slowly above the crown, with palms facing down. Lower the hands slowly, washing the bone marrow as in the 'wash marrow with one hand' stage, clearing out any residual stagnant chi or blockages. At the end relax.

Lightning Source UK Ltd.
Milton Keynes UK
UKOW051142240312

189521UK00001B/56/P

9 780957 130401